Mountain New England
Life Past and Present

A New York Graphic Society Book
Little, Brown and Company
Boston   Toronto   London

Mountain New England
Life Past and Present

William F. Robinson

First edition

The publisher is grateful to the following for permission to quote:
Excerpts from *Kinflicks* by Lisa Alther. Copyright © 1975 by Lisa Alther.
By permission of Alfred A. Knopf, Inc.
Excerpt from *The Dunwich Horror* by H. P. Lovecraft. Reprinted by per-
mission of Arkham House Publishers, Inc., Sauk City, Wisconsin.
Maps on page 34 by d'Art Studio, Inc.

Robinson, William F., 1946–
    Mountain New England : its life and past / William F. Robinson.
        p.   cm.
    "A New York Graphic Society book."
    Bibliography: p.
    Includes index.
    ISBN 0-8212-1670-8
    1. Mountain life — New England — History. 2. Mountain life — New England — History — Pictorial
works. 3. New England — Social life and customs. 4. New England — Description and travel — Views.
I. Title.
F4.R63 1988
974′ .009′43 — dc19   88-3197
                                                                            CIP

New York Graphic Society books are published by
Little, Brown and Company (Inc.).

Published simultaneously in Canada by
Little, Brown & Company (Canada) Limited.

PRINTED IN THE UNITED STATES OF AMERICA

Another one for Peggy

Contents

Fourth of July, 1898, Williamsville, Vermont

Acknowledgments

A writer draws from many sources and, with luck, does not misquote too many of them. He therefore lists the names of those he would like to thank, with both gratitude for their help and fear that any incompetence in the text might be associated with them as well as with him. Be reminded that all mistakes are the author's.

After having given this warning, I would like to thank Bob and Kathy Lotty of Trumbull, Connecticut; Cynthia Ostroff of the Wesleyan University Science Library; Hugh and Betty Montgomery of Phillips, Maine; Russell Handsman and the staff of the American Indian Archaeological Institute; Russell Smith of the Vermont Travel Division; Polly Rollins of the Mount Mansfield Company; Mary Pat Brigham and other members of the Vermont Historical Society staff; the staff of the Calvin Coolidge Birthplace and Homestead; the helpful gentlemen residents along the gold streams of Plymouth, Vermont; Connell Gallagher of the Bailey/Howe Library, University of Vermont; Barbara Burn of the Proctor Free Library, Proctor, Vermont; the staff of the Woodstock Historical Society, Woodstock, Vermont; Bob Moeller of the Northeast Audubon Center, Sharon, Connecticut; the staff of the Seeley G. Mudd Library, Yale University (where Old Blue has effectively buried all their best research material); and Dianne Schaefer, who has so beautifully designed this and others of my books.

I would especially like to thank my editors, Terry Hackford, Lucy Lovrien, Dottie Oehmler, and Patty Adams, also, the many people I have met in my travels through the New England countryside, whose knowledge and suggestions have led me down many old paths of wonderful discovery.

Finally, I would like to give recognition to my father, Cedric L. Robinson, of Windsor, Connecticut, who has always been a constant source of historical knowledge and insight. My wife, Peggy, I thank for all her understanding, love, and especially patience.

Introduction

Any brief introduction to the life of New England's hill country will inevitably fall short of its goal. Any quick description of its essential nature grows ever longer as one comes to know these broad hilltops and nestled valleys. There are the reds and oranges of fall foliage, smooth granite boulders in a mountain stream, drifts of clouds touching the forest hillsides high above the thin stratum of chimney smoke in the valley below, stone walls crisscrossing through a woods, an old white-painted church with attendant dignified houses clustered around a hill-top green, a mill in some shaded valley beside its dam and pleasant waterfall, personal memories of people, hikes, unexpected vistas, and the pervading feeling that here, somehow more than anywhere else in the world, man and nature co-exist in a state of balanced stubborn tenacity — neither allowing the other an upper hand.

The boundaries of New England's hill country are enigmatic. Much of the landscape throughout this six-state northeast corner of America is rolling hills. However, at a certain point, these hills grow sufficiently large to dominate the lives of their inhabitants, shaping both their economy, and their very character.

Various physiographic definitions can also be used. One can say the hill country is the section of New England whose upland forest zone consists of northern hardwoods, hemlock, and white pine, spruce, and fir. Another definition would limit the hill country to all land lying above one thousand feet. This latter, however, excludes much valley land, even far up among the northern New England mountains, which lies well below one thousand feet. This book will follow what seems to be the best geographical definition, the United States Department of the Interior's land surface classification, which draws a line around that part of New England where the heights, not the landscape as a whole, reach above one thousand feet. This region includes the northwest portion of Connecticut, the western third of Massachusetts, most of Vermont, three quarters of New Hampshire, and the northwestern quarter of Maine.

Throughout this section of New England (except for the two complexes of real mountains — the Green and White mountains), the landscape is characterized by relatively steep-sloped rolling hills. In the southern portion of the region, the valleys are narrow and the hilltops are flat and broad little plateaus. As one travels north through the New England hill country, the hills gradually become more peaked and the valleys widen into arable flats.[1]

The best definition, however, is subjective, identifying it simply as that region where the hills and mountains have shaped an economic and cultural unity which sets it off from the rest of America.

It may seem strange to suggest that life in the relatively mild climate of the Litchfield Hills resembles that of the north woods wilderness. Yet, from the time of each place's settlement onward, their histories ran roughly parallel. Until well into the first half of the nineteenth century, self-sufficient agriculture dominated life throughout America, and the story of life in the hills was much the same throughout the region, no matter whether settlers came in the late 1600s in the hill country of southern New England, or early 1800s in the north. In many cases, the later settlements in the north were populated by the excess and restless of the hill country to the south. The basic economies remained similar, differing only in growing seasons and local geography.

These uplands were long a wilderness, even for the Indians, who hunted there but preferred to live in the more hospitable lowland regions.

The white man began settling the uplands late in the colonial era, after the protracted Indian wars had ended. The New England hill country reached its peak in national importance in post-Revolutionary years, as the lands west of the Alleghenies still held hostile Indian tribes, forcing many pioneer families to prefer the bracing hilltops of northern New England.

The nineteenth century opened to a rolling landscape of cleared land and small villages, which soon fell to abandonment as the midwestern Indians were forced into the Plains States, enticing westward movement over the Erie Canal, and the later railroads.

Next the old patchwork of self-sufficient farms became great sheep pastures, producing wool for the new textile mills set up in New England's mountain valleys. These industrial villages were soon joined by little manufacturing shops, turning out the many inventions of Yankee ingenuity.

By Civil War times the "summer folk" were beginning to be an important part of many hill villages' economy, as the old villages' farmers moved down into the valley to work at the mills owned by these affluent vacationers.

Finally the macadam road, Model T, and ultimately the interstate highways opened the land to year-round visitors.

The New England hills are a region of diverse pasts, and its meager resources have given rise to its most famous product, the character of its people. As Daniel Webster said of the Old Man of the Mountain stone face profile in New Hampshire's Franconia Notch,

Men hang out their signs indicative of their respective trades: shoemakers hang out a gigantic shoe; jewelers, a monster watch; and the dentist hangs out a gold tooth; but up in the mountains of New Hampshire, God Almighty has hung out a sign to show that there He makes men.[2]

Mountain New England
Life Past and Present

1 *Landforms*

In its simplest description, New England's uplands comprise three north–south ranges.

Farthest west, the line of the Taconic Mountains straddles the New York–New England border. They are a modest range; their highest peaks reach only some three thousand eight hundred feet, but they create an almost continuous wall, undulating between peaks and high passes, that stretches from northern Connecticut all the way into Vermont. The Taconics' eastern slope is footed by a long ribbon of pastoral valley (called, from south to north, the Housatonic, Berkshire, and Vermont valleys). As seen from these valleys, the Taconics are an impressive sight, and their ridgeline forms a logical divide between New England and the Hudson.

Turning from the westward-looking view of the Taconics to the eastward range that forms the other side of the Housatonic–Berkshire–Vermont valley, the sight is of an ever-heightened jumble of elevations.

This range begins in southwestern Connecticut, almost at Long Island Sound, as low rolling hills. Thirty miles inland, near the famous Litchfield (their namesake in Connecticut) town green, they reach a thousand feet in altitude. They double this height as western Massachusetts's Berkshire Hills. Farther north, they reach their full majesty — Vermont's Green Mountains.

A traveler following any of the many streams that wind through the myriad of valleys that drain these elevations will, whether in the low hills of Connecticut, or the high mountains of Vermont, look up at much the same view, steep slopes and scattered hilltops which seem to display no geographical symmetry as in the grand sight of the Taconic "wall."

Yet, once one is out of the valleys and onto any height with a clear outlook, the vista shows a surprisingly level horizon of flattened ridge after flattened ridge, fading off into the haze.

Far in the distance a few modest peaks stand out to break the monotony of the hilltops' even altitudes. From this vantage point it is easy to think of these high-

New England land surfaces, as defined by the United States Department of the Interior. The surfaces are classified in three ways: Slope, Altitude, and Profile.

Notice that the "Profile Type" (small letters) on the map shows how the hilltops are flat and the valleys narrow in the southern region of New England's uplands, while farther north, the valleys hold the flatter portion of the landscape.

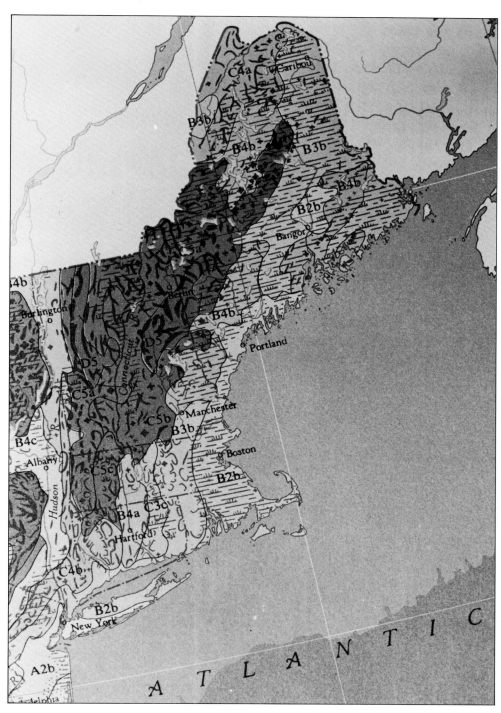

Slope
A. Over 80% gently sloping
B. 50–80% gently sloping
C. 20–50% gently sloping
D. Under 20% gently sloping

Altitude
1. 0–100'
2. 100–200'
3. 300–500'
4. 500–1,000'
5. 1,000–3,000'
6. Over 3,000'

Profile
a. More than 75% of gentle slope is in lowland.
b. 50–75% of gentle slope is in lowland.
c. 50–75% of gentle slope is on upland.
d. More than 75% of gentle slope is on upland.

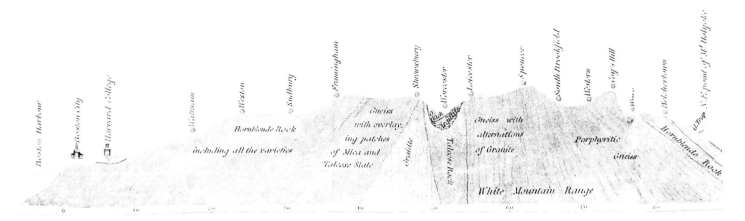

A portion of the "Geological Profile Extending from the Atlantic to Lake Erie . . . Taken 1822 & 3," showing topography across northern Massachusetts.

lands not so much as a range of craggy mountains but rather as an old uplifted tableland which swift-running streams have carved into little plateaus and deep valleys.

The highland's eastern slope drops off abruptly into the Connecticut River valley, New England's richest farmland.

At the eastern edge of the Connecticut River valley rises yet another range of hills. They too begin as modest hills in Connecticut and gradually rise in height as they progress north to reach their maximum altitude as New Hampshire's White Mountains. The range then curves northeast, gradually losing height as it extends far into Maine's north country.

These highlands east of the Connecticut River are a jumbled conglomerate of hills, mountains, and upland patches.

Even the impressive White Mountains strike the explorer as a confusing block of granitic rock raised out of the earth and shaped into individual peaks by the whims of nature.

Geological events began shaping this landscape about four or five hundred million years ago, halfway back through known geological history. According to the present theories of plate tectonics and continental drift, the American continental plate broke off from Europe and Africa. As these two plates drifted apart, a precursor of the Atlantic Ocean appeared, and much of the eastern half of the American continental plate lay submerged beneath a shallow sea. Over millions of years, soil and plant and animal life settled on this sea bottom to form a hard layer of sedimentary rock.

America then swung back back to bump against Europe and Africa. The early Atlantic Ocean disappeared, and the region that is now New England collided against north Africa just south of Gibraltar.

As the continents swung back toward each other, all the sea-floor sediment laid down on that early Atlantic Ocean was squeezed together to fold over like a crumpled rug, ultimately, when the continental plates finally met, to be forced up in a pile onto America's eastern shoreline. This is much as the Himalayas are being formed today out of the old sea floor between Asia and India. In New England this ancient shore ran up through the present-day Litchfield and Berkshire hills and the Green Mountains.

Scientists computing the amount of pressure required to compress the sedimentary rock to its present hard density surmise that some of it lay beneath mountains piled nine miles high. Himalaya's Mount Everest rises only five and a half miles.

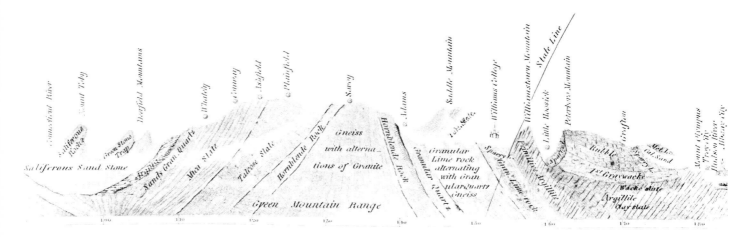

Geologists say these young Appalachians rose to such an unstable altitude that portions of their tops "tumbled off" to form the Taconic Range.

Before the collision, the approaching continental plates also shattered cracks in the earth's crust. Magma welled up beneath the shrinking Atlantic to cool into a chain of volcanic islands.

Continental collision pressed this island chain against the newly formed Appalachians. The eroded cores of these volcanoes are New England's eastern uplands, the crescent of hills and mountains that run from eastern Connecticut to the White Mountains to Mount Katahdin. Geologists call this range the Bronson Hill Anticlinorum (or upward fold of bedrock), after a modest hill in the White Mountains.

The continental plates ultimately drifted apart again. A portion of the African plate broke off, adhering to the American plate. This forms Rhode Island, the eastern thirds of Connecticut and Massachusetts, the southeastern lowlands of New Hampshire and southern Maine, and about half of the Canadian Maritimes.

Since that time, the great span of the New England uplands' geological history has witnessed a series of gradual erosions and uplifts. Water and weather wore everything down to a static, level landscape, or peneplain, interrupted by a few remnants of the volcanic islands and other residual hills of harder rock. These old hills are today classified under the generic term *monadnocks,* from the classic example in southern New Hampshire.

Periodically the flat landscape uplifted; old sluggish streams picked up speed and cut down into the new plateau. However, most New England stream courses predate the upheavals, so they often follow their original lowland meanders. New England rivers thus have the apparently obstinate habit of taking the line of greatest resistance through a range of hills or region of harder rock, rather than curving off to follow the easiest path to the sea.

Then came the glaciers, a few million years ago. Continental collision may have formed the uplands, but it was the ice cap, its journey over the hills, and its subsequent melting, that created the environment which defined the New England hills for man, from Indian, through early settler, to modern Yankee.

The worldwide climate began dropping a few degrees. In the colder lands a bit of snow always remained from winters past to accumulate in patches of ice field.

When their depth piled up to a few hundred feet, its tensile strength could no longer keep the ice solid, and it flowed outward along the edges. The Ice Age had officially begun. More and more snow accumulated; the ice piles made contact with each other, solidified into one great ice sheet, and bulldozed south. In North

America, the ice cap ultimately covered all of Canada, the Midwest, New York, and New England. It extended far across Long Island Sound, then dry because a few hundred feet of the ocean's depth was locked up in polar ice. The ice itself was so thick as to cover all of 6,288-foot Mount Washington.

Whenever the ice pushed down a valley, it ground the valley's original V-shaped profile into a wide U.

As the ice pressed its way over the hills and mountains, it ground off only about twenty feet of altitude, but took away any sharp peaks, leaving the hill country with characteristically smooth and rounded summits.

This moving ice formed many elevations into a distinctive shape. As it pushed up over the north side, it ground a smooth gradually ascending slope. Descending the southern slope, however, the ice plucked away much material as it pressed down and shattered the mountain's bedrock along every fault.

Many New England heights are characterized by this gradual north–abrupt south outline. The precipitous southern faces often form outcrop combinations vaguely similar to human physiognomy. Up in Franconia Notch, New England's most famous symbol for its mountain regions — the Profile, or Great Stone Face, in the White Mountains — came to be when the ice cap shaped Profile Mountain's southern slope into a cliff face. Later freezes tumbled away great blocks of stone, leaving the famous granite face looking down from high above.

The detection of other such profiles throughout the New England hills rose to a high art by the late nineteenth century, leading one tourist to marvel, tongue-in-cheek, at how wonderful it was that nature knew, over ten thousand years ago, the profile of every notable American politician.[1]

The boulders cracked out of the bedrock were sometimes carried miles from their origin. Patches of bedrock, whose overlying soil was scraped away by the ice, often show scoring from the rocks dragged over them.

Farmers plowing New England fields found the land a homogenous blend of soil and rock. No matter how well they cleared, frost heaves pushed up a new crop of stones for the spring thaw. The familiar New England "stone fences" attest to their abundance.

Balanced Rock, Lanesboro, Massachusetts. The boulder is about the size of a tractor trailer and rests against a few square feet of bedrock.

An 1827 rendition of the Old Man of the Mountains, New Hampshire, considered at the time a quite good likeness.

Sometimes the ice picked up boulders the size of a small house. These "erratics" are today favorite local gathering sites where families picnic in their shade and the children scramble over their great bulk.

In some cases, these giant boulders did not settle squarely upon the supporting bedrock. A slight push makes them wobble. These giant "rocking stones" were popular tourist attractions in the nineteenth century. Few, however, still rock today. Enthusiastic vacationers worked their best to see how far they could wobble the boulder before it tumbled over into a stable position.

About twenty thousand years ago, the ice reached its maximum extent. As the climate warmed, there began a melting that cleared the ice cap (at a speed of about 240 feet per year) back to the Arctic, where it lies today.

Even after the true ice cap was gone from New England, local glaciers still existed in a few northern elevations: Mount Katahdin, the Presidential Range of the White Mountains, and two locales straddling the Canadian border — in the region surrounding Jay Peak in northern Vermont, and on the Boundary Mountains in the northwestern corner of Maine.

During this time small local glaciers, not more than a mile in length, carved out the bowl of Tuckerman's Ravine on Mount Washington's shoulder, and in Maine, two glaciers intersected to form Mount Katahdin's Knife Edge.

As the ice cap continued to melt, the water running back into the ocean raised the sea level a few hundred feet. It was an awesome flow. Whirlpools created out of the water's brute speed spun large boulders to grind out undulating curves and drill potholes in the granite streambeds. Maine, Vermont, and New Hampshire (especially the White Mountains) abound in potholes. Some are twenty feet across. A set of slightly less magnitude in Wentworth, New Hampshire, demonstrated the diluvial nature of the melting Ice Age. These fifteen-foot-diameter, twenty-feet-deep potholes angle 45 degrees into a sloping rock face, one hundred feet above the valley floor.

Potholes along the Westfield River, Chesterfield Gorge, Massachusetts.

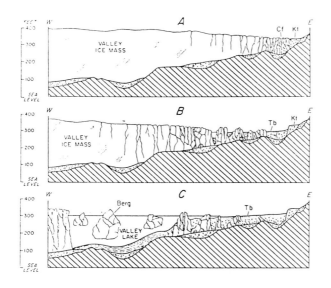

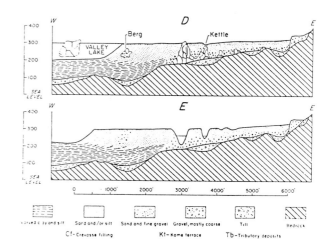

Cross sections showing the formation of hillside and interval topography during the melting of the glaciers.

Peneplains

According to geological theory, much of the New England landscape periodically rose as plateaus, only to have been eroded into deep valleys, leaving the hilltops as the remnants of the ancient high flatlands. The land apparently rose in blocks — low along the shore and higher inland, in a series of about a dozen terraced steps.

Profiles of the peaks across the southern portion of New England's western uplands show this stairlike character to the region's descent seaward. Farther north, the Green Mountains have a good number of summits peaking at the 3,200-foot level.

The terracing is less noticeable in the profile of the highlands east of the Connecticut River. The highest summits of the White Mountains, however, share a generally common altitude. Some geological theories propose that Mt. Washington was once an isolated, low monadnock rising alone out of the peneplain that lay at today's 5,500-foot-high Alpine Gardens, that almost horizontal "lawn" that sits high on Mount Washington's slope.

Peneplain profiles, showing the evenly stepped nature of the upland heights.

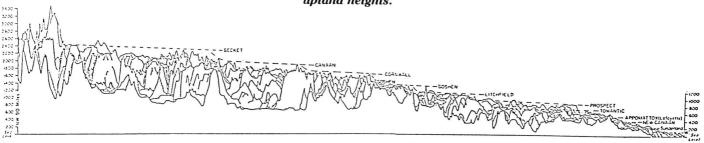

Sometimes the abrading rocks escaped, before being completely ground to sand, and lie as perfectly shaped stone cannonballs, along the upland watercourses.

When the ice melted on the slopes, various bits of dirt and rock settled. This built up into a layer of glacial till over the underlying bedrock. On the hillsides, runoff kept such deposits to a thickness of only about ten feet, but on the flatter hilltops it often lay up two or three dozen feet in depth. This mixed-consistency material, described as a "frozen gravel" by early settlers, formed a tight bond which made it impervious to water. Early farmers sought these areas of hilltop hardpan where water always lay near the surface.

Farther down the hillside, debris from the glacial melt took on a more orderly classification. Where there was a bend or eddy in the outwash stream, boulders of appropriate size and weight would drop, becoming progressively smaller as the stream grade flattened and the water velocity slowed. When the stream slackened current where the sloping valley wall met glacially flattened valley floor, the fine sand usually fell to produce outwash plains.

Often the ice still lay deep along the center of the valley. In these cases, the debris filled in along the sides. When the ice finally melted completely, little plateaus jutted out from the hillside.

At other times debris or another glacial finger blocked the valley's mouth. Here a lake formed, and the fine-ground soil now settled to the bottom in the still water. Once the blockage was breached and the water ran out of the valley, the smooth lake bottom remained. Its dirt — rocks ground to a fine powder off the many varieties of New England bedrock — was a rich growing soil for the settlers who cleared and farmed these flat valley "mountain intervals." The word *intervale,* a flat area between mountains, is more semantically correct, but local usage shortened it to *interval,* originally defined as a space between two ramparts.

The Eruption of Runaway Lake

In the summer of 1810, the citizens of a few neighboring settlements in northern Vermont received an unexpected lesson in glacial geology. Near the town of Glover then lay Long Lake, a beautiful sheet of water a mile and a half in length north to south, and up to three quarters of a mile wide. Near its northern end, its depth reached one hundred and fifty feet.

The land along the northern shore of Long Lake sloped down for about a half-mile to Mud Lake, at least two hundred feet lower. The glacial age had left a great embankment across the valley. Long Lake drained south, and the waters of Mud Lake made their outlet north, along Barton River, a modest stream, to Lake Mephremagog, almost twenty miles north.

The settlers in the little hamlets along Barton River had long discussed the prospect of diverting a bit of Long Lake's water northward, down the slope into Mud Lake, thereby giving the little Barton River enough water to drive their much-needed grist- and sawmills. On June 6, about a hundred citizens gathered with all their tools and set out for the northern end of Long Lake.

The wide, deep trench they dug through the slight rise at the northern end of the lake was not a difficult task. The soil was pure sand, and only a half-foot-thick layer of hardpan atop it sealed in the lake water. Digging back toward the lake, they finally cleared the sand from beneath the hardpan at the water's edge. A scientific visitor who toured the site a few years later gives this report:

As large a piece of the hard-pan, as their pick-axes would reach, was broken off. The water issued at first through the chasm thus made, with a moderate degree of force; but to the great surprise of the workmen, it did not run off into the trench ... the issuing stream, instead of flowing obliquely towards the declivity [down the trench], began to sink perpendicularly beneath the hard-pan.... In a few moments a large amount of the sand under the hard-pan was washed from beneath it, and the portion of the hard-pan was undermined, being unable to sustain the immense pressure, gave way.... This process of undermining and fracturing successive portions of the hard-pan having continued about twenty minutes; a passage was forced through it, down to its lower extremity; and the superincumbent water of the lake, being wholly without support, flowed with such impetuosity towards the northern shore, that it all gave way ... it was but a few moments before the volume of water, a mile and a half in length, about three-fourths of a mile in width, and from 100 to 150 feet in depth, had wholly disappeared.[a]

Plan of Long and Mud lakes.

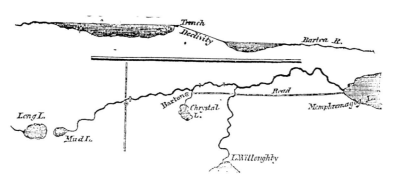

The lake water disappeared northward in a speeding torrent, carrying all in its way.

An inhabitant of Barton, who was standing at the time on high ground, told me, hearing the noise, he looked up the stream and saw the flood marching rapidly forward, opening itself a path through the valley, and bearing a moving forest on its very top; so that those who were with him gave the alarm, that the forest from Glover was coming down upon Barton.

It tore a gash through the valley all the way to the flats just below Lake Mephremagog. Somehow, no lives were lost, this probably because everyone was up watching the goings-on at the lake.

Our scientific visitor, in hindsight, considered the event propitious. While it never did enlarge the flow of Barton River (the owner of the stream's only mill instituted a celebrated lawsuit against his pick and shovel "benefactors" to recoup the cost of building a new mill), the lake flats and the flood path created an easy highway for settlers into the region, and, concluded the scientist, the "eruption" was inevitable, and best that it happen before the valley had been heavily populated.

Today the Old Mud Lake has been rechristened Tildys Pond, and just to the south, Route 16 comes out into a flat, where a picnic area and sign mark the location of Runaway Pond.

Kame terrace along the First Branch of the White River, Tunbridge, Vermont.

Sometimes the rocky debris, or a chunk of unmelted glacier that backed the stream up into a lake, was so high that the water found another outlet before the old was breached, creating a new drainage pattern. Hundreds of thousands of yet-to-be-drained swamps, bogs, ponds, and lakes still dot the New England landscape. Likewise, the hill country's abundance of waterfalls attests to the youth of its streams.

During the warming period just after the glacial retreat, woolly mammoths grazed the Maine tundra. South of the open tundra grew spruce and fir. With the coming of conifer forests — hardwoods appeared during another warming period around five thousand years ago — came caribou, moose, deer, bears, as well as now extinct species, including mastodons and giant beavers. Soon also came the cause of their extinction — early man.

2   *The Indians before the Coming of the White Man*

 As the mammoths and musk-oxen of the tundra moved north with the retreating ice, to be replaced by conifers and the forest-dwelling mastodons, the first humans — Paleo-Indians — entered the region. Current archaeological evidence dates this as occurring about 12,500 years ago, just before the onset of forestation.

Our knowledge of this race is slight, based largely upon the discovery of uniquely crafted spearpoints with hollows along each side running from the back to about halfway up to the point. This "fluted" point allowed the flint to fit more easily into the holding slit at the end of the spear shaft. Such a design differed from the weapon points of later Indians, enabling archaeologists to identify Paleo-Indian settlements.

The most interesting site in New England is the Reagan Site in Shawville, Vermont, in the state's northwest corner, half a dozen miles from the Canadian border. At the time of its occupation, the encampment edged an enlarged Lake Champlain, swollen beyond its present level by glacial runoff (which at one time turned the whole Saint Lawrence Valley into an arm of the sea).

The location of this and the other New England sites suggests that these earliest inhabitants commonly set up camp at the water, be it riverbank, lakefront, or seacoast. The disappearance of glacial lakes — like the one that once filled almost the whole of the Connecticut River Valley — and the rebound of the land from the lifting of the ice cap's weight has left many of these sites on hillsides. There must be others that today lie out to sea, drowned by the refilling ocean.

Modern estimates of New England's Paleo-Indian population suggest a count of about 25,000 individuals, with the majority living in the southern part of the region.[1]

The acidic soil of the evergreen forests through which these people roamed quickly dissolved any of their skeletal remains, their clothing, or remnants of their prey. Much of our impression of Paleo-Indian culture comes from examining their environment.

Reconstruction of a Paleo-Indian shelter at the American Indian Archaeological Institute, Washington, Connecticut — simply limbs and vegetation laid against a rock overhang.

It was an age of constant change. Lakes in dammed river valleys appeared and disappeared. Rivers changed their courses or went dry. The sea level went up as the glacier melted or went down as the land rose after the great weight of the ice was lifted from its back. Temperatures and climate changed. So, too, must have the animals and plant life.

The Paleo-Indians had to be versatile, adaptable, and, above all, mobile during the twenty-five centuries of their existence. They could not have survived had they lived by only certain crops and game animals; likewise, they must have had to shift their homesites not only for the game and edible plant life, but also because one summer's lakefront camp was the next year's hillside camp.

For these reasons, the Paleo-Indians must have relied on a simple complement of tools, all fashioned from flint brought in from the Hudson River valley. Such environmental dictates meant that the Paleo-Indians traveled light and did not create durable artifacts, bowls and other household goods, that could survive to give us a better understanding of their existence.

About ten thousand years ago the landscape again changed. Hardwoods began to replace the conifer forests and remaining tundra. What remained of the great post–Ice Age roaming herds which the Paleo-Indians once followed moved north.

The leafed trees filled in the old sparse landscape with a protective canopy under which, in place of the conifer and tundra browsers, developed a multitude of forest game and their edible vegetation.

The Archaic culture now developed. No longer wandering tribes, the Indians settled down in specific locales. The men became solitary hunters, tracking deer, bear, and smaller game. Fixed villages, usually set along riverbanks or protected coastline, encouraged the creation of specialized tools and implements — bowls, mats, mortar and pestle, stone pendants for fishing sinkers, spear weights, scrapers, drills, adzes, stone hearths — and more permanent dwellings.

By eight thousand years ago the vegetation was essentially stabilized in its modern climatic regions. As the Archaics learned more and more about how to utilize

Soapstone bowls, Litchfield, Connecticut.

the variety of game and plant life around them, their population and technical sophistication steadily grew.

While the Archaics shared many cultural characteristics of the later New England Indians, they still lacked a variety of crafts. The making of clay pottery was unknown; Archaic bowls were laboriously hollowed from soapstone. The bow and arrow had not yet replaced the spear. Neither had the eminently portable birchbark canoe replaced the heavier dugout. These people did not farm, but relied upon constant forays of hunting and wild-food gathering.

Sustenance was abundant, but their complete dependence on the hunt meant that life was a hand-to-hand grapple with the environment. Commonly, they lost the sharpness of their physical resources around the age of thirty-five, and succumbed to the elements.

Skeletal remains of the Archaic people show them as finely boned, with delicately modeled faces and a short — about five-and-a-half-foot — stature. Set over this thin frame was an amazing musculature. Their skeletal joints reveal that they slept curled, in fetal form, against the heavy cold.

In the centuries just before the coming of Christ, the region's Indians received great technological infusions from the Adena, tribesmen of a more sophisticated culture who were then migrating into New England from the Ohio Valley. They brought with them knowledge that transformed the character of New England Indian life: how to mold clay into bowls and cookpots; how to cultivate corn and other crops; how to make food storage pits, rope, bows and arrows; the use of tobacco in pipes; and ritual burials with important possessions of the dead.

And with the material (storable) wealth, brought in through seasonal crops and better hunting, came raiding parties by other tribes less successful at storing up provisions for the oncoming winter. The larger villages were replaced by stockaded fortifications and the hunter-gatherers became warriors. Still, those who avoided enemy weapons could expect an almost doubled life span over their Archaic predecessors.

The infusion of new genes affected the physical stature of later generations. European explorers found them

between five and six foot high, straight bodied, strongly composed, smooth-skinned, merry countenanced, of a complexion something more swarthy than Spaniards, black haired, high foreheaded, black eyed, out-nosed, broad shouldered, brawny armed, long and slender handed, out breasted, small waisted, lank bellied, well thighed, flat kneed, handsome grown legs, and small feet.[2]

Previously, Paleo and Archaic cultures had spread into New England from the west. Now the effect of outside cultural influences lessened, and the New England Indians (though all part of a predominantly Algonkian cultural base) began to split into separate and distinct tribes.

In Massachusetts, Connecticut, and Rhode Island, constant friction between communities created neat political boundaries to separate hunting areas.

The southern Berkshires and the Litchfield Hills were the domain of a number of smaller tribes: the Tunxis, Housatonic, and Wyachtonok. The tribes typically lived along the downriver valleys and used the uplands for tribally owned hunting preserves. Their boundaries typically ran along the ridges. The Abenaki (from the Maine tribe's *Wabanaki,* the "dawn land people") covered most of northern New England. The Eastern Abenaki inhabited most of Maine and a portion of eastern New Hampshire, while the Western Abenaki inhabited the rest of New Hampshire, almost all of Vermont, a stretch of Canada north of those two states, and a north-

A Massachusetts Indian, sketched by the anthropologist C. C. Willoughby from information by F. W. Putnam. Considered to be one of the most accurate likenesses of a New England Indian.

western section of Massachusetts. Ethnologists differentiate the western and eastern divisions by dialect; otherwise, the two groups were quite similar.

While the agriculturally oriented tribes of southern New England burned off the underbrush each fall to produce a hunting landscape marked by great open vistas, the Abenaki lands remained the primeval wilderness of bear, moose, and catamount (mountain lion).

Unlike the tribes of southern New England, the Abenaki practiced virtually no agriculture. The growing season was too short for most crops. Also, the vast territory of upland created such a low population density (about one fifth of southern New England's) that intensive food production was unnecessary. There was plenty of land for hunting and food gathering.

In Maine, the Eastern Abenaki were a confederacy of separate river-drainage peoples banded together under a common treaty of peace: the Pigwacket of the Saco drainage, the Arosaguntacook of the Androscoggin drainage, the Kennebec, and the still-flourishing Penobscot.

They camped along the shore and the lower reaches of the rivers during the warmer months. There they caught or dug up the abundant sea life — from whales to shellfish — as well as the salmon coming up the rivers to spawn.

With the autumn, they broke camp, dismantling their bark-shingled huts, and headed upstream to their assigned territories for the cold-season hunt of moose, deer, bear, and caribou. They also laid traps for beaver, otter, muskrats, and other pelt animals.

Indians clearing land. The Indians cleared land by setting a girdle of fire around a tree and tending it until the trunk had burned through. After that, the dried fallen tree was again set afire to clear the forest opening.

In 1605, Samuel de Champlain wrote of the Indians of eastern Maine:

When they go a hunting, they use a kind of snow-shoe twice as large as those hereabouts, which they attach to the soles of their feet, and walk thus over the snow without sinking in, the women and children as well as the men. They search for the track of animals, which, having found, they follow until they get sight of the creature, when they shoot at it with their bows, or kill it by means of daggers attached to the end of a short pike, which is very easily done, as the animals cannot walk on the snow without sinking in. Then the women and children come up, erect a hut, and they give themselves to feasting.[3]

It was a harsh life. Infant mortality was common, and despite their intertribal amity, these Indians developed a more aggressive personality than their agrarian neighbors in southern New England.

Experts suggest a pre-colonial population of about 12,000 Eastern Abenaki.[4] There was about an equal population of Western Abenaki in Vermont and New Hampshire. In total, the Western Abenaki occupied about sixty inland settlements, the majority of which lay within the Merrimack River drainage of southeastern New Hampshire — Amoskeag at present-day Manchester, Penacook at Concord, Winnipesauke at the outlet of that lake, and Ossippiee just over the height of land to the north. Along the Connecticut River, there was Squakheag, also known as Sokoki, at Northfield, Massachusetts. Cowasuk village lay in the present Newbury, Vermont, area farther up the river. To the northwest, on the other side of Vermont, there were identified villages where a few of the major rivers emptied into Lake Champlain: Missiquois, Lamoille, Winooski, and Otter Creek. The intervening highlands among all these Abenaki valley settlements was winter hunting territory.

Like their Eastern Abenaki neighbors, all able-bodied tribe members left their waterside settlements in midwinter to head inland to family-allotted hunting territories, each about twenty square miles in area. Here the men hunted moose, deer, and any smaller animals they found. At winter's end, the Indians dragged their kill on toboggans down over the hard snow to the valley settlement.

Dogs helped the hunt. In good times these friends of man might receive a few scraps from the family cookpot. Should the hunt go bad, they might be added to its simmering contents.

Come spring, the whole tribe remained in the valley, first catching the spawning fish, then, during the moose mating season of late summer, they hid in canoes among the lakeshore cattails waiting for moose to answer their birchbark moose callers.

Such an environment also neutralized much intertribal friction, and the Abenaki lived as one relatively homogenous unit, communicating with each other by well-trodden paths through the mountains. Wrote one early colonist: "Take these Indians in their own trim and natural disposition and they be reported to be wise, lofty-spirited, constant in friendship to one another, true in their promise, and more industrious than many others."[5]

Their relationship with other Indian nations was not so amicable. The Iroquois to the west in New York State were constant raiders of the Abenaki. The Iroquois were a confederacy of five (later six) tribes, one of which was the bloody Mohawk, which ranged far into New England, preying and destroying. For this reason, the typical Abenaki village stood on a high bluff to the east side of a large stream and was often surrounded by a high palisade.

Iroquois Indian camp. From a mural painted by A. A. Jansson at the American Museum of Natural History, New York.

An Indian bark-sided hut, reconstructed at the American Indian Archaeological Institute, Washington, Connecticut.

Yet for all this threat, the Abenaki did not appear to have lived in a state of preparedness for war. They banded together when such a common enemy threatened, but otherwise lived a relatively peaceful life.

They had a quite stable society. The families lived in long huts divided up into separate sections. The older parents occupied the center, while the married offspring lived in the end portions.

The modest size of the population, combined with a simple set of common needs, promoted the lack of friction. Malefactors were punished by the aggrieved family, either through physical punishment or magic spells.

The Abenaki, like Indians throughout the rest of the New England region, were great believers in the power of the spiritual world and its strong interrelationship with their natural environment. Like the pagan tribes of pre-Christian Europe, most Indian religions had their own equivalents of devils, ogres, wood nymphs, goblins, fairies, and Nordic gods. Their spoken tales of tricksters, personified natural forces, and sentient animals served as an all-inclusive cultural repository.

Many were learning stories, preparing Indian youth for the rigors of the forest and combat. Yet throughout these stories there runs a theme of the great love that the Indians had for their environment. Tales show great care in the laying out of the path of some journey through actual New England locations. Trails, fords, rivers, and mountains are all described with scrupulous accuracy.

Many of the mythic tales take place at the two northern New England locales apparently most beloved by the Abenaki, Mount Katahdin and the North Conway Intervale, where the abrupt eastern slope of the White Mountains rises out of the placid flat of the Saco River valley.

The Indians, while venerating these locations in legend, seem to have avoided scaling the mountains because of the spiritual powers envisioned there. The earliest English explorers of the White Mountains had great trouble inducing the Indians to accompany them into the heights to what the natives considered a certain death. Likewise, a colonist held captive by the Maine Indians around 1700 reported:

I have heard an Indian say that he lived by the river, at the foot of Teddon [Mount Katahdin], the top of which he could see through the hole of his wigwam left for the smoke to pass out. He was tempted to travel to it, and accordingly set out on a summer morning, and labored hard in ascending the hill all day, and the top seemed as distant from the place where he lodged at night as from his wigwam, where he began his journey. He now concluded the spirits were there, and never dared to make a second attempt. I have been credibly informed that several others have failed in like attempts. Once three young men climbed towards its summit three days and a half, at the end of which time they became strangely disordered with delirium, &c., and when their imagination was clear, and they could recollect where they were, they found themselves one day's journey. How they came to be thus transported they could not conjecture, unless the genii of the place had conveyed them.[6]

Indian Legends of the Ice Age

Some Algonkian tales have fascinating similarities with the course of events laid out by archaeologists in the last eras of the Ice Age — tales which suggest the giant animals which populated prehistoric times, and the drying of the land after the ice cap melted.

One story tells of how the great lord Glooskap came into the land of the Wabanaki and created the life therein. According to this tale, first came the elves and dwellers in the rocks, then the Indians, then the animals. Glooskap first made the animals big, but later reduced them in size to protect the Indians. Winter had been eternal in the land, but Glooskap tied a rope to Summer and pulled her north into the wigwam of the great giant, Winter, "And ere long the sweat ran down winter's face, and then he melted more and quite away, as did the wigwam. Then everything awoke; the grass grew, the fairies came out, and the snow ran down the rivers, carrying away the dead leaves. Then Glooskap left summer with them and went home."[a]

Perhaps the most intriguing story was told by a Penobscot to a white anthropologist friend in the 1930s. It is the story of a young brave named Snowy Owl, who lived in the north. In his search for a bride, Snowy Owl came upon "stiff-legged bears" who slept leaning against trees and whose tusks were so long they could pierce seven men at once:

He traveled far to the south, and on the way noticed how the lakes and rivers were drying up. Desiring to learn the cause of the water shrinkage, he ascended the valleys and finally reached a place where he saw what he thought were hillocks covered with brown vegetation moving slowly about. Upon closer scrutiny he learned that these masses were really the backs of great animals with long teeth, animals so huge that when they lay down they could not get up. He saw that they drank for half a day, thus taking up all the water in the basins of the land. Snowy Owl decided that some day he would have to kill them.[b]

Snowy Owl ultimately kills these strange creatures. With their deaths, the great woolly mammoths and the lake-filled landscape of postglacial times pass into Indian legend.

Mastodon skull unearthed in Connecticut.

The Abenaki had a quite sophisticated system of spiritual belief. The modern-day image of a "powwow" is of a peace conference. For the Abenaki it was more of a Black Mass, or Walpurgisnacht, where the tribal shaman would call up spirits to send out on a mission of vengeance.

For the Abenaki, survival required constant placation of possibly harmful forces. The remains of a catch were not casually discarded, but returned to their own habitat, lest the spirits of that species take offense and make further catches of their kind impossible.

As a rule, Algonkian Indians mentally allied themselves to various natural and spirit forces, in hopes of help in their struggle for survival. They assumed that these spirits could see into their very minds and detect weakness or fear. To exist in such a world, the Indian must never express a vulnerable emotion, even in his most inner thoughts, lest the spirits find him unworthy.

With the coming of the Europeans, Indian life quickly changed. The men now hunted beavers for the trading posts, whole tribes succumbed to European diseases, and the land slowly changed from forest to colonial settlements.

Indian hunting game at Bash-Bish Falls, Massachusetts.

3 *Early European Contacts and Settlements*

1524–1675

 The men of Giovanni da Verrazano's 1524 voyage of exploration along America's Atlantic coast were the first Europeans to report sighting New England's mountains. They came up from the south into Maine coastal waters "and distant in the interior [they] saw lofty mountains, but none which extended to the shore."[1] From here, the White Mountains are little more than fifty miles inland, and on clear days their alpine summits are easily discernible at sea.

Verrazano met with the local Abenaki, who apparently had previously had bad experiences with European fishermen coasting down from the Grand Banks. Verrazano attempted to trade, but, said Verrazano, "no regard was paid to our courtesies; when we had nothing left to exchange with them, the men at our departure made the most brutal signs of disdain and contempt possible."[2]

These "signs" remain undescribed. However, when the seventeenth-century colonist William Wood assembled a short Indian vocabulary during his stay along the Maine coast, he included among the names, places, and common terms needed for communication with the natives, only one scatological phrase, "Chickachava." According to Wood, a Puritan, upon hearing this word, has been given liberty to kiss a certain portion of the Indian's posterior anatomy.[3]

Relations between the Europeans and the Abenaki grew even worse over the next century. It became an all-too-common event for the crew of a European vessel, usually English, to rob, enslave, or generally maltreat the coastal tribes. The Abenaki's growing animosity against the English later had profound importance for the whole course of upland New England's colonial history.

For much of the 1500s, however, the Abenaki and their neighbors had other problems greater than sporadic plundering by European vessels. They experienced frequent attacks by the Micmacs (called the Tarrantines by the colonists) from along the Gulf of Saint Lawrence.

To the west, beyond the Mahicans (as differentiated from the Mohawks of New York and the Mohegans of southeastern Connecticut), who occupied the Taconics and eastern shores of the Hudson, lived the Iroquois, a nation composed of a half-dozen tribes of non-Algonkian invaders who had taken over upper New York State. For a long time the various Iroquois tribes effectively neutralized themselves with intertribal slaughter, leaving their Algonkian neighbors in relative peace. About the year 1570, however, two leaders were able to organize the squabbling tribes into a political confederacy, and the Iroquois turned from internal bloodletting toward rampage upon others.

The Mohawk tribe of the Iroquois nation invaded New England. They soon controlled all the Champlain Basin well up into the Green Mountains.

Territorial conquest, however, came second to their main interest — extortion. The Mohawks descended upon village after village clad in arrow-proof armored suits of tree bark, screaming, "We have come to drink your blood!"

Where other victorious tribes might end a conflict with the ritual torture of enemy braves, adopting the wives and children into their own community, Mohawk raids always ended with well-orchestrated atrocities. Slaughtering all, in the most disgusting manners they could contrive, the Mohawks gained their end. The mere discovery of a few warning arrows placed by a Mohawk band near an Algonkian village would set the inhabitants into a panic. Ultimately the Mohawk were able to make annual rounds exacting tribute from tribes as far east as Maine.

Just after 1600, European colonists found themselves choosing up sides in this Iroquois-Algonkian conflict. The French became allies of the Algonkian, the English and Dutch with the Iroquois. In 1604, Samuel de Champlain arrived in the Canadian Maritimes as official geographer for the first French attempt at a northern settlement. Their plan was to win the friendship of the natives and establish a bustling fur trade.

Voyaging down the New England coast, they saw the White Mountains from Casco Bay: "From here large mountains are seen to the west, in which is the dwelling-place of a savage captain called Aneda, who encamps near the river Quinibequy."[4] Champlain's active interest in the Indians and the scrupulous care taken to treat them as friends quickly established good Abenaki-French relations.

After a few aborted attempts at settlements in this area, the French gave up and headed up the Saint Lawrence. There, at the site of Quebec, they made allies of the more northern Algonkian tribes.

In 1609, Champlain explored south from Quebec, accompanying a war party of Saint Lawrence Valley Algonkian and others bent on attacking the hated Iroquois. They reached Champlain's namesake lake: "Continuing our course over this lake on the western side, I noticed, while observing the country, some very high mountains on the eastern side, on the top of which there was snow."[5] According to the Indians in Champlain's group, the Vermont shore had "beautiful valleys . . . with plains productive in grain [Indian corn] . . . together with many kinds of fruit without limit."[6]

While later experts dispute the statement, Champlain says he was told that the Iroquois then dwelt there. With the Green Mountains on their left, the French ex-

*Champlain's drawing of his defeat of the Iroquois at Ticonderoga in 1609. In his **Voyages** (Paris, 1613), he said: "I rested my musket against my cheek, and aimed directly at one of the three chiefs. With the same shot, two fell to the ground; and one of their men was so wounded that he died some time after. I had loaded my musket with four balls." This battle created the French-Algonkian and English-Iroquois alliances that lasted for the whole colonial era.*

plorers made their way south and ultimately met the Iroquois in a battle whose victory was decided by French firepower. The disciplined Iroquois warriors clad in the bark armor advanced in close array, led by their chiefs, who were quickly slain by Champlain's firepower. From that day forth, the French acquired the Algonkian as their beloved allies, and the whole Iroquois nation as their eternal enemy.

Mortal sickness among the New England Indians, ca. 1618.

As the French established themselves in Canada, warfare was breaking out between the Eastern Abenaki and the Tarrantines (Micmacs). From 1607 until 1615 hostilities persisted. In 1614, John Smith arrived in a vessel to fish and trade for pelts along the Maine coast. He listed all the various local tribes, then reported, "Though most be lords of themselves, yet they hold the Bashabes of Pennobscot the chief and greatest amongst them."[7] In 1615 this chief was killed and his people fell to the Tarrantines.

Yet the carnage from these intertribal wars was nothing to the plagues that were simultaneously ravaging the Indians. Improvements in European shipbuilding and navigation at that time allowed Europeans to cross the Atlantic more quickly than the time it took for smallpox and other diseases to complete their infectious period. A sailor could acquire a disease for which the Indians had no immunity before he shipped out of some European port and be still a carrier of contagion when he set foot in the New World.

The effect on the Indians was appalling. The Massachusetts coast was virtually wiped clean of Indians. Inland, tribes vanished like drifting wisps of smoke. The mortality rate for the Eastern Abenaki was 75 percent; for the Western Abenaki it was a horrible 98 percent. The Pocumtuck of the Deerfield River in the Berkshires suffered a 95 percent rate, the Mahicans, farther to the west, had a 91 percent death rate.

By mid-seventeenth century, these tribes, whose populations once ranged from 5,000 for the Mahicans, to 10,000 for each of the two Abenakis, and 15,000 for the Pocumtuck, now had postepidemic populations of 3,000 for the Eastern Abenaki, 800 for the Pocumtuck, 500 for the Mahicans, and 250 for the Western Abenaki.[8]

It was a civilization suddenly vanished. Those who survived suffered continued Mohawk assaults. While there were only scattered Algonkian remnants to raid, the New England Indians had by then converted from sustenance hunting and farming to an economy based on hunting furs for European traders. This made better pickings for the Mohawks.

The Europeans, English, Dutch, and French, all traded with the Indians for beaver pelts. The beaver, stripped of its shaggy longer hairs, shows a sleek undercoat. However, unlike the deer, moose, and bear, the beaver was not the kind of creature to be caught by sheer gunpowder. It required expertise and great patience, items apparently lacking in the English colonists: "These beasts are too cunning for the English, who seldom or never catch any of them, therefore we leave them to those skillful hunters whose time is not so precious, who experience-bought skill hath made them practical and useful in that regard."[9]

In the early colonial age, many Indians abandoned their shore encampments, setting up more permanent villages among the beaver-rich hills and lakes of the interior. They now came downriver only to trade for European goods — guns, needles, cookpots, knives, hatchets, beads, broadcloth — and corn (maize) raised by the colonists of southern New England.

During most of the seventeenth century, the Indians traded with the English to the south, the French to the north in Canada, and the Dutch along the Hudson. Some tribes ran a dual business, catching fur animals, "which they bring down into the [Massachusetts] bay, returning back loaded with English commodities of

Beaver dam, Pinkham Notch, White Mountains, New Hampshire.

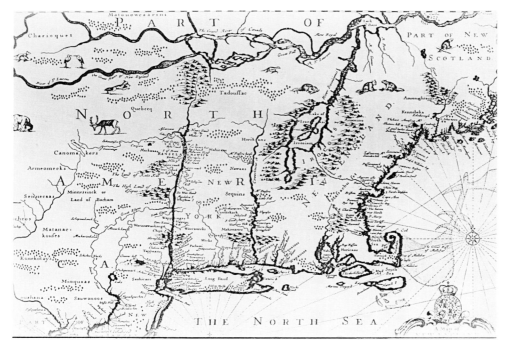

which they make a double profit by selling them to more remote Indians who are ignorant at what cheap rates they obtain them."[10]

Along the Connecticut and Merrimack rivers, the trade was regulated by the English government. William Pynchon received the monopoly for the Connecticut River trade and in 1636 set up a trading post–settlement that grew into Springfield, Massachusetts. The early towns inland around Boston — Lancaster, Chelmsford, and Concord — all started as trading posts. Royalist patents supposedly controlled the Maine coast trade, but these were usually ignored.

There was constant friction over the right to trade for the beaver skins. The English fought the French. The Puritans fought the Pilgrims. The government fought with its own citizens, barring them from venturing into the wilderness to trade on their own. Nevertheless, many English went up into the hills with goods to trade for pelts. Some were agents of legitimate trading posts, others free-lanced.

Little is recorded of these traders and their travels, except when officials period-ically recorded a trader's death after an Indian decided to obtain the "truck goods" by violent means. Records show more deaths of whites killing whites than inter-racial murders. There was even a shootout on the Kennebec at one point between the Plymouth and New Hampshire factions over who would trade on the river.

The need to outflank one's competitors did encourage forays of exploration into the wilderness. While the English knew the New England shore and fishing grounds with great familiarity, their knowledge of the interior was most rudimen-tary. They knew of mountains inland, and heard from the Indians of a great lake to the west, which the English supposed was some kind of beaver El Dorado. Like-wise this "Lake of the Iroquois" was reportedly well stocked with delicious fish, surrounded by countryside abounding in edible fruits and nuts. Secure islands would provide excellent places for safe habitation, and of course the whole region abounded in game.

Unfortunately the Puritans could not yet differentiate Lake Winnipesaukee from Lake Champlain from the Great Lakes, combining all descriptions into one lake.

The First Explorations of the White Mountains

In the spring of 1642, Darby Fields became the first person to ascend the White Mountains' highest peak. Wrote John Winthrop, governor of Massachusetts Bay Colony:

One Darby Field, an Irishman, living about Pascataquack [Piscataqua, near modern Portsmouth, New Hampshire], being accompanied with two Indians, went to the top of the white hill [Mount Washington]. He made the journey in 18 days. His relation at his return was, that it was about one hundred miles from Saco, that after about 40 miles travel he did, for the most part, ascend, and within 12 miles of the top was neither tree nor grass, but low savins [juniper], which they went upon the top of sometimes, but a continual ascent upon rocks, on a ridge between two valleys filled with snow, out of which came two branches of Saco river, which met at the foot of the hill where was an Indian town of some 200 people. Some of them accompanied him within 8 miles of the top, but durst go no further, telling him that no Indian ever dared to go higher, and that he would die if he went. So they staid there till his return, and his two Indians took courage by his example and went with him. They went divers times through thick clouds for a good space, and within 4 miles of the top they had no clouds, but very cold. By the way, among the rocks, there were two ponds, one a blackish water and the other reddish [Lakes of the Clouds]. The top of all was a plain about 60 feet square. On the north side there was such a precipice, as they could scarce discern to the bottom [Great Gulf]. They had neither cloud nor wind on the top, and moderate heat. All the country about him seemed a level, except here and there a hill rising above the rest, but far beneath him [monadnocks above the peneplain]. He saw to the north a great water which he judged to be about 100 miles broad, but could see no land beyond it. The sea by Saco seemed as if it had been within 20 miles. He saw also a sea to the eastward, which he judged to be the gulf of Canada: he saw some great waters in parts to the westward, which he judged to be the great lake which Canada river comes out of. He found there much muscovy glass [mica], they could rive out pieces of 40 feet long and 7 or 8 broad. When he came back to the Indians, he found them drying themselves by the fire, for they had a great tempest of wind and rain. About a month after he went again with five or six in his company, then they had some wind at the top, and some clouds above them which hid the sun. They brought back some stones which they supposed had been diamonds, but they were most crystal [quartz].[a]

Field's expeditions caused quite a stir, and Winthrop reports in October of 1642:

Mention is made before of the white hills, discovered by one Darby Field. The report he brought

View from the top of Mount Washington, looking north. Photograph by Franklin White, April 10, 1861.

of shining stones, etc., caused divers others to travel thither, but they found nothing worth their pains. Amongst others, Mr. Gorges and Mr. Vines, two of the magistrates of Sir Fernando Gorges his province [the eastern half of Maine] went thither about the end of this month. They went up Saco river in birch canoes, and that way, they found it 90 miles to Pegwagget, an Indian town [Fryeburg, Maine], but by land it is but 60.... From the Indian town, they went up hill (for the most part) about 30 miles in woody lands, then they went about 7 or 8 miles upon shattered rocks, without tree or grass, very steep all the way. At the top is a plain about 3 or 4 miles over, all shattered stones, and up that is another rock or spire, about a mile in height, and about an acre of ground at the top. At the top of the plain arise four great rivers, each of them so much water, at the first issue, as would drive a mill; Connecticut river . . . Saco river . . . Amascoggen [Androscoggin] . . . and Kennebeck. The mountain runs E. and W. 30 or 40 miles, but the peak is above the rest. They went and returned in 15 days.[b]

Their maps show this supposed lake not far in from the coast, and a number of English expeditions had been sent across the Atlantic with orders to sail up Maine and New Hampshire rivers for its discovery.[11]

These explorations revolved around what was called the Laconia Grant, a track of land extending inland in the general region of the New Hampshire–Maine border, bounded by the Kennebec on the east, the Merrimac on the west, and the "River of Canada" (Saint Lawrence) on the north. The English Royalists under Sir Fernando Gorges, a wealthy man of Plymouth, England, believed that their fabulous lake lay within these bounds.

In 1632 an exploration party under Walter Neal, captain of the Laconia Company's little settlement along the New Hampshire shore, set out to explore the interior. Historians argue as to their actual itinerary.[12] The best argument theorizes that the English headed north toward the "Crystal Hills" (White Mountains). Making their way through this range, they were dismayed to look down on a land "daunting terrible, full of rocky hills as thick as mole-hills in a meadow, and clothed with infinite thick woods."[13] They pushed onward for a while longer, but ultimately turned back for lack of provisions, convinced that they had almost reached their goal, reporting that "the [lake's] discovery wanted but one day's journey of being finished."[14] Neal apparently also made further explorations within the bounds of the Laconia Grant, but there is little description of his finds.

The New England beaver trade did not last more than a few decades. Unlike migratory animals, which repopulate back into overhunted territories, beavers, once their dens are emptied, are no more.

The Indians pushed farther and farther into the hills, but by the 1640s, the number of pelts exported from New England had dwindled. Canada, the Great Lakes region, upstate New York, and the Midwest became the prime fur areas. The Abenaki and other tribes had abandoned their old life-styles for an economy that, within a few decades, had consumed itself.

In 1637, a group of Abenaki appeared at the French trading station in Canada, hoping to buy furs with wampum. It seems that the English offered better rates for the pelts. The French preferred that the Saint Lawrence Algonkian remain ignorant of this, so the French rebuffed the Abenaki, seized their arquebuses, and sent them back south.

A Jesuit priest among the Indians.

Yet while the business element of the French in Canada stayed hostile to Abenaki visits — in 1649 a group of thirty came up and were allowed to leave with twenty bundles of beaver pelts, but with the warning "not to come again or their goods [would] be plundered if they return[ed]"[15] — the French Jesuit missionaries began to take an interest in these tribes of northern New England.

The Jesuits had at first left New England alone; it lay within the French-defined province of Acadia, where missionary efforts had been allotted to the Capuchin order. However, in 1642, a few converted Canadian Indians visited and preached to the upriver Kennebec tribes. One Abenaki chief, impressed with what he heard, accompanied the missionaries back to Canada for baptism.

That same year, Canadian Algonkians made prisoner of an upper Connecticut River valley Sokoki. When the Jesuits heard of his tortures, one French and one Indian missionary set out in a canoe to effect his rescue. The French priest died on the journey, but the Indian missionary was soon able to send the Sokoki home with glad news of how one of these "Black Robes," as the Jesuit priests were called, had sacrificed his life to free the Sokoki and bring him the word of God.

With word spreading among the Western Abenaki, and Eastern Abenaki delegations coming up to the Saint Lawrence to reproach the Black Robes for not send-

"Penobscot Belle," from a daguerreotype, ca. 1848.

ing missionaries to teach them the path of eternal salvation, the Jesuits were eager for official permission to move into northern New England. It soon came.

By mid-seventeenth century, Iroquois victories against the French and the subsequent slaughter of their Canadian Algonkian allies drastically reduced French fur territory. The French desperately needed the Abenaki in the struggle against the Iroquois.

In August 1646, the Jesuit priest, Père Druillettes, embarked on a one-year mission among the Eastern Abenaki. He had a fourfold task — to visit the many English and French trading posts along the upper Maine coast, break the Indians away from their practice of trading furs for alcohol, make peace among the various squabbling tribes, and wrest the Abenaki souls from the jealous grip of their medicine men.

The Indians built him a chapel upriver from the Plymouth Colony's trading post at present-day Augusta. Druillettes returned to Canada the next summer, and the natives grieved, but converts continued his efforts.

In 1650 Druillettes again set out in a bark canoe, portaged over the height of land, crossed Moosehead Lake, and descended the Kennebec. This time his mission had even greater importance for the French. He was to cement an alliance against the Iroquois, not only between the various Abenaki tribes but also between the English Puritans and the French.

He succeeded with the Indians, but not with the English. Though he journeyed far down the coast, appealing to the Plymouth Colony to protect the Indians within the Kennebec trading region, which they then held in possession, and spoke with the leading Puritans of Boston, the English were not inclined to poke a stick into the Iroquois hornet's nest.

Druillettes did, however, enact a treaty between the Saint Lawrence River Algonkian, the Mahicans along the New England–New York border (which included the Housatonic of the western Berkshires and, to the south in Connecticut, the Wyachatonok), the Pocumtuck of the Deerfield River drainage in the Berkshires, the Sokoki of the Connecticut River valley, and the Penacook of the Merrimack River valley. The Eastern Abenaki apparently stayed out of this alliance, a decision that would later serve them well.

In 1664, the Dutch surrendered their control of the Hudson River to the English. The Mohawks quickly signed a treaty of alliance with the English, which declared English neutrality in any Mohawk hostilities against Algonkian tribes along the northern flank of New England's colonial settlements.

Within a few decades, the Mohawks swept through northern New England, decimating the Jesuits' confederacy. By the early 1670s, the Pocumtuck were scattered from their Deerfield River home and the Sokoki abandoned their Northfield, Massachusetts, stockade and retreated about a hundred miles up the Connecticut River to a fort in Newbury, Vermont. The Penacook too were broken, and their remaining population congregated down the Merrimack within the Massachusetts Bay Colony. While not actually part of the conflict, even the Eastern Abenaki received some damage at Iroquois hands. Only the Mahicans in the border area of western Connecticut and Massachusetts, and eastern New York still held out against the Mohawk Iroquois.

For the rest of the Western Abenaki, the few survivors gradually migrated north to the Saint Lawrence and the Jesuits' missionary settlement of Saint Francis, leaving the lands of the Western Abenaki virtually uninhabited.

4 *Indian Wars and Colonial Settlements*

1675–1763

For almost the first fifty years of colonial settlements in New England, most towns and villages hugged the shoreline or larger river valleys. Only a few trading posts had appeared within the bounds of the upland region. However, by the 1660s, the steady depopulation of the inland region, from Mohawk depredations against the Western Abenaki, enticed Puritan authorities to contemplate "plantations" among the interior hills. Some of these settlements flourished, others were transient affairs, for New England was about to undergo almost a hundred years of sporadic warfare between the English settlers and the French and Indian alliance in Canada.

One of the earliest upland "plantings'" was midway along the Bay Path, that old Indian trail through the hills of central Massachusetts, connecting the Connecticut River valley with Massachusetts Bay. In a valley intervale along the course of the Quaboag River, in the modern town of West Brookfield, Massachusetts, lay fertile meadows cleared by the Nipnet Indians. Steep hills rose up a few hundred feet to enclose the valley.

In 1665, six families from Ipswich arrived to begin the settlement. The colonists laid out their plots of land along the flat crest of an oblong hill at the northern edge of meadows, near where the Bay Path ascended out of the valley to wind around the north side of the hill. Quabaug Plantation was a classic hill town. It commanded a fine lookout in most directions, looking out over the valley below toward the hills beyond. It stood far above the river's seasonal caprices, kept the homes out of the marsh and mosquitoes of the lowlands, and left the damp, fertile soil for better uses than houselots.

The village was simply a line of houses, all facing south for the sunlight. The town grew slowly, and ten years after the first settlers arrived, a traveler looking up toward the ridgeline would have seen only some dozen farms, a meetinghouse, a burial ground, and a tavern for travelers along the Bay Path. Just opposite the houses, along the south side of Town Street, were the barns and other outbuildings.

Each "planter" family owned a relatively narrow strip of land stretching north to the Bay Path and south down into the Quaboag meadows. These long thin lots contained from twenty to ninety acres and were the typical division of land in early New England settlements.

Some homes were imposing clapboarded "garrisons," those antique homesteads with a slight overhang of the second story in front and with a long slope in back down to the rear lean-to. Others were simply one-room shells of rough plank, with roofs of local thatch. For many settlers, the barns of their cattle were more substantial than their own simple domiciles.

Quabaug Plantation, lacking the twenty families needed to qualify as an independent town, came under Springfield's jurisdiction. As on any frontier, it was a rough-and-tumble life, with problems of "unseasonable night meetings," illegitimate children, profane men, and scolding wives, all in a population of fifty-odd.[1]

For the most part, however, the people of this small huddle of brown houses along a wilderness trail spent their lives following the plow, herding their cattle, hunting the woods, carrying their corn to the mill, making the homespun garments, bartering for wovenwork with the Indians at their lakeside camp less than an hour's walk down the valley, and resting on the Sabbath.

The late 1660s and early 1670s had been a relatively peaceful time for New England colonists, but by the mid-1670s, Metacomet, styled King Philip by the English, convinced his Narragansett Bay tribe that it was now or never to rid themselves of the ever-growing English settlements, and in the summer of 1675 began raiding colonial villages in southern New England. The Wampanoag were quickly joined by other tribes, including many Abenaki groups. These more northern tribes were motivated by a sense of insult from English treatment and an eye for the possible plunder that might come of their surprise raids.

The war reached Quabaug on Sunday, August 1, 1675.

On that day, a party of troops arrived from Massachusetts Bay Colony to inform the village that war had broken out with King Philip of the Wampanoag and they should attempt a treaty of peace with the local Nipnet. Scouts set out and arranged a rendezvous some miles north of town. The expedition set out and found no one at the site. Three Quabaug men, convinced that ten years of amity with the Nipnet could not dissolve in a day, insisted the troops push on toward the Indian camp. They were the first to die in the ensuing ambush.

The troops retreated to Quabaug and gathered everyone they could into the tavern, the village's most substantial building.

The full attack came a few hours later:

The barbarous heathen pressed upon us in the house with great violence, sending in their shot amongst us like hail through the walls, and shouting as if they would have swallowed us up alive; but our good God wrought wonderfully for us, so that there was but one man wounded within the house. . . . There was the same day another man slain, but not in the house; a son of Sergeant Prichard's adventuring out of the house wherein we were, to his Father's house not far from it, to fetch more goods out of it, was caught by those cruel enemies as they were coming towards us, who cut off his head, kicking it about like a foot-ball, and then putting it upon a pole, they set it up before the door of his Father's house in our sight.[2]

The one hundred whites spent the next three days returning shots and dousing fire arrows. All the while, the attackers

continued their shooting and shouting, and proceeded in their former wickedness, blaspheming the name of the Lord, and reproaching us, his afflicted servants, scoffing at our prayers as they were sending in their shot upon all quarters of the house and many of them went to the town's meeting house (which was within twenty rods of the house in which we were) who mocked, saying come and pray, and sing psalms, and in contempt made a hideous noise, somewhat resembling singing.[3]

Help finally arrived. Some cattle drovers, who had just entered the town during the initial attack, had returned east to sound the alarm.

A troop of sixty men arrived, attacked the Indians from the rear, and then dashed through to join their besieged comrades. The Indians burned the town and retreated to the woods.

The villagers quickly abandoned Quabaug Plantation and once again, the hills belonged to the wandering Indian. The story of Quabaug-Brookfield became a common litany for New England's next eighty years, although the endings usually did not have the cavalry arriving in time.

On February 10, 1676, the Indians destroyed the frontier town of Lancaster, Massachusetts. Mary Rowlandson described the death of her townsfolk:

There were twelve killed, some shot, some stabbed with their spears, some knocked down with their hatchets. When we are in prosperity, oh the little we think of such dreadful sights, to see our dear friends and relations lie bleeding out their hearts-blood upon the ground. There was one who was chopt in the head with a hatchet, and stript naked, and yet was crawling up and down. It was a solemn sight to see so many Christians lying in their blood, some here and some

Frontispiece of A Narrative of the Captivity, Sufferings and Removes of Mary Rowlandson (Boston, 1778).

there, like a company of sheep torn by wolves; all of them stript naked by a company of hell-hounds, roaring, singing, ranting, and insulting, as if they would have torn our very hearts out; yet the Lord, by his almighty power, preserved a number of us from death, for there were twenty-four of us taken alive and carried captive.[4]

King Philip took the captives and his followers west, to avoid English pursuit. He stopped short of the Berkshires, however, for the Mohawks were still attacking New England tribes.

Mary Rowlandson and her fellow captives were finally ransomed back to the English, and her written account had little good to say about Puritan military competence. Philip's "army" included hundreds of baggage-laden squaws, children, and few provisions. The Indians' "flight" was more of a mass forage, while their mounted pursuers balked at every river crossing.

The enemy in such distress for food that our men might track them by their rooting the ground for ground-nuts, whilst they were flying for their lives. . . . But what shall I say? . . . I cannot but admire to see the wonderful providence of God in preserving the heathen for further affliction to our poor country. They could go in great numbers over [a river], but the English must stop.[5]

Triumphal march into Plymouth, Massachusetts, with King Philip's head.

Within a year, King Philip's severed head looked down from a pole at Plymouth. While the southern tribes surrendered, the northern tribes kept up their raids on isolated settlements, stripping the homes and fields of whatever they could carry away, and seizing hostages for later ransom.

The English finally gave in and asked for peace. It was a defeat. The Eastern Abenaki agreed to cease hostilities and release all captives, but the English promised them a yearly tribute of corn — one peck for each English family living within the tribe's claimed territory.

While the war drove the English to abandon most of the Maine coast and many of the interior settlements of southern New England, it did stimulate further expansion, although sometimes short-lived. The removal of defeated tribes opened new regions. Descriptions of Indian trails, fertile valleys, and cleared lands in the captivity stories such as Mary Rowlandson's gave patchwork glimpses of New England's interior.

When peace came in 1678, many newly discovered places became infant settlements. Yet few survived, for King Philip's War was just the opening battle in a series of conflicts that spanned almost ninety years.

Peace lasted only a decade. In 1689 an Iroquois army of some 1,500 warriors massacred the village of La Chine, not far from Montreal. The French, convinced that the British had inspired the raid, initiated organized warfare against English settlements along the whole New York–Maine frontier. From 1689 to 1763, when the French finally surrendered Canada, every European conflict witnessed the French and Indians carrying the battle to the Puritan frontier.

In all, there were four colonial wars fought as part of European conflicts and two sparked by English-Indian conflicts that were strictly American. There were King Philip's War (1675–1678), King William's War (1689–1697), Queen Anne's War (1702–1713), Lovewell's or Dummer's War (1722–1725), King George's War (1744–1748), and the French and Indian War (1754–1763) — almost forty years of actual conflict.

Life in the New England interior became the repeated litany of settlements suddenly attacked, the houses burned, the cattle shot with arrows, the men killed, and the survivors wringing their hands and crying for God's mercy as they "walked the woods," in the harrowing march to Canada and slavery.

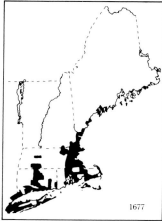

Pushing the frontier into northern New England, from the beginning of the Indian Wars to 1812, after L. K. Matthews, **The Expansion of New England** *(Boston, 1909).*

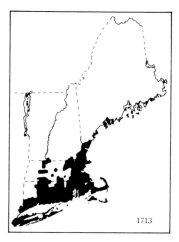

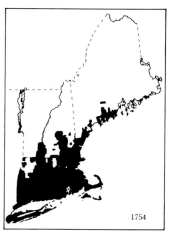

In a 1754 raid against Charlestown, New Hampshire, Indians captured seven settlers, among them the Johnson family. On the way north to Canada, the mother delivered a child, who was named Elizabeth Captive Johnson. Forty years later, the mother returned from Canada to what had become Cavendish, Vermont, and had a stonemason mark the site of her encampment, from which she had walked a half-mile up a brook to deliver the child. A second stone was to be placed at the site of the birth, but instead it, too, was placed at the encampment site.

The Indian proved a master at his style of warcraft. Wrote a Jesuit among the Abenaki:

The manner in which these people make war, renders a handful of their warriors more formidable, than would be a body of two or three thousand European soldiers. As soon as they have entered the enemy's country, they divide themselves into different parties, one of thirty warriors, another of forty, &c. They say to each other, "To you, we give this hamlet to devour," (that is their expression), "To those others we give this village &c." In this way our two hundred and fifty warriors spread themselves over more than twenty leagues of country, filled with villages . . . on the day designated they made their attack together early in the morning, and in that single day swept away all that the English possessed there.[6]

With the destruction of many southern New England tribes and the migration to Canada of those Western Abenaki that survived the Mohawk War, by 1700, the Eastern Abenaki found themselves the largest remaining upland New England tribe.

Many had congregated to villages with Jesuit missionaries. The most famous Catholic apostle to the Abenaki was Sebastien Rale (1658–1724), who in 1693 took over the chapel at Norridgewock, on the Kennebec River. It was an important location in colonial times, for the river marked the boundary between English New England and French Acadia. The river also provided an avenue north to a low pass over the hills to the Chaudière River, which flows north into the Saint Lawrence, a good route to control in times of war.

Since 1646, Jesuits had come to Norridgewock, a hundred-acre tongue of intervale, bordered on three sides by the curving Kennebec. The village itself, a half-mile road of wigwams, sat on a risen section of the meadow. Just upriver, falls provided salmon and other fish during the spring runs. Fields along the river here added to the large arable plot of the intervale itself. Like many other major Indian villages, Norridgewock had a most scenic surrounding. Edging the valley land, hills rose to provide an inspiring panorama.

In Rale's day a stockade, 150 feet on a side, rose in the center of the village street. At either end of the street stood small prayer chapels, one for the men going on a hunt, the other for women going to tend crops. The women's chapel was always adorned with bits of bright cloth and other ornaments.

Site of the Norridgewock, Maine, settlement as it appeared in 1849. The monument at right commemorates Fr. Rale. It was later pushed over.

What really set Norridgewock off from most Indian villages was the large church rising in its midst, built, according to one account, by Boston carpenters in reparation for another burned in previous hostilities.

This edifice, according to Rale,

possessed a beauty which would cause it to be admired even in Europe, and nothing has been spared to adorn it. . . . I have, indeed, thought it my duty to spare nothing either in the decoration of the building itself, or in the beauty of those articles which were used in our holy ceremonies. Vestments, chasubles, copes, and holy vessels, all are highly appropriate, and would be esteemed so even in our Churches in Europe. I have also formed a little choir of about forty young Indians, who assist at Divine Service in cassocks and surplices.[7]

Bayberry, abundant along the seashore, provided candles to illuminate the interior with a blaze surpassing even the greatest cathedrals of the Old World.

Rale himself spent his days in a hectic schedule of mass, prayer, catechism, visiting the sick, receiving visiting Indians of other tribes, and answering the constant spiritual questioning of his converts. Unfortunately, Jesuit missionaries like Rale also sometimes served as "chaplains" on Indian raiding parties, and generally stirred up anti-English sentiment. By the early 1720s the Puritans had put a price on Rale's head.

The French had previously begun the practice of offering payment for scalps as well as hostages, and now the English also began paying scalp money. Little English militias appeared, braving the wilderness not so much for church and country as for the purse. In 1721, the Kennebec Abenaki declared war to push the many new English settlements back down the river. This conflict was known as Dummer's or Lovewell's War. In 1724, the English made a successful surprise attack on Norridgewock. When it was over, Rale lay dead and scalped. The survivors buried him beneath the ashes of his chapel, then either went east to join the Penobscots at Old Town, or made the journey north to Saint Francis, on the Saint Lawrence River. It was Saint Francis that became, as it is still today, the primary location of the Abenaki population. Here the Indians were ministered to by the Jesuits, from here they set out upon their southern raids, and here they returned with their English captives. Saint Francis lies at the mouth of the Richelieu River. From here, the mixed parties of French raiders and Indian braves could paddle upstream to Lake Champlain, then head up tributary rivers for short portages before making downstream runs to fall upon English settlements of the Mohawk, Hudson, and Connecticut River valleys.

For almost two hundred years thereafter, differing versions of the Rale story were passed down among New Englanders to justify their rabid anti-Catholicism, and by Catholic missionaries to the Algonkian, to fuel anti-Protestant feeling among the Indians.

A few years before Rale's death, a group of emigrants from northern Ireland came up New Hampshire's Merrimack River valley to settle. The Abenaki at Norridgewock made plans to massacre them. Rale, however, assumed them to be Catholic, and uttered the wonderfully enigmatic injunction for the Indians to leave these settlers alone, for "they would certainly go to hell if they meddled with the Irish."[8]

These frontier people were in actuality Scotch-Irish, that rugged breed of Presbyterians who had first been shipped across the Irish Sea to Ulster in the seventeenth century, only to decide again for a start in the New World in the early eighteenth.

Contemporary illustration of the Norridgewock raid and the death of Fr. Rale, from the broadside by James Franklin (Ben's older brother): **The Rebels Rewards or English Courage Displayed. Being a full and true Account of the Victory obtained over the Indians at Norridgiwock, on the Twelfth of August last, by the English Forces under the Command of Capt. John Harmon (Boston, 1724).**

They were quite a different breed from the more socially cohesive Puritans of New England, and soon became New England's first real frontiersmen.

When they first arrived in New England, their individuality and independence dismayed the Massachusetts Bay authorities, especially when they combined their voice with more upstart members of the old families in favor of less control by the Puritan authorities. In 1720, the Commonwealth of Massachusetts proclaimed:

That whereas. It appears that certain families recently arrived from Ireland, and others from this Province, have presumed to make a settlement ... [it is] ... ordered, that the said people be warned to move off within the space of seven months and if they fail to do so, that they be prosecuted and by the Attorney-General by suits of trespass and ejectment.[9]

A few of the Scotch-Irish families stayed within Massachusetts, allowed by the authorities to live in Worcester and other frontier towns, establishing Massachusett's western hill-country outposts of Rutland (1716), Blandford (1735), Colrain (1735), Pelham (1738), and Western (1741, now Warren).

Others went north into New Hampshire to settle along the upper Merrimack and slowly push west up into the hill country. Here, settlements like New Boston and New Ipswich adjoined Antrim, Dublin, Londonderry, Derryfield, Dunbarton, and Fitzwilliam.

The men and women who made up this Scotch-Irish breed along the frontier did not carry the abhorrence of the wilderness ingrained in generations of Puritan farmers, in whom a love for the woods was once even considered sinful and a punishable crime.

Over the first half of the eighteenth century, these men set off exploring and hunting in the New Hampshire forests. Some died at Indian hands, although the toll was less than in other stretches of the frontier.

The Saint Francis tribes (as they were called) also roamed the New Hampshire wilds, and captured young John Stark (1728–1822) trapping along the southern edge of the White Mountains. Brought to Canada and sold as a slave, he quickly assimilated all the wilderness cunning of his captors and ultimately rose to prominence among the Abenaki. When he finally returned to his New England homelands, he spread his formidable knowledge among his frontier companions.

While the Puritans sent the Scotch-Irish north toward a questionable fate, their own population spread west, into the Litchfield Hills, where their namesake village was settled beginning in 1720. In Massachusetts, families came over the Berkshire hills a few years later to occupy the lush Housatonic Valley. In the 1730s, Massachusetts authorities laid out townships for occupation along an old Indian path from Springfield, on the Connecticut River, over the southern Berkshires down to Great Barrington, in the Housatonic Valley. This path, for much of the colonial period, was the white settlers' only route through the hills. Here too the first settlers were the Scotch-Irish, settling towns like Blandford and Otis.

Farther north in the Berkshires, the land was still unsettled. The only sign of human life was the well-trodden Mohawk Trail, over which this tribe made their annual round of tribute collection. The whole trail actually extended almost to the Canadian Maritimes. Such was the extent of Mohawk vassalage.

Today, "Mohawk Trail" is the term still used to designate that section running through the northern Berkshires. It runs up the flat wide intervale of the Deerfield River until the valley becomes a deep meandering canyon, swinging north. The trail then ascends west over what the early settlers called Forbidden Mountain, the High Hoosac Mountains, crosses the ridge, and descends to follow the Hoosic River valley west to the Hudson.

It was in this intervale at the base of Forbidden Mountain that white settlers first came to build homes.

In 1735, Boston was allowed to sell, "for support of their poor and their free schools,"[10] Boston Plantations numbers One, Two, and Three, tracts which ultimately became Charlemont (the Deerfield River intervale), Colrain (mentioned above as a settlement of Scotch-Irish), and Pittsfield, respectively.

The plan was that, within five years, the townships should have a population of at least sixty families apiece — each living on a minimum of five cleared acres in a house no smaller than eighteen by eighteen feet with seven-foot ceilings. There was also land to be set aside for church, school, and minister's farm. Each was envisioned as a classic Puritan village: a tight hamlet around the town street and church.

In the case of Boston Plantation Number One, this never happened. Boston sold it lock, stock, and barrel to a speculator. He resold it to two others. They subdivided the tract and offered pieces to all comers. Real estate speculation had replaced the New English Canaan.

It wasn't until 1741 that a settler, Moses Rice by name and not a land speculator, bought land in Boston Plantation Number One.

Rice had reconnoitered the area, sleeping, according to family accounts, beneath a great dapple-trunked sycamore which hung over the streamside trail. He liked what he saw: a wide intervale with hills rising almost a thousand feet to the north and south, a good stream flowing down out of the hills that promised an excellent millsite, and, like Brookfield's location on the Bay Path halfway between the towns of Massachusetts Bay and the Connecticut River, Rice's site lay halfway along the two-days' journey from Deerfield Village to the far Massachusetts outpost west over the mountain.

Rice soon moved in with his family, and, within a year, two other families came to Charlemont. They, too, picked the best pockets of intervale land, leaving the town to consist of three far-spread homesteads, strung along the river valley. Although Rice soon built a gristmill, Charlemont was virtual wilderness. The deer, which prefer the low valleys to the hills, were abundant. One settler even built a low fence along a modest ledge in a nearby meadow. He enclosed the rest of the meadow with a high wall. Deer would jump the fence to browse in the dawn hours, but find themselves trapped within. This deer pound supplied easy meat for the valley family.

It wasn't long before Moses Rice saw a goodly traffic passing up the trail for the open lands west over the mountain. These were soldiers and workmen, en route to build a line of forts between the Connecticut River and the Dutch outposts of the Hudson River valley.

In the 1740s, the Massachusetts government established a string of forts along the northern border of that colony. It was 1744, and King George's War had come to the American colonies.

Along its northern border west of the Connecticut River, Massachusetts had six forts: Fort Dummer, which had been built earlier, before a readjustment of the boundary line left it in what was to become Vernon, Vermont; Burke's Fort, in the flat plain of Bernardston, an ancient streamed of the Connecticut River, which

Scenery near the site of Fort Massachuset. Photograph by Arthur Scott, ca. 1899.

now flowed down a channel farther east, over some low hills; Fort Morrison, in the intervale of Colrain, a half-dozen miles west of Bernardston; Fort Shirley, up in the hills north of Charlemont in what would become Heath; Fort Pelham, again in the hills in what would be Rowe; and, the most important of all, Fort Massachuset, over in the valley west of the Berkshires.

This outpost lay over the mountain in the flats of the Hoosic River valley and guarded the main north-south ford across the river. Some of the forts were of squared pine logs, laid one atop the other and held together by dovetailed ends and dowel connectors to produce a square enclosure sixty feet on a side and twelve feet high. The walls had no gunports: the force within commanded the surrounding area from towers built at the corners. Fort Massachuset housed a garrison of ten to twenty men. Fort Pelham, in the heights of Rowe, was the only larger construction. It complied with our image of the classic western cavalry fort; it was a high palisade of pine trunks, set upright against each other to form a two-hundred-by-four-hundred-foot stockade.

These forts served as a line of sentries, positioned about six miles apart, from which scouts would depart with provisions and dogs in the hopes of returning to exchange an Indian scalp for the hundred-pound bounty.

By 1745, the colonists had finished and manned Fort Massachuset, the farthest outpost, lying in the Berkshire Valley. The fort stood in the east-west valley of the Hoosic. To the south, Mount Greylock rose gradually to its great height. North across a ford, the ledges of Pine Cobble Mountain looked directly down into the fort's interior.

On August 19, 1746, an expedition of over 500 French and 200 Indians attacked the fort's 22 men, 3 women, and 5 children.

The colonists held out for a day and a half until they were almost out of ammunition. When the French offered terms, the English surrendered. That afternoon the French flag was raised over Massachusetts soil. Soon only a tumble of burned logs marked the site of Fort Massachuset. The only sign of its former habitation was a paper nailed to a charred post:

A fortified house.

The Captivity of Titus King of Charlemont

On a summer morning in 1755, six Abenaki from Saint Francis waited in the woods edging the Rice family fields. When the family came out to work their crop, they carried arms, but soon stacked them against some logs. When the Indians saw that the men had moved a comfortable distance from their muskets, they attacked. Moses Rice and another man were killed, and two others escaped, but Titus King and Rice's grandchild were captured and taken north through the wilderness. From King's account of the flight north (the spelling has been modernized by this author):

13 [he was captured on June 11] was up Early this morning having Little to Eat went on our way we had got So far now that the Indians began to give their Holler as their manner is to Signify how many they have Killed & taken The mountains were Very high Very hard to Pass them Sometimes I Felt So Faint that I Could not hold on one moment Longer but the great goodness of God I was Carried through all the Trials & Difficulties that he was Pleased to assign for me.

14 We now Ate up all our Provision this Day the Indians got as many Roots as they Could: in afternoon as we was on top of a Very high mountain there Came up a black Cloud & it Rained as Freely as Ever I Saw it the Clouds Seemed to almost meet the mountaintops they Pealed Some Bark and made a Little Shed & told me to Sit under it [the Indians] Pealed Elm bark and Flung Down to me Gave me a Knife to Scrape out the [insides] Which when I Ate it Seemed to Do me

Some good We got Some greens & boiled [them] that night & Drank the Soup we Lodged at the foot of this great mountain this night.[a]

King and the boy were taken up Lake Champlain to Canada and the Indian village of Saint Francis. King joined other English captives there. Many were children. The Indians hoped that these youth could be converted to Indian ways and grow up to swell the ranks of the Indians' gradually vanishing population.

Wrote King:

... An awful School this is for Children When We See how Quick they will Fall in with the Indian's ways nothing Seems to be more takin in Six months' time they Forsake Father & mother Forget their own Land Refuse to Speak their own tongue & Seemingly be

Wholly Swallowed up with the Indians: then the French Priests take great Pains to School the English Children in their Religion meeting Every morning at Nine of the Clock at the tolling of [the] bell Where they go with the Indian Children & are Catechized according to the Romish Principals.[b]

The boy lived six years with the Indians. King himself spent about two years in Canada before returning home by way of Europe.

August 20, 1746. These are to inform you that yesterday, about nine of the clock, we were besieged by, as they say, seven hundred French and Indians. They have wounded two men and killed one Knowlton. The General de Vaudreuil desired capitulations, and we were so distressed that we complied with his terms. We are the French's prisoners, and have it under the general's hand that every man, woman, and child shall be exchanged for French prisoners.[11]

Hostilities ended this time in 1748, not from any great victory, but from a cessation of the conflict in Europe.

Conflict resumed in 1754. This last and decisive confrontation between the French and English in America was the seven-year struggle called the French and Indian War.

Mindful that the uphill forts north of the Deerfield River never saw action, the Massachusetts military authorities abandoned them, leaving the Deerfield Valley folk to set up their own fortifications. Charlemont's Taylor brothers turned their two houses to face each other, ran walls to enclose the space between the houses, erected firing towers, and surrounded the whole with a palisade. The Rice family were a little less ambitious, simply putting up a stockade around the house.

In the summer of 1755, six Saint Francis Indians attacked the Rice family, killing two, and taking Titus King, who had moved in with the family during the Indian threats, and Rice's grandchild on the march to Canada.

While King and the boy unwillingly made the long march to Canada, by 1759, two Colrain men went voluntarily, with no Indian captors. They were member of a fighting unit called Rogers' Rangers. They marched north as avengers, to destroy, once and for all, what generations of New Englanders had seen as Satan's earthly abode.

The story of Major Robert Rogers and his expedition north to raze the Indians' refuge of Saint Francis is a classic fireside tale. By the late 1750s, the wars between the colonies and Canada produced a new breed of New Englander, known as the ranger. Developed out of the necessities of frontier life, this man could hunt and shoot like an Indian, and while his ability to ignore hunger and privation did not match that of his foe, still, the wilderness held no fear for him as it did for the Puritan farmer.

Many of these men joined up under Robert Rogers to become a welcome addition to the British regulars defending the Champlain-Hudson passageway between Canada and the colonies at New York.

The garrisoned redcoats suffered as much from small Indian raids as the colonists they defended. The Rangers' sallies against the enemy, in their own Indian style, strengthened morale in the British ranks. It also provided the high command with glowing reports to supplant their own lackluster activities in formal warfare.

On September 13, 1759, apparently after two British officers were added to a seemingly endless list of civilian captives seized by the Saint Francis Indians, two hundred men were ordered north under Rogers to wipe out the infamous village. "Take your revenge," urged the commanding general, Jeffrey Amherst, in his orders, but he added that, despite all Indian barbarities, "it is my orders that no women or children are killed or hurt."[12]

After enduring 150 miles of swamp, loss of provisions, bad weather, and enemy pursuit, they reached Saint Francis on October 5, 1759. The town was unguarded. The next morning, a half-hour before dawn, Rogers's men crept forward for the slaughter. Indian after Indian staggered from his bed in alarm only to meet swift death. The hacking and shooting ceased just after sunrise, and Rogers ordered the

whole village, save for three storehouses, burned. He wrote: "The fire consumed many of the Indians who had concealed themselves in the cellars and lofts of their houses. About seven o'clock in the morning the affair was completely over, in which time we had killed at least two hundred Indians."[13]

He also spared twenty women and children, releasing all but five children, and liberated five English captives. "We found in the town hanging on poles over their doors, &c. about 600 scalps, mostly English."[14]

Among the Rangers, there was only one dead and seven wounded.

Fearing a swift counterattack, reported Rogers, "I called the officers together, to consult the safety of our return, who were of the opinion there was no other way for us to return with safety but by [trekking due south to Fort] No. 4 on the Connecticut River."[15]

The party took booty and provisions and began their march south to the head-waters of the Saint Francis River valley. Eight days later, with supplies almost gone, they reached Lake Mephremagog, on the present Vermont border. Rogers divided the band into small groups, telling them to meet forty miles south at Coos Inter-vale, where the Ammonoosuc River empties into the Connecticut.

Many of the parties were overtaken by the enemy and met bad deaths; a few made it to the meadow, "after so many days tedious march over steep rocky mountains or thro' wet dirty swamps, with the terrible attendants of fatigue and hunger."[16] Deliverance still escaped the survivors. At Saint Francis, Rogers had dispatched a scout to creep back through enemy lines to Lake Champlain and arrange supplies to be sent up the Connecticut to the Coos Intervale. The rescue party waited only two days, then returned downriver,

taking all the provisions back with him, about two hours before our arrival. Find-ing a fresh fire burning in his camp, I fired guns to bring him back, which guns he heard but would not return supposing we were an enemy.

Our distress upon this occasion was truely inexpressible; our spirits, greatly depressed by the hunger and fatigues we had already suffered, now almost en-tirely sunk within us, seeing no resource left, nor any reasonable ground to hope that we should escape a most miserable death by famine.[17]

Leaving his men to subsist on boiled groundnuts and lily roots, Rogers, two men, and a captive boy set out on a raft down the river. They reached Fort No. 4, in lower New Hampshire, on October 31. Within a half-hour, rescue was on the way.

For weeks thereafter survivors straggled in at outposts both along the Connecti-cut River and Lake Champlain, telling tales of Job-like escapes from massacres, or of how they survived by cannibalizing the mangled remains they had found of another small group of fleeing Rangers that had been attacked by the pursuing Indians. Of the some 150 men who marched away from the ashes of Saint Francis, 49 never emerged from the wilderness.

Despite the grim toll, New England celebrated the victory. The Saint Francis raid became instant legend. No matter the costs, circumstances, or actual effect on the outcome of the war, the destruction of the Saint Francis Indians heralded the end of New England's long fear of Indian raid. The northern New England wilderness was now open to peaceful settlement.

A remnant of the old Crown Point military road, constructed by a company of Rangers under the direction of Colonel John Stark, in 1759. The road ran from the region of the Massachusetts–New Hampshire–Vermont border from Fort No. 4 diagonally northwest across Vermont to Crown Point on Lake Champlain, allowing movement of supplies and troops over the Green Mountains. This portion can be seen as a line of snow ridge slanting down through the woods in Weathersfield, Vermont.

Fort No. 4, as it has been reconstructed as a museum at Charlestown, New Hampshire.

5   Settling the Hills: The Revolution and Postwar Problems

1763–1791

With Canada in English hands and the Saint Francis Indians no longer a threat, the New England wilderness lost its ominous nature. Life changed completely in the frontier villages. Women and children no longer hovered by fortified doorways and men no longer plowed the field with an eye for their distance from their loaded firearms stacked nearby.

The New England hills now became a beckoning land, ready to accept all the pent-up extra population of the old lowland and shoreline communities. Likewise, it promised a ready escape for those too restless for life in the structured Puritan community. People seemed to pour into the hills. From the end of hostilities in the early 1760s, to 1776, New Hampshire founded some 100 new towns, Maine 94, and Vermont 74.

The new settlers did not, as in previous times, simply carve townships from the frontier edge, methodically extending the patchwork of New England farms and villages outward from the older communities. Instead, the pioneer families ventured far into the woods, laying out communities totally surrounded by wilderness. Sometimes the land was good; at other times the geography too hostile, but only after a protracted struggle did the people desist and try again elsewhere.

The speed with which many New Englanders embraced the idea of moving to the hills reflected both a philosophy of the era and the economic realities of the times. It was an age of terrible roads, muddy, rutted, usually only passable on horseback or during the winter freeze. Bulk transportation of perishable goods for any distance over ten or twenty miles was virtually impossible. Farmers made little attempt to grow more than they needed for family consumption, and took little interest in anything more than a marginally effective farm, which typically consisted of

one miserable team, a paltry plough, ... three acres of Indian corn, ... as many acres of half-starved English grain from a half-cultivated soil, with a spot of potatoes, and a small yard of turnips, [which] complete the round of his tillage, and the whole is conducted, perhaps, by a man and a boy. . . . All the rest of the farm is allotted for feeding a small stock. A large space must be mowed for a little hay for winter; and a large range for a little feed in summer.[1]

America was then a place with more land than people. Population was low, and even in the settled villages, there were usually outlying tracts that were unfarmed. Comparing American and British agriculture, George Washington commented on the problem that resulted from this imbalance:

The aim of the farmers in this country (if they can be called farmers) is, not to make the most from the land, which is or has been cheap, but the most of the labour, which is dear: the consequence of which has been, much ground has been scratched over, and none cultivated or improved as it ought to have been; whereas a farmer in England, where land is dear and labour cheap, finds it his interest to improve and cultivate highly that he may reap large crops from a small quantity of land.[2]

Land was cheap and obtainable, but there were few ways to profit from improved production. With nothing to sell, no one had money or need to hire farm laborers, and with land inexpensive, there was no reason to work for someone else when you could easily have our own farm. Even a village's few artisans, the miller, blacksmith, and others, also devoted a great percentage of their time to their own fields and the minor portion of their day to their crafts. In those days, one was expected to be a farmer. The professional class — the doctors, lawyers, ministers — were, according to some sources, those whom fate deemed unfit to become independent yeoman farmers. The following, we hope, is a bit exaggerated:

Now if among the growing family, one son has been unfortunate, — if a shoulder has been sprained, or a leg broken; if disease have debilitated the constitution for the rough labors of husbandry, or some hereditary ailment predisposed the victim to a shorter life; nay, if he be imbecile or idle, thriftless or lazy; he is the Levite of the flock, set apart for the profession[al career].[3]

The only extra hands that the farmer and his wife could count upon came from the constant production of little New Englanders, which they practiced, observed many an English visitor, with a husbandry far superior to the attention they gave their fields.

By the mid-nineteenth century, this era of farm self-sufficiency became "The Age of Homespun": "The house was a factory on the farm, the farm a grower and producer for the house."[4]

This constant reinvestment of the population into farming gradually pushed many out of the settled towns. "Our Lands being thus worn out, I suppose to be one Reason why so many are included to Remove to new Places. . . . As also that they may have more Room, thinking that we live too thick," wrote Jared Eliot in his classic 1760 essay on New England farming.[5]

In the wilderness, the thick humus required only the forester's ax and the warm sun to become an abundantly fertile soil. In the years just before the Revolutionary War the migration north became an exodus:

Those, who are first enclined to emigrate, are usually such, as have met with difficulties at home. These are commonly joined by persons, who, having large families and small farms, are induced, for the sake of settling their children com-

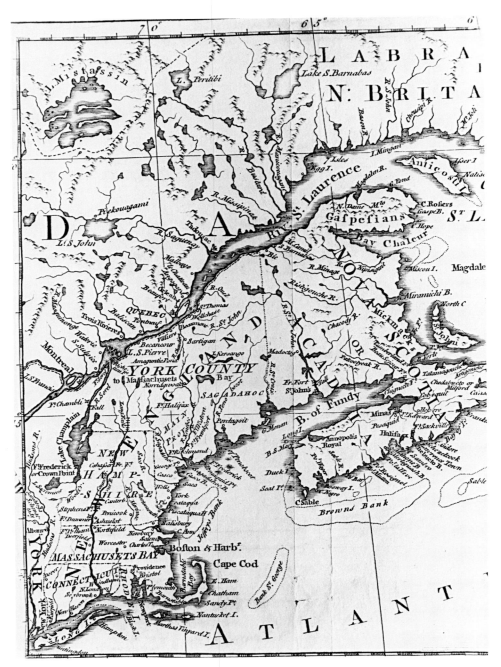

Detail from A Map of the British and French Plantations in North America (1755). Vermont is shown as a part of New Hampshire. In other maps of the same period, New York extends over Massachusetts to the Connecticut River.

fortably, to seek for new and cheaper lands. To both are always added the discontented, the enterprising, the ambitious, and the covetous.[6]

Any settler's predilection toward covetousness paled in comparison to that of the colonial governments. Each colony existed as a semiautonomous region, answerable to England, but not the others. As with children when the parent is away, there was a degree of sibling bullying. All during the colonial period, for example, Massachusetts had bitten off more and more of New Hampshire, which was, for much of this period, a governmentally weak region, under Massachusetts's domination. Ultimately the Crown stepped in and established a firm boundary between these two colonies in 1740. After that, New Hampshire used the increased authority given it by the British government to lay claim to the vast wilderness west of

Hoisting a Yorker, and applying the "Beech Seal" to others.

the Connecticut River that would someday become the state of Vermont. New York also claimed this land as part of their colonial grant.

When their citizens clamored for the new territory, the authorities of both New York and New Hampshire happily combined the adages "Possession is nine-tenths of the law" and "All sales final," and both sold the same land to settlers, who then fought it out among themselves and with the squatters who had preceded them.

In 1764 King George III thought he had resolved matters when he declared the disputed land part of the colony of New York. Not much changed, however. When the people who had previously bought their land from New Hampshire found that New York would not honor their titles, the fireworks really began.

New York tried time and again to bring in its settlers, only to be run out by what came to be known as the Green Mountain Boys, a group of heroic ruffians adept at whipping, removing the roofs of Yorkers' houses, and hoisting chairs high in the air from tavern signs with enemy sympathizers tied to their seats. These settlers were a sort of Minutemen, ready to assemble immediately at the call of their leaders: such legendary names as Ethan Allen (1738–1789), his brother Ira (1751–1814), their cousin Remember Baker (1737–1775), and Seth Warner (1743–1784).

Like many of their fellow immigrants to the Green Mountains, these men were all Connecticut-born. The influx of these men was so great that Vermont, when it finally gained independence, was originally to be called New Connecticut. Today, Vermont has forty town names that are Connecticut namesakes.

By the Revolution, the population of Vermont covered a U shape — filling the hills across Vermont's southern third, and pushing north on opposite sides of the Green Mountains, along the Champlain lowlands and the Connecticut River valley.

In hindsight, it appears that the more conservative element came up the river to settle along the Connecticut Valley, while the more scrappy went over the mountains into the lush Valley of Vermont, stretching up from Bennington into the wide plains along Lake Champlain.

While the conservative Connecticut River valley leaders ultimately took control of Vermont's history, the lively early years are a reflection of the more unusual personalities, and the battles between the "New-states-men" (who wanted to create an independent state of Vermont), Yorkers (who had bought land from New York and recognized that colony's authority), and assorted self-sovereign groups.

The Revolutionary War found the Vermont region in a quandary. Legally, it remained New York's rebellious outback. In January 1777, an assembly met to declare themselves an independent state.

Throughout the Revolution, Vermont remained in uproar: Tory fought with patriot, Yorkers fought with Green Mountaineers. The Vermont authorities initiated a protracted discussion with the English about their joining with Canada (with the intent, most historians hope, to defeat the need for a British occupation — which would be countered by a Continental Army occupation — which might end with New York's annexation of Vermont); the surrounding states of Massachusetts, New York, and New Hampshire offered to resolve the problem by partitioning Vermont among themselves; various adjoining territories in those states periodically seceded and declared their allegiance to Vermont; and George Washington offered to march the Continental Army into Vermont and hang them all.

Not until 1791, full ten years after Cornwallis surrendered at Yorktown, did Vermont make peace with itself and the United States of America to become the fourteenth state.

The actual events of the Revolution that took place in the hill country involved three theaters of operation: the old battleground of the Hudson-Champlain valleys,

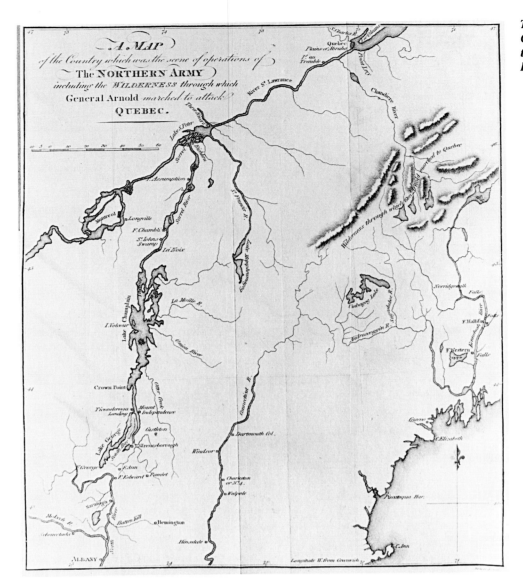

the route of Rogers' Rangers' retreat through northern Vermont to the safety of the Connecticut River, and the path of Benedict Arnold's assault party up through the Maine wilderness to attack Quebec.

After the capture of Fort Ticonderoga in the spring of 1775, where Ethan Allen demanded surrender "In the name of the Great Jehovah and the Continental Congress!" (neither of whom actually gave Ethan such authorization), Benedict Arnold, the nominal commander of the assault party, enjoyed great esteem. His abilities and popularity marked him as the man to lead a force up Maine's Kennebec River, over the height of land and down Canada's Chaudière River to its mouth and a surprise attack on Quebec, just across the Saint Lawrence.

Arnold led about 1,100 volunteers, picked from the revolutionary troops then besieging the British at Boston. They departed north up the coast on September 12, 1775. They regrouped at Augusta and began their journey up the Kennebec by bateaux on the twenty-fifth of September. By the middle of October a ragged army was strung out up the river, carrying their provisions and vessels around the many falls. It was a rugged journey, requiring endless portages through cold and rain.

Food ran short; men ate a stew of moccasin and dog meat. The half not dead, deserted, or lost in the woods reached the Saint Lawrence in mid-November. High winds, however, kept Arnold's men from crossing the river until a week later, giving Quebec ample time to prepare for a now-futile assault.

Another trail into Canada was run from the upper Connecticut River, at Newbury, Vermont. In 1776, General Jacob Bayley and a crew of 110 men began a road from the Connecticut River northwest toward Canada, as a possible invasion route. It was a highroad along ridges and hilltops, but only twenty-five miles were completed before word came of Arnold's defeat and evacuation from Quebec. Later, in spring of 1779, the road was again continued, now under the direction of Moses Hazen. In late summer, with fifty miles completed and thirty still to go, Hazen learned that British scouting parties lay ahead. The Bayley-Hazen Military Road was quickly abandoned, and the road makers retreated south.

The route was never used for any great assault into Canada. While it became, after the war, a line of settlements into northeastern Vermont, during the war it became an easy path for Tory and Indian raiders down from Canada.

Remnants of the Abenaki Indians still lived up in Canada and in fifty-odd little encampments of a tribe of about 700 Indians strung out on a fifty-mile line along the northern border between Vermont's Lake Memphremagog to Lake Umbagog on the Maine–New Hampshire border. They made sporadic raids on the northern settlements. Apart from a few well-celebrated exceptions, the English did not encourage the atrocities common in the French wars. While the Indian attackers might shoot the men, they left the women and children alone. When the alarm of an attack sounded, the men usually took to the woods, leaving their families to watch the looting.

The major military events of northern New England occurred in the old battlegrounds of the Hudson-Champlain valleys, where English once fought French. In the summer of 1777, Burgoyne's forces moved south down the lake. On the seventh of July, a detachment moved down the Valley of Vermont, defeating the rearguard of the revolutionary troops retreating from Ticonderoga. It was the only battle on Vermont soil.

By mid-August, British victories had carried far ahead of their supplies. Burgoyne sent a party of 700 men to capture the Americans' military stores at Bennington. The tide now turned. The Indians accompanying the British troops had committed atrocities against the backwoods farmers and now this once-neutral population rallied to help the Continental Army.

Members of Arnold's expedition carting their bateaux up through the Maine wilderness on their ill-fated foray against Quebec.

Some 2,600 Minutemen met the British in New York, just west of Bennington. The Indians informed their British commander that "the woods were filled with Yankees" and fled for their lives.[7] They were right; in the ensuing battle, virtually every British soldier was killed, wounded, or captured. Burgoyne's reinforcements also suffered defeat.

The British fell into dismay. They had expected the New England frontiersmen to either join them or at least remain neutral. Instead, wrote Burgoyne soon after the battle, "the Hampshire grants in particular, a country unpeopled and almost unknown in the last war [French and Indian War], now abounds in the most active and most rebellious race on the continent, and hangs like a gathering storm on my left."[8] The Vermont and New Hampshire troops soon joined with the main revolutionary forces in New York and combined to defeat Burgoyne a month later at Saratoga.

With the end of hostilities, southern New England families again poured into the northern hills. Typically a town consisted of about forty families, who often emigrated as a group. As the settlers cleared pockets of wilderness, the land took on a new face. At first it was either deep woods or scar. Hastily built log homes sheltered the families, and sapling barracks afforded some protection for the domestic animals. The house yards and hillsides were marked by dead tree trunks, bare of branches and blackened by the fires that had killed them. Beautiful sugar maples, the treasure of later generations, stood girdled and slowly withering in the sun.

The marks of improvement that signified that a farm had come to civilize the wilderness were acres stewn with decaying timber, undergrowth, and old windfalls. Nearby in the woods still prowled the wolf, catamount (mountain lion), and bear.

A French traveler through New England in 1780 described seeing

for the first time, what I have since observed a hundred times; for, in fact, whatever mountains I have climbed, whatever forests I have traversed, whatever byepaths I have followed, I have never travelled three miles without meeting with a new settlement, either beginning to take form, or already in cultivation. . . . Any

Peacham, Vermont, in a snowstorm, as seen from along the Bayley-Hazen Road.

man . . . may go into the woods and purchase a portion of one hundred and fifty to two hundred acres of land. . . . There he conducts a cow, some pigs, or a full sow and two indifferent horses. . . . To these precautions he adds that of having a provision of flour and cider . . . he begins by felling all the smaller trees, and some strong branches of the large ones; these he makes use of as fences . . . he next boldly attacks those immense oaks, or pines . . . he strips them of their bark, or lays them open all round with his axe . . . the next spring . . . their trunk becomes a hideous skeleton. . . . This object completed, the ground is cleared; the air and sun begin to operate on that earth which is wholly formed of rotten vegetables, and teems with the latent principals of production. The grass grows rapidly; there is pasturage for the cattle the very first year; after which they are left to increase . . . and they are employed in tilling a piece of ground which yields the enormous increase of twenty or thirty fold . . . [by selling his cattle to other newcomers] . . . at the end of four or five years, he completes the payment of his lands, and finds himself a comfortable planter. Then his dwelling, which was first no better than a large hut formed by a square of the trunks of trees, placed one upon the other, with the intervals filled by mud, changes into a handsome wooden house.[9]

Almost always, the pioneer settlers chose the more elevated locations for their homesites. An early Vermont historian explained:

The first settlers of this state seemed inclined to select for the center of their towns, the highest situation. This has been the case also, more or less, with the early settlements of other mountainous districts. Indeed it is a common trait in man, that he needs to do a work once, in order to know how to do it in the best manner. He wants the advantage of seeing where he was mistaken.[10]

It was to the elevations and swells that the men came to clear their homesites, for here more acreage could be cleared with less labor. A 1785 traveler through the Green Mountains explained:

Mushrooms, moss and similar vegetation grow in great abundance. Often large fallen trunks are so rotten they collapse under the weight of one person. The dankness of the woods, where the sun's rays rarely penetrate, is such that a very large tree falls of its own weight, tearing up all its roots. The ground, which has never been cultivated, is virtually impenetrable beneath the shallow layer of humus, so the trees preferably extend their roots horizontally.[11]

Such shallow roots could be more easily cleared than those pushed deep into the valleys' rich intervale soil.

Once the land was cleared, the hilltops also promised a longer growing season than in the valleys, where the steep slopes kept the land in shadow a good portion of the day.

Psychological reason also argued for the hilltop location, as life on a hilltop overlooking the wilderness was more appealing than the claustrophobia of a small valley clearing. Unfortunately the emigrants from climatically milder southern New England did not learn about the fierce winter winds straight out of the Canadian Arctic until it was too late.

The settlers first found a rough life. Elias Smith, of Lyme, Connecticut, told how at age thirteen, he accompanied his father to their half-built future home in the hills of South Woodstock, Vermont. Elias had been told his new home resembled "the land of Canaan; a land of hills and valleys, flowing with milk and honey. The

The Allen Clan

The Allens had grown up in Connecticut's Litchfield Hills, and in no way reflected their birthright in "the land of steady habits." Ethan, among other activities, wrote blunt, ungrammatical, but appealingly down-to-earth tracts espousing "Deism," the belief in a personal, rather than clerically supervised, relationship with God. Such blasphemy put the lower New England colonies in an uproar. Even after his death, he long remained the Antichrist to many devout New Englanders. A Connecticut minister recorded, passing by Ethan Allen's grave, "An Awful infidel one of the wickedest men that ever walked this guilty globe. I stopped & looked at his grave with pious horror."[a]

Ethan's philosophy found good soil in the minds of many who were to come to settle the future state of Vermont, leading our minister to complain, "About one quarter of the inhabitants and almost all of the men of learning are Deists — would chuse to have no Sabbath — no ministers — no religion — no heaven — no Hell — no morality."[b]

The Allens began filtering north from their home state in the late 1760s. Ira, with brothers Heman

and Levi, spent the fall and winter in the Berkshire Hills, fattening a herd of 350 hogs on the beechnuts that covered the wilderness floor. The only sign of humanity here was a few cabins in the whole of the region and rudimentary trails, marked by tree blazes. Ira, then eighteen, wrote how he remained to watch the herd, living in the cabin of a family of Scots:

It is remembered that hogs are strange animals. If not attended to they will, in a few days, get as wild as the beasts of the field. But by being seen once in a few days, and salted like cattle, they may be kept tame, and will grow or fatten as fast on beech nuts, as on any food that can be given them.[c]

Another spirited Vermonter was Congressman Matthew Lyon, considered in his day "a strange offensive brute. Too wild to tame, too base to shoot." In 1798 he responded to disparaging remarks by Connecticut Representative Roger Griswold about Lyon's war record with a gob of spittle in Griswold's face. A few weeks later Griswold went after Lyon with his cane on the House floor. Lyon grabbed a pair of firetongs, and the rest was history. Lyon was soon jailed by the opposition under the Sedition Act. The Vermonters reelected him while he was serving his sentence.

first part I found true." As his father cleared a path for the ox team up the mile-long slope to the cabin, the boy went on ahead to see his new home,

which struck a damp in my spirits, as it appeared only an abode of wretchedness. . . . I determined myself to return to Connecticut; thinking it better to be there to dig clams for my living than to be in such a place. . . . Though I was some over thirteen years, I cried. . . . I went down to the team, and passed by the team down the steep and dismal hill as fast as possible.

Only by the stern command of his father did he return to his fate:

The dwelling place stood on the north side of a very large hill. . . . Around the house (as it was called) there were twelve acres of land. The trees were cut down

Early the next year, Ira drove portions of the herd over the mountains to Albany for a profitable sale. On the return trip, he lost his horse near the New York–Massachusetts border. Although it was Sunday, Ira kept on walking, in search of his horse. When he put up for the night, it was his misfortune that the landlord was also the local minister and justice of the peace. When he saw the color of Ira's money in the morning, he ordered Ira to pay a fine for traveling on the Sabbath. After some argument, and a threat of force from both sides, Ira paid the fine:

I put on my hat in order to go, when the Justice began to give me a lecture for disorderly behavior, ordering me to take off my hat and attend to what he had said. To which I answered that all travellers had a right to wear their hats in the bar room of a public house, and if I had broken any law, I had paid my fine and was at liberty. The Justice continued his lecture, when I observed that I paid [the Reverend] Mr. Lee of Salisbury for preaching.[d]

After more argument, Ira was ultimately set free. This was certainly not a New Englander of the old Puritan style.

Ira later joined with his cousin Remember Baker and went off to survey in Vermont, reconnoitering and getting hold of whatever was the best land. In the fall of 1772, he surveyed a tract of land high in the hills that he had been a partner in purchasing, the present towns of Stowe and Underhill. Discovering that there was not enough usable land to make "one good farm," he returned to Connecticut, planning to get out of the deal and still make a profit. "A great proportion of the [blazes marking the] corners of said lots were made on spruce and fir timber, and if I described them as such, it would show the poorness of the town." Instead, Ira called them gumwood in his reports. When the other investors asked what gumwood was, "I told them tall straight trees that had a gum, much like the gum on cherry trees." While everyone was looking over his reports and maps, Ira drew the brother of one of the investors aside and "in secret" tried to buy their land rights to this new town. The wily Yankees rose to the bait, wrote Ira: "I was urged to sell back to the proprietors the twenty rights I had bought, which I did, and obtained the ninety pounds for the survey, &c., which [amount] I considered of more consequence than the whole town."[e]

Many citizens of the lower New England states breathed a sigh of relief when the Allens and their ilk set off to populate the northern frontier.

During the Revolution, the Allens took a great part in secret negotiations with the British, ostensibly to keep them out of Vermont. This ultimately damned them in the eyes of many, who considered that the Allens had more interest in keeping hold of the more than 300,000 acres they held as the Onion River Land Company, than in any ideals of American independence — although it should be remembered that the great slogan of the patriots themselves was the two-headed cry of "Liberty, Property!" According to one source, Ira informed a British agent that "he and his Family have large fortunes which they do not intend to lose, if there were a possibility of saving them. At all risks, he is determined that Congress shall not have the parceling of his Lands to their avaricious Minions."[f]

Some of this may have been bluff for English ears, but there is probably some underlying truth to Allen's statement.

---

and laid in different directions, excepting a small place where the house stood. There was no way to look, to see far, without looking up, as the trees around prevented seeing any house or cleared land, in any direction whatever. The house was made of split bass-wood logs, locked together at the corners. There was no floor to the house, nor was there any roof to it. The grass had grown up within these wooden walls, and there was one large stump in the middle of the house, which to heighten my trouble my father said would do for a light stand.[12]

By the next day, the horse had grazed the interior flat, and neighbors had come to help "finish" the house with a bark roof and split-log floor.

The story is typical.

Many difficulties could befall a family in the years before they achieved self-

sufficiency; the greatest danger was starvation. After a bad harvest, a Congregational minister wrote: "Several women I saw had lived four or five days without any food, and had eight or ten children starving around them, crying for bread, & the poor women had wept till they looked like ghosts."[13] The men were probably off in the woods desperately searching out the ever-dwindling supply of game. For many, the life in the "dark, dirty and dismal"[14] mud-packed log hut lasted even ten or fifteen years.

With the early years of settling-in so often harsh, there were many who preferred to find some way of amassing a little money in the settled region and then coming north to buy some cleared acreage. This demand brought into existence a class of transient settlers who constantly followed the frontier, preparing the way for others. These people saw a relatively quick profit in buying wilderness, cutting and burning the forest into ashes, then selling the cleared land.

The ashes themselves added to the financial gain of this occupation. They were boiled into potash, potassium carbonate, the then-common source for the lye needed to make fertilizers, glass, mortar, bleaches, dyes, and soap.

Every settlement had one or two potash houses, where large, double-bottom tubs — the upper bottom having holes to make it a sieve — were stored. The upper area was filled with straw or hay with a foot layer of ash packed over it. Water poured over the ash leached out the lye and dripped down to collect in the bottom chamber. The liquid was drawn off by a cock,

and if it should not yet have attained a sufficient degree of strength, poured again over the ashes. The lye is deemed sufficiently strong when an egg swims in it. This lye is afterward boiled [to remove the liquid] in large iron cauldrons. . . . This salt [remaining] is of a black color and called black potash. *Some manufacturers leave the potash in the cauldron, and encrease the fire, by means of which the oil is disengaged from the salt in a thick smoke, and the black potash assumes a grey colour, in which state it is packed up in barrels for sale.*[15]

Stages of a "Green Mountain Boy." Photographs ca. 1860s by A. F. Styles.

THE MOTHER PERISHING WITH COLD.

IN December, 1827, Mr. Blake, with his wife and infant daughter, while traveling in a sleigh over the Green Mountains in Vermont, were overtaken by a snow storm. The storm was so thick and furious, that their horse refused to stir. Mr. B., realizing his dangerous position, after protecting his wife and child as well as he could against the storm left them, intending to seek for aid at the first house he could find. He was soon benumbed by the cold, and fell, and found himself unable to rise. His wife, as is supposed, alarmed at his long absence, left the sleigh in order to find him. When within thirty rods of her husband, she was overcome by the cold. Knowing her fate, she stripped herself of the thickest part of her clothing and wrapped up her infant daughter. Mr. Blake was found alive the next morning, with his hands and feet badly frozen: the body of his wife was found lifeless and cold: and lifting up the infant from its snowy bed, the hearts of the beholders were rejoiced to see it smile.

"The Mother Perishing with Cold." (John W. Barber, Historical American Scenes.)

It took a great amount of forest to make a little potash, but then, cleared land was an important by-product. Likewise, if the ash-producing fire also happened to burn the rich humus of the forest floor as well, so much the more ash. If the potash could not be trundled out in barrels, it was put in a bag to be carried out tens of miles to market on the seller's back.

The character of the men clearing the wilderness was distinct from that of those who came to make the new lands their permanent home. Wrote one Vermont traveler:

A considerable part of those who begin the cultivation of the wilderness may be denominated foresters or pioneers. . . . These men cannot live in regular society. They are too idle, too talkative, too passionate, too prodigal, and too shiftless to acquire either property or character. . . . At the same time, they are usually possessed in their own view of uncommon wisdom . . . after censuring the weakness and wickedness of their superiors, after exposing the injustice of the community in neglecting to invest persons of such merit with public office . . . and under the pressure of poverty, the fear of jail and the consciousness of public contempt leave their native place and betake themselves to the wilderness.

Here they are obliged to either work or starve. They accordingly cut down some trees and girdle others; they furnish themselves with an ill-built log house and a worse barn, and reduce a part of the forest into fields, half enclosed and half cultivated. The forests furnish browse, and their fields yield a stinted herbage. On this scanty provision they feed a few cattle, and with these and the penurious

The Wilderness Animals

THE COMMON WOLF

The early settlers faced a variety of wildlife.

Wolves typically avoided human contact unless driven by extreme hunger. Weighing up to one hundred pounds, they arrived in packs to prowl the settlements on winter nights. They did not come stealthily but announced their arrival with "such horrid and prolonged howlings as were calculated not only to thrill terror through their timorous victims, but to appall the hearts of the inhabitants of the neighborhood."[g]

Yet the most feared creature of the forest was the catamount, or mountain lion. Growing to about two thirds the size of its African cousin, it has a strength and fierce nature that were legend. It has a peculiarly horrible cry which carries for miles. It preys by night, hence wilderness travelers built great fires when camping. Many tales were told of two great eyes reflecting the firelight at the edge of the darkness, and the desperate choice between ignoring the creature or trying for a killing shot between those glowing pupils. While there have never been a great number of these creatures in the

THE CATAMOUNT.

New England wilds, the thought of one dropping out of a tree for the fatal blow kept many a traveler on his guard.

This fear, however, usually produced more casualties than the catamount itself, for there was another more common inhabitant of the night forest, the screech owl. This diminutive bird produces a noise all out of proportion for its size. Many a Green Mountain citizen, wrote one old Vermonter, "as he has been passing through a wood in a dark night has felt his hair rise, his heart leap, and himself flying as upon wings of the wind, at the terrific scream of this little bird, perched on a tree just over his head."[h] Flight was usually only a short run, as trees were numerous.

THE BLACK BEAR.

Bears were not so vicious as the catamounts and wolves, but they too gave problems. In the spring, when the corn shoots were tender and juicy, or "in the milk," the bears came in packs at night to join the raccoons to feast on the crop. A farmer would spend many a night with his musket, cutting down bear after bear as they ambled into the clearing. Afterward, the family had a good store of grease, meat, and fur. The bears also raised problems with the herds of pigs, which were usually taken into the woods each fall to fatten on the fallen nuts, and it often took an Ira Allen to handle such encounters. The bears also made nuisances of themselves in

THE SCREECH OWL

the farm cabins. The lumbering creatures were sometimes known to break down a flimsy door and make themselves at home within. If a musket was not immediately at hand, the regular inhabitants retreated up a ladder to the sleeping loft above. Here they watched the methodical destruction of their worldly possessions as the bear searched for edibles, forced to await his ultimate departure before descending to salvage the remains. After that they put up a stronger door.

As the frontier advanced, many of the larger creatures slowly disappeared. The deer were first to go, and one of the Vermont legislature's initial acts was to put a six-month season on deer. Soon also the wolf and catamount became scarce, and the moose population retreated into the northern areas. Even the raccoon population dwindled.

Of all the woodland creatures, only the skunk stayed put. He exchanged forest den for cabin crawlspace, and all too often disputed habitation rights with many an unfortunate farm dog.

THE RACCOON.

products of their labor, eked out by hunting and fishing, they keep their families alive.

A farm thus far cleared promises immediate substinence to a better husbandman. . . . The proprietor is always ready to sell, for he loves this irregular, adventurous, half-working, and half-lounging life. . . . The forester, receiving more money for his improvements than he ever possessed . . . willingly quits his house to build another like it.[16]

Another incentive for the continued existence of this ever-migratory farmer was the immediate richness of newly cleared land. No matter how intolerable the plowing, the first plantings of the old woodlands produced a bumper crop of garden vegetables. Even better, the newly cleared land produced a natural harvest of grass — sometimes chest-high and always nutritious to the grazing cattle.

When the new land's original fertility waned, it was time to sell the farm to the more permanent settlers and move on.

Except for the few military roads built through the region, most routes were simply blazed trails fit only for a person on foot or perhaps on horseback. The paths kept to the high ground, and the pioneers found themselves alternately climbing "over the steep ascent and ridges; and then descending into the deep valleys, apparently for the pleasure of mounting the corresponding hill."[17]

In regions of scattered settlements, it was usually the roads themselves that gave warning of the imminent frontier. Here, remarked one traveler on horseback, "the roads were less wrought; the bridges were less safe; and all the inconveniences of traveling were both multiplied and enhanced."[18]

The roads were a gruel of humus, rocks, and stumps, worn into a channel with roots shooting in from the sides. Bridges were simply slippery logs. And the underlying stones appeared to bring forth the proverbial remark that here a horse had never put its foot upon the ground.

Winter's freeze provided a three-month period of easy travel, allowing the movement of bulk goods down to navigable waters to shipment away downriver in the spring. The farmer hitched his oxen and sledded out his potash, shingles, hides, and other products of his rudimentary environment. He often journeyed as far as Portland or Boston to market his wares. The snows drifted high along the open roads, and the constant passage of teams over it produced a solid crust:

But this bridge of crusted snow is narrow, and a slight deviation at either hand will give the passenger a plunge; that is, his horse will sink and flounder. . . . As the warm weather and rains of spring weaken this crust, these become treacher-

"Panther" (mountain lion) killed on the slopes of Mount Ascutney, Weathersfield, Vermont, and the dog that went into the den after him. (Photograph by A. A. Baldwin.) The last mountain lion was killed in Vermont in 1881. It now graces the entry to the Vermont State Museum.

The Sovereign District of Guilford, Vermont

In the southeastern corner of the state lies Guilford, an upland town of hills and small valleys. It has only one rugged elevation of about 1,700 feet, called Governor's Mountain. It was so named by prospective settlers when they set aside this most untillable place in the whole township as Governor Benning Wentworth's five-hundred-acre slice of the pie. As the grant for the township called for a government by a committee appointed by the townspeople, answerable only to Parliament itself, the Massachusetts people who moved in soon began to show an even more obstreperous nature.

The first settlers came around 1761. They simply followed a footpath tramped out up from the Connecticut River alongside a stream, past the once-far frontier outpost of Fort Dummer, and walked up to their hilltop allotments. This soon became a familiar trek for the pioneer shouldering a bag of corn for the fifteen-mile walk back down to the mill in the wide valley. By 1764, the newcomers were pouring in so fast that Guilford had the largest population of any town in the state. Unlike other settlements consisting of a few dozen families, Guilford's wilderness gave way to a patchwork of fifty- to one-hundred-acre farms, each with its five- to ten-acre clearing and smoking little cabin. This approximately six-by-seven-mile grant soon became one of the most populous towns in Vermont.

For twenty years the settlers kept flooding in. In 1772, the town committee declared themselves a part of New York. In 1776 the Vermonter faction took control, only to lose out again to the Yorkers in 1778. By this time, Guilford had become a haven for Yorkist sympathizers ejected from other parts of the state as well as many attracted by the independent nature of this township republic. With over 3,000 settlers, it had the greatest population of any town in Vermont. In 1781 the town committee voted to arm and "defend themselves against the insults of the pretended state of Vermont."[i] The town now consisted of one great "village" of little farms, each with its rude cabin. Two town committees existed in hostile tolerance, one Yorker, one Vermonter, each ready to take over the other when it had enough power.

By 1783, conditions became intolerable. Each faction governed where it could, and interfered where it could not. Doctors could not visit the sick without passes from both sides. Soon open warfare broke out. Vermont called out the militia. Ethan Allen left his estate to lead a force of a hundred Green Mountain Boys into Guilford. Upon his arrival he made this short proclamation: "I, Ethan Allen, declare that unless the people of Guilford peaceably submit to the authority of Vermont, the town shall be made as desolate as were the cities of Sodom and Gomorrah."[j]

The Yorkers took the hint. Many left to resettle upstate New York. Other Guilford families moved north to other Vermont towns. Guilford's great population boom died, and its era of fame ended. The whole character of the town changed. Wrote a historian of the 1850s: "Where one farmer now occupies and improves, formerly lived half a dozen, or more, and you now see one respectable dwelling instead of as many log huts."[k]

---

ous, not to say dangerous *passways. What are here called times of* slumping *and* plunging *now come; and disasters sometimes follow.*[19]

Yet for all the frontier's hardships, the people who came developed a most amazing character, combining the intellectual heritage of their southern New England birthrights with a strength developed out of adversity. Marveled Nathan Perkins, the strict Connecticut Congregational divine, who had little enthusiasm for freethinking Vermont:

When I go from hut to hut in the wilderness, the people with nothing to eat — to drink — or wear — all work, & yet the women quiet — serene — peaceable — contented, loving their husbands, their home — wanting never to return — nor any dressy clothes — I think how strange! I ask myself are these women of the same species with our fine ladies? Tough they are, brawny their limbs — their young girls unpolished — & will bear work as well as mules. Woods make people love one another & kind & obliging and good natured. They set much more by one another than in the old settlements. Leave their doors unbarred. Sleep quietly amid fleas — bedbugs — dirt & rags.[20]

6 Hill Town Portraits during the Golden Age

1790–1840

 The fifty years between 1790 and 1840 were the upland region's golden age. The people who came to push the frontier out of the New England hills during this half-century brought the region its golden age of national importance in many fields, such as politics, invention, and intellectual thought. Most visible was the example it gave of pioneer determination, and what it could do in domesticating the wilderness.

Wrote a Vermonter in the early 1840s:

In looking back from 1842 to 1790, the eye sees many marks of improvement and general, progressive prosperity. The reign of the wilderness has been turned back from the rivers and vallies and lakes to the mountains. The dead trunks "with singed tops," standing frequently on lawn or hill-side, like the naked masts of ships . . . have disappeared in many parts. . . . The stumps and far spreading roots, have been drawn up and the surface smoothed over. The eye is no more pained at the sight of the lofty sugar maple, girdled and withering in the sun; or of fallen timber and logs of the first growth; decaying, and disfiguring your prospect; impeding and turning aside your feet. The underbrush and the windfalls are cleared away. . . . The plow and the roller; the scythe and the sickle have followed the axe and the fire. . . . Where growled the bear and howled the wolf and gnashed the catamount, are seen the gambols of domestic flocks and herds. . . . The log and hasty tenements of early days; the hovels and barracks for wintering of their herds and flocks have given way to neat, substantial, convenient, well-finished houses and barns.[1]

By the 1790s, the whole of New England's upland region began to take on a homogeneous character. From the affluent hilltop town of Litchfield, in Connecticut, to the modest little communities in Maine and upper New Hampshire, there were solid homes, vistas of cleared land, white churches, and active mills.

The southern New Englanders had come north and, as they were again to do a few generations later in the Ohio Valley, actively re-created the culture of their

home states. Academies sprouted up in every county seat: ornate buildings, whose impressive facades promised an Athenian future for our young nation. The academies shared the village center with churches of many denominations — Baptist, Methodist, and Episcopal — whose parishioners came north to escape the taxes levied to support Congregationalism, then the state religion in Connecticut and Massachusetts.

Old homestead on the heights, Weathersfield Center, Vermont.

The hills were not entirely Arcadian in the years just after the Revolution. Unresolved land problems, the economic and judicial chaos of the Articles of Confederation, and a growing separation between the old seacoast population and the new upstart culture in the hills to the west, all threatened the stability of the infant nation.

State governments, often controlled by old mercantile money in the seaboard cities, saw no reason to adjust taxes or voting laws to accommodate the new population of hill dwellers. The disenfranchised farmers of western Massachusetts were among the worst hit. To quote the historian Samuel Eliot Morison:

In that State the case of the farmers was really deplorable, and they lacked the political power to obtain relief. Farm produce was a glut on the market, owing to the stoppage of the West India trade [with whom American could no longer trade now that it was out of the British Commonwealth], and taxes were heavier than elsewhere. The commercial interests . . . rigged the State constitution . . . succeeded in shifting the weight of taxation on to land and polls. Courts were clogged with suits for debt . . . and lawyers were more grasping than usual.[2]

In 1786, rebellion broke out in the Massachusetts interior. The backwoodsmen, many of them Revolutionary veterans, marched on the courthouses at Springfield and Worcester to prevent further legal actions of foreclosure. Ultimately a Revolutionary officer named Daniel Shays (1747–1825), of Pelham, became their leader, and the hostilities became known as Shays's Rebellion.

It was an ineffectual campaign. The affluent gentry of eastern Massachusetts Bay raised money to form a militia, and their sons at Harvard organized a cavalry regiment "to terrify the common folk."[3]

With few munitions of their own, much of the "rebellion" consisted of Shays leading his men around western Massachusetts, with the militia in pursuit, in much the same manner as King Philip's maneuvers of a century earlier.

Ultimately the rebel force was captured, although Shays and some other ringleaders escaped to Vermont. While most of the rebels' demands were later quietly passed into law, the whole affair made it clear to the people of America's hills and frontier that the interests of the old established seaboard lowland regions were not the same as their own.

New Hampshire had some minor insurrections similar to Shays's Rebellion, but its greatest problem in the post-Revolutionary years was boundary disputes. The far northern tip of that state experienced some forty years of uncertainty as New Hampshire and Canada argued over its possession.

Shays's forces meeting the militia at Springfield, Massachusetts.

Throughout this whole era, settlers moved constantly in and out of New England's upland region. Families settled and resettled, sometimes moving a short distance to better land, at other times packing up and beginning over again and again, following the frontier first northward, and then westward out of New England.

While this north and westward expansion laid the foundation for a great future nation, its short-term effects were more negative. Wrote a British visitor in the 1810s:

It prevented the inhabitants from thinking of any improvement; if their farm was not sufficiently productive, the easy remedy to a restless people was to sell it, collect their effects and go five or fifteen hundred miles (the distance, greater or less, was not thought of) in pursuit of a richer soil. It was not by the employment of greater skill, but by change in location, that they sought to improve their condition.[4]

For all the continuing migrations, the pioneer farmers still clung to the upper slopes in the hill country. The dense growth in the lush valleys precluded an easy foothold there, although the hilltop location left them far from whatever mills appeared later at the falls, and uncomfortably exposed to the winter's blast. Today, the hill country contains many high settlements which reflect this first era of town-making. Many others, however, have long ago passed into abandonment, ruin, and oblivion.

In the half century after the Revolution, New Englanders considered (as they still do today) Litchfield, Connecticut, to be the classic ideal of a hill town. Nathaniel Hawthorne, on a visit in 1838, sketched the town's character:

In Connecticut (and also sometimes in Berkshire) the villages are situated on the most elevated ground that can be found, so that they are visible for miles around. Litchfield is a remarkable instance, occupying a high plain, without the least shelter from the winds, and with almost as wide an expanse of view as from a mountain-top. The streets are very wide, two or three hundred feet, at least, with wide green margins, and some times a green space wide between two road tracks. Nothing can be neater than the churches and houses.[5]

A visitor to the Litchfield of today will quickly echo Hawthorne's impressive description. The old plain along the ridgetop is still a village of wide lanes, stately trees, and even more stately mansions.

Founded around 1721, Litchfield grew quietly for much of the century. The turning point came with the Revolutionary War. As the British then controlled the seas and occupied Manhattan, the colonists had to trek along inland roads with their troops and supplies.

The old path through Litchfield between Hartford and the American-held West Point fortifications on the Hudson suddenly became a part of this national road. The route north from Litchfield also served as a safe passage up the Berkshire Valley to the outposts on Lake Champlain.

Far enough in the hills that no marauding redcoats could attack, but convenient to the Continentals' encampments, Litchfield found a ready market for all the cattle, cheese, and grain it could produce. Outlying hill towns, such as Norfolk and Goshen, also sent their largess to Litchfield, where carters and drovers delivered it to Washington's troops along the Hudson.

The wartime demand for finished products drew many away from agrarian pursuits toward a full-time occupation with activities which they had once practiced

Cutting firewood on the Litch-field, Connecticut, Green, ca. 1850.

Sheldon's Tavern, Litchfield, Connecticut, built 1760.

Hill Town Portraits during the Golden Age   **65**

because of the rigid self-sufficiency of farm life — turning leather into saddles and boots, forging horseshoes, cookpots, and other ironware from the iron mined in the hills to the northwest, making combs from cow horns, fashioning hats, and making clothing.

Litchfield village became known simply as the Hill. It adopted a ritualized obeisance to the source of its prosperity and virtually deified Washington, Lafayette, and other heroes of the conflict. Any chair or bed used by Washington was immediately set aside as an object of veneration.

The village's principal Revolutionary figure, Colonel Benjamin Tallmadge (1754–1835), chief of Washington's spies (a group that included Nathan Hale), made it a matter of principle after the war to wear clothes of the Revolutionary era long after three-cornered hats and buckled knee-breeches had become a humorous anachronism.

By the end of the war, Litchfield Hill had grown into a handsome town of some fifty houses grouped around the wide village streets.

With no military contracts to continue its prosperity, a couple of its merchants founded the Litchfield China Trading Company. Each year for fourteen years, a long caravan of oxcarts loaded with all the goods of the region's farms and shops followed the dusty paths to New Haven, where they would be loaded for a voyage to China.

By 1810, many of the town's 4,600 inhabitants worked in the town's fifty-odd shops and mills. It was "a handsome town, situated on an easy, beautiful slope, scarcely declining from north to south, and descending a little more rapidly to the east and to the west. The houses are well built, and the courthouse is handsomer than any other in the state."[6]

The Hill looked out on a beautiful vista, "consisting of open extensive valleys, hills gracefully arched, rich hollows, and groves formed of lofty trees interspersed everywhere at the most pleasing distances."[7]

Litchfield Hill fulfilled all the ideals the new nation had for its interior communities. There were mansions, built from profits of the overseas trade, constructed from designs brought over from England. There was a law school, which for some forty years was the only real law school in the whole of the English-speaking world. Organized by Tapping Reeve (1744–1823) around 1782, it produced in its little classroom building over a thousand lawyers, some of whom became vice presidents, Senators, Supreme Court justices, governors, and college presidents. It closed in 1833, when Yale and other colleges began teaching law.

About ten years after Reeve began his law lectures, Litchfield also became the site of the nation's first school of higher education for ladies. At that time, "the country was preferred as most suitable for females' improvement, away from the frivolities and dissipations of fashionable life" in the cities.[8]

The female seminary was run by Miss Sarah Pierce (1767–1852), a Litchfield native. Opened in 1792, it continued until 1832, graduating some 3,000 ladies. There were, of course, many social events tied to the law school, especially frequent balls. The young men and ladies shaped much of the town's character at this time. Many of the men lived in hotels and boardinghouses in the village. The girls promenaded in good weather.

In 1832, a young man wrote of his visit to Litchfield on a beautiful summer's day. Entering the town just before sunset, he discovered "a long procession of school girls, coming down North Street, walking under the lofty elms, and moving to the music of a flute and flageolet. The girls were gaily dressed and evidently enjoying their evening parade, in this most balmy season of the year."[9]

The modest 1784 schoolhouse (left) of Tapping Reeve's Litchfield Law School. Reeve's home is at right.

Litchfield's shop industries had also grown by this time, sending their products down the turnpikes for the New York trade. There is a story of Colonel Tallmadge bringing his best boots to a local cobbler for repair. The colonel informed the man that he came to the shop with great apprehension, as these had been the choicest boots in a New York store. Replied the shoemaker, "I made these boots in Litchfield, and sold them to the New York trade. I guess I can mend them!"[10]

Litchfield's success lay in its fertile surroundings and access to outside markets. At first only two routes led through the town, one north-south, the other east-west. In the years after the Revolution, many states began encouraging private corporations to construct turnpike roads. Connecticut, especially, gave preferential treatment to such endeavors, to the point of requiring towns to construct rights-of-way, which were then turned over to the toll companies.

With all the traffic fanning out from the Hill, it was not long before every direction had a tollbooth set up not far down the way. The turnpikes included the New Preston & Litchfield; Litchfield, Goshen & Cornwall; Canaan & Litchfield; Torrington; Litchfield & Harwinton; and the Straits. Until the coming of the railroad, such routes out of the hill towns assured economic success to these elevated locations.

Farther north, other settlements attempted the Litchfield ideal, though with more modest results.

Paris Hill, in southern Maine, stands as another exemplar of hill-town gentility. The first settlers came to its heights in 1779. With the incorporation of Oxford County in 1805, it became the shire town, or county seat. While the little plateau upon which it sits is only 831 feet in altitude, it commands a full panorama of the low surrounding hills. An English visitor in the early 1830s commented that Paris was "a place as little resembling its European original as a cottage does a palace. At the same time it may be said, that to the extent it falls short of its great prototype as to architectural beauty, does it exceed it in the beauties of nature, being surrounded by a circle of mountains of the most imposing and romantic features."[11]

The village, while not filled with the grandeur of Louis XIV, grew to some sixty buildings on the hilltop. It became a Greek Revival hamlet, all set around a triangular green. When the county seat moved down into the valley at South Paris, Paris Hill was left to remain just as it had been in the early nineteenth century, a little Mount Olympus of Maine culture.

Today, one region which still retains much of the flavor of the post-Revolutionary era is the hill country of Vermont's northeastern corner. Here, in the decades after the Revolution, little agrarian communities came to bud along the wilderness path of the Bayley-Hazen Military Road.

A visitor today will puzzle over the elegant mansions, ornate academy buildings, and dignified churches standing along some ridgetop in what modern description would relegate to a region of "nothing but farms." Yet this anomaly itself shows us the affluence and importance of a successful agricultural community in the national economy of that day. Except for the farms, there *was* nothing else in the American interior.

The first farms and homes in this area of the hills were cleared out of the wilderness close by the path itself. Driving up a backroad section of the path today, one finds the quiet road abruptly lined on each side by stately trees and a handful of "old colonial" houses, seemingly transplanted out of the Litchfield Hills. This is the community of Hardwick Street, first settled in 1795.

Except for the harshness of winter, the countryside is reminiscent of the Connecticut hills. The more slender-trunked sugar maples may have replaced the elm, but the elevation difference between heights and valleys of Vermont's Piedmont region to the east of the Green Mountains is similar to southern New England hills. A Litchfield resident could find comfort in a Vermont sunset.

The only noticeable difference is that where the Litchfield Hills are marked with a number of actual individual hills, and the Berkshires tend toward a series of

Milestone along the New Preston & Litchfield Turnpike, the old route that led west from the busy center of Litchfield, Connecticut, to the Hudson River and, during the Revolution, to the soldiers of George Washington's Continental Army: "33 Miles/To Hartford/ 102 Miles to New York/ J. Strong/AD 1787."

Paris Hill, Maine, drawn from a photograph taken January, 1858, which "has as much scope as could well be obtained by the camera, on account of the sharp elevation of the hill and all the neighboring points. The foreground of the picture indicates the mode of the artist's arrival," according to A. J. Coolidge and J. B. Mansfield, A History and Description of New England, General and Local (Boston, 1859).

Sugarmaking

"Sugaring off," boiling maple sap into syrup, seems to have been the fondest memory of the hill-country childhood. Sugaring took place in early spring, at a slack time of year. People were just coming out from their winter isolation and relished the chance for social contact. Children especially enjoyed the nights in the woods attending the fires boiling the sap down to a thick syrup. It was a welcome change from the farm family's endless cycle of daily chores.

Wrote Charles Dudley Warner of sugaring off in the Berkshires:

"American Forest Scene. Maple Sugaring," by Arthur Fitzwilliam Tate, lithograph by N. Currier (1856).

Sometimes this used to be done in the evening, and it was made the excuse for a frolic in the camp. The neighbors were invited; sometimes even the pretty girls from the village, who filled all the woods with sweet voices and merry laughter and little affectations of fright. The white snow still lies on all the ground except the warm spot about the camp. The tree branches all show distinctly in the light of the fire, which sends its ruddy glare far into the darkness, and lights up the bough shanty, the hogsheads, the buckets on the trees, and the group around the boiling kettles, until the scene is something out of a fairy play.[a]

They often poured the hot sugar onto the snow, cooling it to a waxy consistency. When someone gobbled too large a ball, it set in the mouth and, until it melted a few minutes later, locked the teeth. The boys had great fun in snaring dogs with this sweet trap.

parallel ridges, Vermont's eastern Piedmont is more of a haphazard ocean chop in topography.

The two classic villages of the Bayley-Hazen route are the hilltop hamlets of Peacham and Craftsbury. These two villages, along with nearby Danville, give a good sense of the character of the old village centers, huddled on a windy hillcrest.

Peacham was one of the earliest settlements, founded in 1775, along the first portion of the route cleared under Bayley's supervision. It is today very much what it has always been: a little cluster of fine homes, a church, academy building, and old tavern.

Craftsbury Common, Vermont, from the valley below.

Craftsbury Common was settled later, in 1788, by refugees from Shays's Rebellion. It stands a short distance off the farther, Hazen-built, section of the old path. Unlike Peacham, where, over the years, the community center has migrated down the lee slope to protect the village from the winter blasts out of the northwest, Craftsbury's center remains squarely set upon a flat hilltop rising almost five hundred precipitous feet out of the surrounding intervales. In the days of the early hilltop settlements, it was an ideal location. Wrote a visitor in 1823:

The village is built on a table-land, rising abruptly in the center of a deep valley, which surrounds it on all sides, and separates it, at a moderate distance, from hills generally of the same height with itself, but occasionally aspiring to a greater elevation. This table-land is about three miles in length, and one and a half in breadth. The valley surrounding it was once probably a lake, and the table-land a large island in its centre. At present it is almost an island: one river winding more than half round it, in its progress through the valley, and a second nearly completing that part of the circuit which the first had left. Its situation is more than commonly beautiful and picturesque; and, in connexion with other more solid advantages, bids fair to render it one of the most pleasant and flourishing villages in the state. . . . The village is well-built, and every thing indicated good order and general prosperity.[12]

The village, today set around a wood-fenced common, still conveys the feel of a community little changed since the 1830s, when it had some thousand residents (about twice today's count).

For all its graceful image, Craftsbury's early years were one long hard struggle. The winter winds soon drove the farmers off the northern slopes. There was no way to build a fire sufficient to warm a house from the freezes sweeping down from Canada. If one tried, such roaring fires were sometimes driven by gusts to reverse themselves, rolling out into the kitchen to incinerate home and family. Those who held out erected ingenious barriers and wind hurdles near the houses in a vain attempt to stay the gusts.

Sometimes, as in 1816, when it snowed every month, families were reduced to a forage of field mice and boiled beech leaves. Only the potash from the dwindling forests promised any reliable income when trekked north for sale in Montreal. Writes Craftsbury's town historian:

Until the 1820s there was much hardship and starvation; there was hardly enough food to go around even in the best of years, and families were obliged to share food throughout the community. . . . The hardest things for the settlers to bear were the loneliness and isolation in Craftsbury. Roads were horrendous and one's closest neighbor could be miles away. People have told me that the suicide rate was once very high and that the month of March [mud time] was worst.[13]

By the 1830s, the farmers were realizing a modest profit from their farms by carting butter, cheese, hogs, and maple syrup to the Montreal market. Yet there was never any great affluence in the village. Life was hard. Everyone worked. The modest unpainted houses hung along the Vermont hillsides much as they do today: one-story affairs with low sloping roofs. Behind each house, the hillside slopes up abruptly so cattle can be seen grazing over the shingled roof. In front a little porch bends under the weight of the washing hung between its simple columns. A muddy wagon track follows the contour of the hill in front of the house, with a line of bucketed sugar maples separating the lane from the wheel-rutted mire that is the front yard.

The people of Craftsbury in the early half of the nineteenth century worked awfully hard to make ends meet. Virtually every necessity was produced at home, and everyone performed a myriad of professions in his or her daily round. Those who survived childhood usually lasted to about fifty, before the neighbors added the profession of pallbearer to their own lists.

Yet for its struggling existence, Craftsbury had an academy constructed on its common in 1829. The men who settled the town had been well educated in the lower New England states, and they felt it a duty to provide the same benefits for their children. Here high on the hill above where Abnaki still periodically haunted the woods, still brandishing their resentment for past injuries, seventy of the town's youths, both girls and boys, learned a mixture of arts, letters, and practical business. These academies flourished throughout northern New England at this time, and many still carry on the old tradition as prep schools, teachers' colleges, and town high schools.

The life of the mind in the hill country was a curious mixture of richness and deprivation. There had always been a high premium placed on literacy. A traveler through southwestern New Hampshire around 1810 found his journey constantly interrupted as his stage driver slowed to toss out a newspaper, causing the traveler to observe: "There is scarcely a poor owner of a miserable log hut, who lives on the border of a stage road, but has a newspaper left at his door."[14] Foreign visitors sometimes complained that the New England farmers seemed too greatly educated for their situation.

If the struggle to wrest a living from the hard climate left few evenings for contented reading, then there was the traditional Sunday sermon to be contemplated.

The richest portion of hill life was the village's social communion. While the farmer, his wife, and children might find themselves maddeningly isolated from their neighbors in their day-to-day activities, the people developed a sense of unity from the constant need to combine together to complete activities larger than single families could handle. The use of the word *bee* to describe a group or community activity entered the printed page as an Americanism in the early nineteenth century.[15] It was a deliberate reference to the social labor of the beehive. Today we think of the spelling and quilting bees. There was also the husking bee, where everyone gathered in a barn to strip the husks off the harvested corn. Barn raising was also called a bee in early times. When winter snows finally melted to isolated patches of dirty white in the spring, everyone gathered at the sugar camp to boil the maple sap down into sugar. There was the logging bee, to clear brush and forest in late spring, the brush being burned off in late summer, giving a greater haze to a sultry August sky. All these were typically family affairs. In the outdoor work, the men and older boys joined together in the task. The women and older girls prepared food or "beed" at some other activity. For the youngest children, it was a picnic. As the country became more domesticated, there was a day of working on the town roads due from each able-bodied man. The annual town meeting also brought the community and its wits together; humor at such times was more visible than money. Such was the character of life on the New England hilltops in the early nineteenth century.

7   *The Move Downhill: Newfane, Vermont, and Harrisville, New Hampshire*

 The movement of settlers onto the hilltops, ridges, and plateaus waned in the early decades of the nineteenth century. After that, more and more people chose to establish their businesses and farms in the valleys below. Even many of the hill farmers themselves came down off the windy slopes. One commentator on Vermont in the 1840s wrote:

Have you not observed one and another of your acquaintance retreating from elevated, windy positions into the lowlands; and taking shelter in the vallies and cavities; behind projecting mounds and clumps of trees? Have you not seen and known one building after another taken down and rebuilt in a more retired, quiet place? ... Do we not hear it said by one and another, and our elders too, "I have lived on this hill long enough?" "I mean to move down to the foot of it." — "The snow drifts have burrowed me up here often enough."[1]

The same commentator went on to lament that much of the pioneer lands were returning to wilderness:

If these are to be deserted, where will be your means of sustaining the increasing population of the Green Mountains? ... Will you suffer your comparatively favorable circumstances to enervate your energy and resolution and make you a puny race, afraid to ascend and overlook the summits of your mountains; turn your backs upon the winds that roar among your forests; and cover your faces and hide from the driving snow storm? Shall the healthful, blooming complexion once so common on your hills ... become pale and wan?[2]

The answer was an emphatic yes. The people drifted down into the valleys, leaving many once-important villages isolated and forgotten on the hilltops. Sometimes they actually packed up the community buildings and carried them down with them.

In southeastern Vermont, the idyllic upland villages of Windham County — Newfane, Jamaica, Saxtons River, Townsend, Grafton — owe their present character to this second period of town arrangement.

Newfane Common, Newfane, Vermont.

Virtually all of these communities were first settled on the heights of the township. Today only a few forgotten hamlets still cling to these exposed situations. The town of Windham, the county's namesake, still remains on its hill site. With its population of about 150, it sits high in the hills, with unpaved roads leading into the village. To reach the center, the traveler must climb steeply up past a few houses whose foundations are buried on the uphill side but leave plenty of room for a full door into the basement on the downhill side. At the crest of the slope is the Windham Congregational Church, which since 1802 has stood looking out over the surrounding valleys. At an elevation of about 2,000 feet, it is the second highest steeple in the state. Even here, however, the town center has slipped a small distance down the slope. The church no longer commands the highest point on the hill, but has moved one steeple's height down from the windy summit. This is the case of most surviving hill centers. They have moved just down the hillside, usually along the eastern slope, to escape the fierce winter blasts.

The community of Newfane, Vermont, not far to the southeast of Windham, was also first established on a hilltop location.

The first settler came to Newfane in 1766, but a real community did not appear until 1776, when families under New York grants came to settle the lands on Newfane Hill.

In 1787 Newfane had grown to become the shire town (county seat) of Windham County. On the hill around the commons stood

a court-house, jail, meeting house, three stores, two hotels, a variety of shops . . . and about twenty private residences. The village stood upon the summit of the hill, and afforded a prospect as extensive and picturesque as any in New England. From the summit, near the meeting house, might be seen not less than fifty townships, lying in Vermont, New Hampshire, and Massachusetts.[3]

By the 1820s, the logic of planting on the hilltops left such settlements isolated from the mills, roads, and lush farms down in the valleys. In 1825 the hilltop inhabitants literally dismantled their village and transported its buildings two miles and 1,060 vertical feet down into the valley to reassemble Newfane village in the intervale. An 1840 traveler on the old high road which passed through what was once Newfane Hill observed that the old village buildings

are now gone; the court-house, the jail, the merchants' establishments, the business shops; the hotel; the commodious houses and the house of God itself; and you see a mere desolation and waste compared with what it once was. The academic building stands, but deserted, dilapidated; the old tavern stand is there; but no longer clustered with the shivering crowd of December court. The winds whistle unheeded; the northern blast finds few dwellings there to rack; and fewer occupants to wake from their midnight slumbers, clinging to their bed posts.[4]

By 1860 only the old graveyard remained to mark the site of Newfane Hill.

The Newfane of today is the valley town that came into existence as the hill town died. The central common and its white-pillared courthouse, churches, hotel, and other buildings "form a beautiful situation protected by adjacent hills from the piercing winds of winter. In the summer, its fertile, well cultivated fields; and its level even surface, and spacious common on which you can plant your foot with the horizon and stand perpendicularly to it without bracing, you find one of the pleasantest villages in Vermont."[5] Today, almost one hundred and fifty years after this was written, the words still ring true.

The movement downhill was not just *away* from the winds. It was also *toward* mills, roads, and the improvements springing up along the valley floor.

As the towns reestablished in the valleys during the early nineteenth century, turnpikes appeared, encouraging a better link between seaboard merchants and

Old cemetery at the original hilltop site of Newfane, now Newfane Hill, Vermont.

inland producers. Ports like Hartford, New Haven, Providence, Boston, Portsmouth, and Portland all sent turnpikes radiating into the hills. In winter, sledges hauled farm produce out over the frozen roads. In the summer and fall, herds of cattle and other livestock would be driven overland to the city markets. The most curious sight was the turkey drovers. Every evening, they could be found resting beneath a roadside tree, with the flock slumbering comfortably in the branches above.

New England's more than 300 turnpikes typically adhered to the maxim that the cheapest distance between produce and merchant is a straight road. Reminisced one traveler in 1874:

Our grandfathers had a species of indominatable directness in making roads and making love that was wonderful to see. They did not believe in the line of beauty; there was nothing curvilinear about them, either in word or deed. They went by square and compass, and life and religion were laid out like Solomon's Temple. And so, straight over the hill, and right through the big timber, and plump into the swamp, and bounce over "corduroy," went the old road.[6]

Sometimes new communities grew up along the turnpike route. Elsewhere, untrafficked routes were abandoned to the grass and scrub. Such cleared ways through the forest became the once-familiar "long pastures."

The turnpikes offered profit for the export of only certain types of hill-country produce — livestock which could transport itself to market, foodstuffs sufficiently imperishable that it could wait for winter before transport, and items of such great value that the long trip to the city did not eat up all profits.

This last category neatly encompassed all the labor-intensive products of home industry, made in spare moments, or during long afternoons of winter twilight: the brooms, nails, hats, garments, buttons, wooden tools, baskets — all the innumerable household necessities crafted of inexpensive materials which made a farm family almost entirely self-sufficient.

Making cloth, from Edward Hazen's Popular Technology *(New York, 1850). In colonial times, all aspects of the work were done by hand. Later, little mills supplied the thread for home weaving, and ultimately the business became completely mechanized, spelling the end of cottage industries.*

The farmers soon found greater profit working in cottage industries beside their wives than devoting full time to the farm. Soon a whole town's livelihood entailed sitting at home in such occupations as weaving palm-leaf hats, tying straw brooms, or whittling buttons out of cattle bone.

A year's production was then sent to the coastal merchants, or, more likely, loaded aboard a wagon to be peddled door to door throughout the nation, by the itinerant Yankee peddlars.

When some inventive mind, bored with the tedious work, figured out a way to drill out the buttonholes with a novel piece of machinery, it hatched the industrial economy of New England's next century.

All over the hills, little shops appeared to adapt machinery and waterpower to traditional handcrafts. Creativity abounded like family Bibles in the New England uplands; it lurked in the mind of every Yankee farm boy, the natural result of growing up among the region's peculiar combination of resources and shortcomings.

The outward appearance of this great vessel of change was quite modest.

You would have seen a short boy, barefooted, with trousers at once too big and too short, held up perhaps by one suspender only, a checked cotton skirt, and a hat of braided palmleaf, frayed at the edges and bulged up in the crown. It is impossible to keep a hat neat if you used it to catch bumble-bees and whisk 'em; to bail water from a leaky boat; to catch minnows in; to put over honey-bee's nests, and to transport pebbles, strawberries, and hen's eggs,

wrote Charles Dudley Warner (1829–1900) of his own youthful appearance while he was growing up in the northern Berkshires.[7]

A boy's life was one constant chafing between skylarking and chores. Although his clothes were typically one mass of patches, carrying proud evidence of many adventurous scrapes, on paper, at least, a hill farm boy had no time of his own, or, as Warner termed it, he was "like a barrel of beer, always on draft."[8]

It was the boy's task to follow everyone about, ready to give a hand or clean up after. There he stood, at beck and call, with idle time to plan future exploits or ways to avoid the laborious drudgery of farm life:

There was another notion I had about kindling the kitchen fire, that I never carried out. It was to have a spring at the head of my bed, connecting with a wire, which should run to a torpedo which I would plant overnight in the ashes of the fireplace. By touching the spring I could explode the torpedo, which would scatter the ashes and cover the live coals, and at the same time shake down the sticks of wood which were standing by the side of the ashes in the chimney, and the fire would kindle itself. This ingenious plan was frowned upon by the whole family, who said they did not want to be waked up every morning by an explosion.... A boy's plans for making life agreeable are hardly ever heeded.[9]

Since earliest Puritan days, childhood fancy did not sit well in the New England psyche.

These drudging aspects, however, had their foil in the many positive qualities imparted by a hill-country upbringing. The jack-of-all-trades dexterity required on a self-sufficient farm inbred both the idea and hands-on practice of being able to master any problem.

It made the stuff at which, half a century later, Mark Twain would marvel, and which he would immortalize. Mark Twain embodied this ingenuity in a character so adept at making do with whatever he might find that he could be set down anywhere, even over a thousand years into the past, and still be the organizing, inventing, curious personality so common during New England's nineteenth century: *A Connecticut Yankee in King Arthur's Court.*

Yet, in reality, this genius was often only a transient flame, and often quickly suffocated. A farm boy's "best of all times" came in the summer of his tenth year. After that, a dawning recognition that he too was destined to inherit the drab repetition which defined his parents' life began to sap his youth. For all the invention that went on in the little shop villages, virtually none of it related to the improvement of hill country farming.

As Stephen Douglas, Lincoln's great debating adversary, observed of his boyhood state, "Vermont is a fine state to be born in, provided one immigrates early." Douglas, born in 1813, left for the Midwest around the age of twenty.

The spirit of emigration, which brought settlers to the northern hills, now acted to drain them off westward, to the dismay of many.

Hill farmers unhappy with their lands simply headed west down the Erie Canal to turn the new lands of Ohio, Indiana, and Illinois into a patchwork of little communities with churches and greens so strikingly of New England character that one would think that the western settlers had floated the whole original village in disassembled parts down the Erie Canal.

Some towns folded up and moved west as a group; others bought tracts of land they had seen only on maps. Land speculation was a big and chancy business. Wrote one humorist of an old childhood companion:

Ed May ... is now the owner of a large town in the West. To be sure, there are no houses in it except his own; but there is a map of it and roads and streets are

Great Falls, Westfield River, Russell, in the Berkshire Hills of Massachusetts, ca. 1840.

laid out on it, with dwellings and churches and academies and a college and an opera-house, and you could scarcely tell it from Springfield or Hartford, on paper. He and all his family have the fever and ague, and shake worse than the people in Lebanon; but they do not mind it, it makes them lively, in fact. Ed May is just as jolly as he used to be. He calls his town Mayopolis, and expects to be the mayor of it; his wife, however, calls the town Maybe.[10]

In 1841 the Boston-to-Albany railroad connected through the southern Berkshires. By 1850, New England had almost three thousand miles of right of way, with two lines cutting up from Boston, northwest through the New Hampshire hills and the Green Mountains, to curve west after making their way around the northern end of Lake Champlain.

With the two-hundred-mile trip between Boston and Albany reduced to a seven-hour ride, the little towns along the way began to succumb to the vices and virtues, fashions and follies, of city life.

At first the railway proved a benefit, reducing the price of finished goods once carted into the hill towns, and providing a nearby outlet for farm produce. But this did not last. The vast flat regions of the Midwest produced crops in such abundance that staples could be raised and railed back east to be profitably sold at a price lower than any New England farmer could afford to ask.

As the many railroads traced their network into the hill country, more and more farmers gave up and left their farms. Those close to railside clear-cut their land, selling the wood to fuel the locomotives and using the money for their fares west.

Trestle across the Quechee Gorge, Woodstock, Vermont, built 1875, 280 feet long, 163 feet high. Built on a 13-odd-mile branch line to connect Woodstock with the main through line at White River Junction.

Sometimes only the buildings and old folks remained after "western fever" struck:

The town of Tuftonborough [by New Hampshire's Lake Winnipesaukee], through which we drove [around 1840], has nearly fallen into decay. Ancient houses; ruined tenements, black and battered with the storms of fifty winters; huge mansions, exhibiting the English architectural style of the seventeenth century; half buried remains of forts and block-houses, built for the protection of the inhabitants against the hostile incursions of the Indians; and the antique chairs, tables, bedsteads, bureaux, and a variety of other chattels of a former age, daily exposed for sale in the windows of the shops, or on the counter of the auctioneer ——— give to it an aspect of antiquity, very rarely met with in any part of our country. The people too seem to partake of the character of the place. There are more old ladies who peer over their spectacles as you drive through the long dilapidated street; more old gentlemen who stand leaning on their canes, "chewing the cud of sweet and bitter fancies," than I ever saw any where else.[11]

The Merino

The prized merino ram of midcentury was a ludicrous creature. It had a dark greasy coat (wool was sold by weight, so the oils added more dollars to the price) with folds and folds of skin overlaid by undulations of wool — as much as twelve pounds a shearing. Every American sheep raiser now demanded the famed "Vermont strain." With not enough to go around, the wily Yankee introduced the application of a "Cornwall finish," a paste of linseed oil, lampblack, and burnt umber, to less impressive rams. The treatment lasted a surprisingly long time, and it took a few good downpours before a western rancher would realize that somewhere, back east, a bunch of Yankees were laughing.

Besides those going west, others migrated only a short distance downhill to the water-powered manufacturing villages along the waterfalls and to handcraft shop villages along the railway lines. They turned the local raw material, like wood and animal hides, into a variety of hats, shoes, chairs, brooms, and so on.

In southern New England, many little factories and shops became the seeds for large industrial cities, producing guns, clocks, hats, brass items, silk, and especially cotton — brought up from the South by ship. Northern New England's manufacturing establishments remained predominantly modest in size, except for the woolen mills.

Before 1800, America's native breed of sheep was a small creature with thin, short wool.

For many generations having little care, their best shelter in winter being the stacks their poor fodder was tossed from, and their fare in summer the scant grass among the stumps of the clearings and the shaded herbage of the woods, by the survival of the fittest they came to be a hardy race, almost as wild as deer, and almost as well fitted to withstand the rigors of our climate and to elude capture by wild beasts or their rightful owners.[12]

With the coming of automated weaving technology in the early nineteenth century, a new breed, the merino, was imported from Spain. Napoleon had invaded that country, and a few specimens of this once-guarded stock were shipped to America. Some died in the crossing; others were ignominiously served up as mutton roasts.

By 1810, wool growers recognized the quality of the sturdy, long-haired sheep, and imported them by the thousands. They soon became the standard hill-country breed.

Within twenty years, woolen mills grew beyond their colonial functions of simply treating the wool for weaving on home looms. They now turned out finished cloth, although many hill-country establishments still simply took in the local farmers' wool and, for a fee, worked it into material, to be returned to the individual farmer. These would become the then-characteristic suits of "Vermont gray," which set the rural highlander off from his city cousin.

Over the next few decades, these little mills grew into factory villages, where

a mountain-rivulet, rushing over a rocky bed, between hills covered with groves of forest-trees, and high rocks which stand out here and there, to mark the stages of descent, turns the wheel of a little mill, perched upon a steep rock, or the high bank of the stream, accompanied with a little cluster of cottages, shaded with oak and maple,[13]

wrote a Manhattan journalist on an 1847 tour of New England's industrial villages.

The description matches the modern scene at Harrisville, in New Hampshire's southwestern corner, not far from the rocky heights of Mount Monadnock. The village lies in Goose Creek Ravine, the spillway outlet to a chain of highland lakes. Here, lining the precipitous walls of a gorge where the bouldered streambed drops over one hundred feet in less than half a mile, are mill buildings, stores, homes, and boardinghouses, set on steep yards or flat terraces shored up by high stonewalls built up from the hillside. House doors look out over the neighbors' roofs just across the narrow lane. At some places the valley is so narrow that the mill buildings themselves must straddle the falling stream.

Only up near the lake's lip does life return to the horizontal. Here, facing in on a rectangle of paved lanes, the village appears: the church, post office, mill build-

ings, homes, a small library — all in fine brick, and all facing, instead of the expected town green, a millpond, the impounded connection between the lake's wide surface and the tumbling outlet that gave Yankee ingenuity the opportunity to harness nature.

When Bethuel Harris arrived here to begin work in 1820, there were only a few farms in the area. The stream itself formed the town line between Nelson and Dublin. In 1830 Harris began the construction of his first great brick mill. As the business grew over the next few decades, Harris, now joined by his sons, built more mill factories. A traveler in 1843, coming around the lip of the lake wrote how he was "surprised and delighted . . . to see a little city . . . well built of substantial two-story brick houses, a very handsome brick church and school-house, two woolen factories, a large store, machine shop, and . . . some 10 or 12 dwelling houses. . . . The Messers. Harris must have expended something like $75,000 in this village."[14]

The character of these factory villages depended greatly upon how benevolently despotic the mill owner styled himself. The people who worked the mills came as transients, young men and women hoping to amass money for transportation west, a piece of land, or a dowry. They had no ties to the community, and unless the mill owner took a hand in beautifying the village, the laborers' own investment in their impressive personal adornment provided a striking contrast against the dirt-packed dooryards, grimy factories (termed by one writer "castles of Giant Despair"), and shabby tenements backed by pigsties and cowsheds.[15]

Stream and forest floor, Berkshire Hills, West Granville, Massachusetts

Mount Mansfield, Stowe, Vermont

Old Flour Mill, Clarendon Gorge, Vermont

Western Connecticut countryside

Old Academy Building (Town School), Gilmanton, New Hampshire

Late autumn, Hill, New Hampshire

Deerfield Valley, looking east from Florida, Massachusetts

Conway Intervale with Presidential Range in distance, New Hampshire

Store dating from the summer-folk era, Norfolk, Connecticut

Covered bridge — Slate Bridge, 1862, Swanzey, New Hampshire

Newfane Customs

The people of early Newfane, population 1,688 in 1810, revealed an interesting cross section of the character of the hill-country settler. They had their peculiarities. The legal turmoil involved in Vermont's quandary over its sovereignty led its citizens to take some interesting precautions. In 1789, when Major Moses Joy proposed marriage to the widow Hannah Ward, there was some question as to whether, by marrying the widow, Joy also took on the debts of the deceased husband. To signify that the new husband took just the lady, the couple devised a curious ceremony. While the wedding party stood assembled in the parlor, the bride went into a closet, and, with the help of a maid, "stripped her of all her clothing, and while in a perfectly nude state, she thrust her fair round arm through a diamond hole in the door of the closet, and the gallant major clasped the hand of the widow, and was married in due form."[a]

New clothes provided by the groom had been placed in the closet beforehand, and the lady

Just up a side valley from Newfane, Vermont, stands the Round Schoolhouse in Brookline, built in 1822 by a "Dr. John Wilson," who arrived one day in town and offered to be the village schoolmaster. After his death in 1847, suspicions grew that the townsfolk had put their children in the educational care of a retired British highwayman.

"came out elegantly dressed in silk, satin and lace."[b]

Propriety was not always the catchword in some of the stories of the early pioneers. In nearby Jamaica, Vermont, there came great hue and cry in 1798 when the town's first minister, John Stoddard, sold his (apparently not unwilling) wife to neighbor Henry Jones. The town got itself a new minister, Henry got the wife, and the Jones couple went on to have six children.

The Harrises, however, had bricks made at a clay bank some four miles from town and erected homes and mills which copied the best of the great cotton textile centers along the shore. By 1850, the village of some 25 homes had a population of about 120 persons, of whom 40 were factory "operatives." The mills made doeskin cloth (a firm-bodied, soft-napped material) and consumed the yield of about 7,500 local sheep.

During the mid-nineteenth century, wool raising had become the hill country's leading industry. The hillsides stood bare of both forests and plowed field. It was all a smooth green of high clover, broken only by the stone fences of vanished farms. Vermont especially became one big pasturage.

Almost every Vermont farmer was a shepherd, and had his half-hundred or hundred or thousands of grade sheep or full bloods dotting the fenny pastures of the hill country.... From old Fort Dummer to the Canada line one could hadly get beyond the sound of the sheep's bleat unless he took to the great woods, and even there he was likely enough to hear the intermittent jingle of a sheep-bell chiming with the songs of the hermit and wood thrushes, or to meet a flock driven

*Harrisville, New Hampshire,
mill building, mill owner's
house, town buildings, and
pond "green."*

*Sheep grazing on heights over-
looking Lowell Lake, Londonderry, Vermont.*

*clattering over the pebbles of a mountain road; for a mid-wood settler had his
little herd of sheep to which he gave in summer the freedom of the woods . . . and
[which] were sheltered from the chill of winter nights in a frame barn bigger than
their master's log house.*[16]

One and a half million sheep grazed Vermont's hills by the early 1840s. Maine
and New Hampshire counted a half million each.

Ultimately the small farm flocks gave way to consolidation. The old values had
reversed. Once, the land was cheap and extra hands to work it a dear commodity.
Now the land had great value, but the import of produce and the small crew
needed to tend the sheep almost eliminated the demand for agricultural labor. All
this increased the emigration to new lands. Intoned an 1834 editorial, "Beware of
the 'western fever' and above all, *sell not your farms to your rich neighbors for
sheep pastures.*"[17]

Driving the hills today, one comes on solid brick houses, with slate roofs and granite lintels. Do not think this the homestead of dirt farmers; it appeared when the scattered farmhouses were torn down to make way for the vast barns and neat fields of "sheep money."

The large profits from wool raising and manufacture in the hill country lasted until the late nineteenth century. Remote factory towns like Harrisville grew until the 1870s. At this time Harrisville had a population around 400. In 1878, a rail line passed by just downhill, leaving a little station seemingly dropped in the valley's semiwilderness. Yet the railroad did more to harm than to help the remote village mills. By then the New England woolen manufacture had passed to a few large mill centers, dependent on shearings railed and shipped into New England from as far away as Australia.

Sheep raising then also moved out from the hills, westward to the prairies and plains. While the stock degenerated after a few generations away from the harsh New England winters, it simply meant that a few breeding farms remained, periodically sending rams of the old blood to western ranches.

As the "sheep craze" died, the hillsides slowly returned to forest. For the little woolen villages, the future held a hundred years of slow economic decline. Harrisville, set in a deep ravine which left little room for further construction beyond the original mill-town layout, persevered as a model hill-country mill village, retaining all the pragmatic beauty with which the Harrises first envisioned it.

Religion in the Hills

Religious peculiarities seemed to be the hallmark of the hill country in the first half of the nineteenth century. There were many social and religious experiments during this time. A spirit of evangelical revivalism swept the land, especially among those who moved away from the established order of their ancestral communities. Many religious groups found good foundations in the hill communities. Joseph Smith and Brigham Young were born in the Vermont hills. The Scotch-Irish Covenanters (believers in a covenant with each other to sustain their religion and dedicated to the idea of living their life isolated from the sins of humanity) founded communities in the hills. Similar, but differing in their strict celibacy, were the Shakers, who also founded their self-sustaining communities in the northern region. Many Baptists and members of other denominations also came north to live by their own creeds. In Porter, Maine, travelers on a back road can find an old Bullockite church, the last memory of an early Baptist group.

Yet the serious efforts of such people were at times overshadowed by the more bizarre activities of other "religions." As one example, there were the Millerites. These people followed the declaration of William Miller of Poultney, Vermont, that Christ's Second Coming would occur on October 22, 1844. By the appointed day, Miller had some half-million believers, dressed in white, standing in their churches, on hilltops and rooftops (there was some argument as to whether one should be upside-down to ascend right-side-up into heaven). When the appointed hour passed without incident, many gave up the faith, but others kept the belief and developed into the Seventh-Day Adventists of today.

The somber Shakers and Covenanters also had their stranger counterparts. The intellectual freedom of the new settlements allowed many to succumb to theological pitfalls around which the old Puritan divines had put taboos. One such principle was put forth by Vermont's John Humphrey Noyes (1811–1886), Dartmouth class of 1830. In 1836 he established a Bible school in Putney, Vermont. Here, among his disciples, Noyes made the final step in the old Calvinist creed of the infallibility of those elected to be "God's chosen saints." The Puritan divines traced their authority to being the Lord's "select," who, after their conversion, could do no wrong. Yet their strict upbringing called for a pro forma conscience and morality. Noyes, however, concluded, "Whatsoever is not of faith is sin; but for him who believeth all things are lawful."[c] What this boiled down to was that after one's "conversion," anything that came into one's head should be considered an immediate order from God. If a woman of this "Perfectionists'" community entered the house of another family, and

THE HYPOCRITE'S LOOKINGGLASS.

EXPLANATION OF THE PLATE.

The Tything-Man Unmasked;

OR

The Devil's Herald mounted upon Hell's Hobb, in the execution of his Infernal Offices,

Armed with a spear stained with the blood of innocence, and representing robbery and extortion.

THE DEVIL IN HIS REAR, STIMULATING HIM TO ACTION, BY RECOMMENDING " HYPOCRICY AND PRIEST-CRAFT."

while they were at dinner, announced that the Lord told her to take the husband over to her house and crawl into bed with him — well, the Lord's will be done. The Perfectionists deplored monogamy as disruptive to their communistic ideals and considered sexual union something like our modern custom of having everyone in church turn and shake hands with his or her neighbor.

The Putney citizens never tarred and feathered Noyes, but they were not heartbroken when he, out on bail from arrest for promiscuity in 1848, skipped town and took his followers to resettle in Oneida, New York. There the community expanded and flourished, through converts and a systematic selective interbreeding among its members, all underwritten by their manufacture of an excellent quality leghold trap.

An attack by Isaac Eddy of Vermont in 1815 on the Congregationalists' practice of tithing their parishioners. A long explanation accompanies this wonderful picture. Eddy is also known to have illustrated a Vermont-printed edition of Fanny Hill.

Besides the small religious communities scattered throughout the region, there were many traveling preachers bringing the word of God to the backwoods towns. The Baptists and others maintained circuit riders who went from village to village, holding services wherever the congregation was too poor to support their own minister.

The greatest of all the traveling preachers was Lorenzo Dow (1777–1834), a man of such bizarre and compelling nature that it is virtually impossible to distin-

guish between his own deeds and the Paul Bunyan yarns that grew up around him. Connecticut-born, Dow became an itinerant Methodist preacher, "on trial" in 1798. The Methodists soon got a whiff of his style and declined his application, but that did not keep Lorenzo from spending the rest of his life roaming most of North America and the British Isles, giving blood-and-thunder sermons that usually began, "Crazy Dow is with you once again!" A modern church historian wrote: "Without formal education, Dow nevertheless possessed an intelligence so sharp that its edge became ragged."[d] Dow preferred his own dreams, visions, and savvy over established doctrines, and his sermons raised both the roof (if he were not outside, preaching from a treep stump) and the congregation's religious fervor.

One of the best stories attached

LORENZO DOW,
Itinerant Preacher,
in the United States, Canada, England & Ireland.

FROM AN ORIGINAL PORTRAIT
formerly in possession of J.W.Barber. – Engraved by A.Willard . Hartford. Conn.
Painted by Lucius Munson in South Carolina in 1821.

Born in Coventry
Connecticut
Oct, 15th. 1777.

Died in Georgetown D.C.
Feb. 2d. 1834. Æ. 56.
Buried at Washington, D.C.

One of the first
Protestant Pioneer
Preachers,
in the West & South West
States and Territories,
Distinguished for his
Labors & Eccentricities.

Lorenzo Dow, preaching on the steps of the South Portico of
the State House New Haven, Conn. June 30th 1832.

to Dow is his own account of a snowy night's lodging in a northern Vermont log cabin. The lady of the house at first refused to let him in, saying her husband was away drinking. After he identified himself and made repeated entreaty for shelter from the blizzard, she let Dow come in and told him to sleep in a little corner of the shack boarded off into a room. He soon discovered that his hostess was entertaining a gentleman friend on the other side of the flimsy partition. The plot thickened with the drunken husband's noisy approach. The lady's suitor hid in a barrel of spinning flax, and the wife tried quieting the husband by saying that they should not wake the great Lorenzo Dow. The husband immediately began yelling for Dow to come out and do what everyone said Dow could do: raise the very devil. Dow gradually acquiesced. He told the husband to open the door and stand back. He then dropped a lit candle into the barrel of highly inflammable fiber. The sudden blaze was quickly accompanied by an unearthly howl, as the "devil" rose up in a sheet of flame, made a fiery streak for the open door, and disappeared into the snowy night.[e]

When Dow finally died after some thirty-five years of camp meetings and stump preaching, the Methodist fathers mourned the passing of a good, moral, and useful man, yet concluded, "One such character in half a century is enough."[f]

8　*Lumbering and Mining*

Along with the farms and factory villages, the hills had two other economic bases of life: mining and lumbering.

While prospectors had been climbing the mountains since colonial days in search of the legendary "Great Carbuncle," a massive precious stone, it was the more plentiful timber that first created nonagricultural income for the New Englanders.

Colonial and early nineteenth-century woodcutters made their living off the white pine. At mature growth, it stood about one hundred and fifty feet, with a base six feet in diameter. This was the tree made famous during the colonial era by the skirmishes between backwoodsmen and the Royal Navy's surveyor general, who reserved the best specimens for warship masts.

To the settlers, this tree was known as the "pumpkin pine," for its lightweight, knot-free, virtually grainless wood made it as easy to carve as a pumpkin. Its size permitted extremely large beams for house or bridge. It split into shingling with ease. Molding makers carved it into ornate doors, paneling, and mantelpieces. It took paint evenly. With varnish and a little age, it mellowed to a beautiful reddish hue. Today, the image of a classic New England old colonial house's interior is rooms decorated by carved white pine in all its possible uses.

This most ideal of timber typically grew in clustered stands in flatlands, ravines, and along the snaking glacial ridges, or eskers, commonly called horsebacks.

As the southern and coastal New Englanders depleted their white pine, foresters entered the wilderness to settle near virgin tracts. Timothy Dwight, in his travels around the year 1800, observed that even after a few generations of farmers had worked the land, the general layout of a town still showed whether foresters or farmers had been the original settlers. If it had been originally a farming settlement, there would be the central green, with churches and town buildings. The farms would be laid out in an orderly pattern. Not so in a community grown up around a woodcutters' camp. Puritan Dwight was not impressed with the less orderly life of the woodcutters, either, whose "course of life seduces them to prodigality, thoughtlessness of future wants, profaneness, irreligion, immoderate drinking, and other ruinous habits. The farmers of New England have never willingly resided among people of such a character."[1]

A New Hampshire historian of the same era concurred, adding, "They are always in debt, and frequently at law. Their families are ill provided with necessar-
ies, and their children are without education or morals."[2] In actuality, they later
became much worse.

By the mid-nineteenth century, logging had cleared the forests north into Maine
and the upper halves of Vermont and New Hampshire. Except for its coastal lands
and modest inland farming regions, Maine was still wilderness, although since
1830 it had exported three quarters of America's white pine.

Throughout the northern hills, the semipermanent foresters' villages gave way to
seasonal winter camps for the chopping crews. Despite Timothy Dwight's statement about farmers and foresters not mixing, the early crews were made up of
hard-pressed farmers, looking for extra cash during the winter months.

In Maine, wood harvesting became the state's dominant industry. By 1850, the Penobscot River watershed alone had some 10,000 men engaged in the lumber trade.

Each fall, timber hunters set out in twos or threes to tramp the wilderness. Periodically ascending a tall spruce (its numerous limbs gave an easy climb), they scanned the horizon for the telltale sight of an esker, or a stand of white pine towering high above the surrounding forest.

Once they had found their trees, the timber cruisers then began their tasks of calculating the harvest, planning logging roads, and siting the camps.

Next came the return downstream to obtain logging rights. Virtually all of Maine's north woods had been divided up into grants and purchases during the early nineteenth century. The state gave some tracts to colleges; speculators bought the rest. Not all this land was actually Maine's to give, however. Until the determination of a final boundary in 1842, the state claimed more than 5,500 square miles of modern Canada. The Maine state militia and Canadian forces almost clashed over the disputed territory just before the problem was settled through diplomacy. The conflict became celebrated as the mostly oratorical "Aroostook War."

With logging rights purchased, a small crew would go upriver to build the camp. It was not a delicate task. Winter freeze had yet to extinguish the insect population. The camps almost always lay along buggy riverbanks, rather than the less infested upland conifer forests.

Even worse, the oxen which hauled the logs to the riverside were to be fed with the wild meadow hay which often grew in thousand-acre tracts. These marshy flats were pest-ridden hells.

Eumenides came in three species. There were the black fly and the mosquito, which could be avoided by working in rains or high winds or using protective clothing and smoky fires.

Such defenses were nothing for the midge, or "midget": "so small as to be almost imperceptible to the naked eye. The black fly and the mosquito can only reach the exposed parts of the body, but to the midget every portion is accessible. He insinuates himself under the collar, the wristband, and through the texture of the garments, and the whole region between the shirt and the skin is a field for his operations."[3]

The crew's job was to cut the hay, and carry it to high ground stacked across a two-pole litter:

While thus employed, with both hands engaged, millions of these little invisibles insinuate themselves under the garments, and, whatever interest or ambition may fail to do, by way of producing energetic motion, the irritating smart of their bite abundantly makes up. Nolens volens [*willy-nilly*], *the men thus employed dance to the tune of* "midget's meadow-hay jig;" *and when no longer able to resist the earnest invitation to scratch, which the irritating bite holds out, drop down the poles, hay and all!*[4]

With the coming of winter, the full timber crew arrived to occupy the camp set up by the preliminary group: a narrow rectangular log cabin shed about twenty feet in length. One of the long walls stood about eight feet high and the roof sloped down to the sleeping-side wall, which was only about two feet high. The common bed consisted of a pile of hemlock, cedar, and fir boughs. At one end, near the fire, was the furniture, a bench made from a spruce trunk; its legs were

Crosby's Camp, Rangeley Lake, Maine, ca. 1880. A fishing camp built in the style of a logging camp.

Mills at Goodrich's Falls, Bartlett, New Hampshire, ca. 1870s. Photograph by John P. Soule.

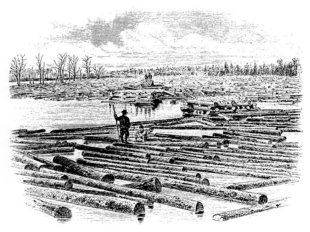

"Down at the Boom," ca. 1877.

stumps of limbs extending from the bark-covered underside. Another log structure sheltered the oxen, and a smaller one served as the cookhouse.

The crew spent the winter felling trees and sliding them over icy ground to the riverside. Come spring breakup, the men floated the logs downstream to the tidewater mills.

Any land cleared by logging soon attracted settlers who raised cattle and hay for the loggers and oxen. Thoreau, in *The Maine Woods,* the account of his 1846

travels through this wilderness, tells of visiting a settler's clearing on the shores of Chesuncook Lake, a few dozen miles west of Mount Katahdin. Here he found Ansell Smith, living in a one-story-high, eighty-foot-long, one-room-deep, "loggers' hotel,"

designed and constructed with the freedom of stroke of a forester's axe, without other compass and square than Nature uses. Wherever the logs were cut off by a window or door, that is, were not kept in place by alternate overlapping [at the corners], they were held one upon another by very large pins.... These logs were posts, studs, boards, clapboards, laths, plaster, and nails, all in one. Where the citizen uses a mere sliver or board, the pioneer uses the whole trunk of a tree. The house had large stone chimneys, and was roofed with spruce-bark. The windows were imported, all but the casings. One end was a regular logger's camp, for the boarders, with the usual fir floor and log benches. Thus this house was but a slight departure from the hollow tree, which the bear still inhabits, — being a hollow made with trees piled up, with a coating of bark like its original.[5]

Nearby stood a cold cellar, a blacksmith shop, and a very substantial barn — part of which was actually constructed of sawed planks — to hold hay and the root vegetables Smith raised to supply the loggers.

The scarcity of white pine by the Civil War era turned the lumbering industry toward the felling of spruce. Logging techniques, however, changed little until the end of the nineteenth century. By this time, logging of the vast timberland around the Great Lakes had taken away New England's national preeminence in lumbering.

Until the turn of the century, the dominant use of New England logging production was wood products, from furniture to firewood. Around that time, however, the emphasis shifted to timbering the spruce for paper. Employing a chemical process developed around the time of the Civil War, the Maine lumbering industry transformed itself from a series of sawmills along the falls near tidewater reaches to large factory towns that produced paper in all its varieties.

At first, paper companies were reticent about establishing mill towns in northern New England, fearing they could not attract labor to this "Arctic" climate. Many mills appeared in western Massachusetts — Crane near Pittsfield, Woronoco along the Berkshire's Westfield River, or at Holyoke dam to take up the logs floated down the Connecticut from far upriver, like the mills at Bellows Falls, Vermont. Soon, however, large paper towns appeared in the north, at Berlin, New Hampshire, and Millinocket, Rumford, Livermore Falls, and Madawaska, Maine. By World War I, the transition had been made, and Maine mills had become America's leading source of paper.

As technology and the amenities of lumber-camp life improved, the character of the logging crews changed. The "sober" farmer, in search of extra cash for his land and family, could no longer be seen in the north woods. He had either given up and gone for a job in the paper and pulp mills, or headed for better lands west:

The woodsman of today [1901] is quite a different person from him who swung the axe forty or even thirty years ago. In the old days the calling was much more respectable — that is, men of family and good character generally went into it, and they earned better wages than are now paid. Now-a-days the camps' crews are made up of Tom, Dick and Harry from all around.[6]

For a while, the woodsmen were French Canadians, Penobscot Indians, and immigrants of various nationalities imported by the lumber companies (there was even a colony of refugee Tibetans in the 1960s), but these, too, ultimately headed for better pastures.

By the early decades of the twentieth century, the usual lumberman was someone who did not agree with society or was currently at odds with its laws. Today we romanticize these woodcutters of over half a century past who settled arguments with their fists or their even harder skulls, destroyed half the town when paid at the end of the river drive, and then returned north to medicate any venereal problems with tobacco juice.

While the Maine uplands are drained by over 5,500 named streams, and over 2,500 bodies of water sufficiently large to be called ponds, certain areas, especially the northwest corner of the state, have rivers too filled with rapids for driving logs. Here and in other places, the logging companies turned in the 1890s to steam locomotives for harvesting logs from the deep backwoods. Most ran on semipermanent trackage, and, around 1900, a few ran on roads. These were the Lombard log haulers, modest engines with a set of steerable sled runners up where the cowcatcher usually stood, and with the driving wheels linked together with treads, like those on a caterpillar tractor.

Some of the railroads branched off from main lines, and in doing so connected a remote region to the outside world. Local mills and factories could now sell their products to a much larger market. Sportsmen and vacationers could sample the wilderness.

By the early decades of the twentieth century, Maine's lumber industry had begun to consolidate. By 1930, 32 individuals or corporations owned 85 percent of the state's forest lands. There was quite a lot of forest in northern New England by this time, as the abandonment of many farms during the preceding half-century had actually increased the amount of land reverted to wilderness. At that time, 78 percent of Maine and 76 percent of New Hampshire was wooded.

Today, the lumber industry is still Maine's leading business. In New Hampshire and Vermont, however, many of the old timber stands and mills have given way to newer industries, especially tourism. Old mill towns have become ski villages, the factories broken off into condos, the old rolling stock now a tourist attraction.

The story of mineral diggings in the New England hills is much the same tale as the story of farming: modest resources being worked, not so much for their intrinsic wealth, but for their accessibility, ultimately to be abandoned when greater resources were opened up west of the Alleghenies.

The region has seen much activity, from quarrying for limestone, slate, granite, and marble, to mining for lead, copper, iron, and small mineral deposits.

New England mining has had a long history of conflict, in which old Yankee owners, well entrenched in the political hierarchy, were pitted against immigrant labor. When new discoveries out west cut the value of the ore produced, failing finances inevitably set miners against mineowner.

The copper mining village of Ely (later Copperfield) in Vershire, Vermont, had the worst incident. Here, around 1880, the miners and their families took over the whole town after being told that the bills of credit they had received in lieu of pay were worthless and that unless they accepted drastic pay cuts the mine would fold. When armed troops arrived to quell the riot, the miners besieged them with tales of privation and grievance. The national guardsmen were soon dispensing their own rations to the hungry families.

From earliest colonial times, explorers have set out to prospect New England's hills for precious metals. During the mid-seventeenth century, the authorities of Connecticut's New Haven colony investigated what seemed to be Hebrew petroglyphs found in hills to the north, and at first developed a Lost Tribe theory, then concluded that the inscriptions were claim markers, recalling that one of the gold prospectors who had passed through the colony had been Jewish.

Gold has actually been found in New England hills. It occurs as placers, or streambed nuggets, in the clear upland stream, and sometimes as veins in the bedrock.

Berlin, New Hampshire, north of the White Mountains, as it looked in the 1930s, when it had a population of 20,000. Its lumber mills then made it the fourth largest city in New Hampshire.

Miners in the shafts of the Vermont Copper Mine, Vershire, ca. 1880.

Looking down on the mining village of Ely, Vermont, ca. 1880s.

While gold panning today centers around the Swift River in northwestern Maine, and around the adjoining towns of Bridgewater and Plymouth in central Vermont, over the years other scattered finds have included Indian Stream, Pittsburgh, New Hampshire, Baker River, Plymouth, New Hampshire, and the so-called Ammonoosuc Gold Field around Lyman and Lisbon, New Hampshire. In the 1880s, a whole string of some fifteen mines was dug along valley slope just west of Hurd Hill in South Acton, Maine, to bring out a small, but profitable, silver lode.

Gold, however, has always been the magic word, and when it was discovered in central Vermont in the early 1850s, many a California forty-niner turned homeward to try his luck.

In 1855, Abiel H. Slayton found gold while fishing in a Stowe, Vermont, stream. Slayton had been in California and knew how to go about things. He bought the farm through which the stream (later to be named Gold Brook) passed, then hired men to work the sluice. His ultimate strike consisted of enough gold for a hundred-dollar watch chain and a few other pieces of jewelry.

A grander tale is the Plymouth, Vermont, gold rush and its aptly named Large Rooks Gold Mining Company, situated along Buffalo Brook.

A vein of gold had been discovered in 1851 in Bridgewater, just north of Plymouth. This region of central Vermont had long been mined and worked for its various mineral deposits. Iron furnaces had smelted local ore since 1837. Visitors had been breaking off the stalagmites and stalactites of the limestone Plymouth Caves since the discovery of the passage down into this series of room-sized chambers in 1818. Elsewhere in town, limestone had been burned in kilns to make powdered lime. The town by this time also had modestly sized quarries of talc, soapstone, marble, asbestos, and granite.

The gold find attracted many former California prospectors in the 1850s, and men came to work claims which typically netted a few hundred dollars at best.

The Great Carbuncle

Indian tales told of a shining jewel, set somewhere in the heights of the White Mountains. This firestone, legend said, could be grasped by no man, and when approached, brought dark mists in which the explorer would be hopelessly lost. This tale lasted as a belief well into the mid-nineteenth century. Wrote a White Mountain historian of that era:

This tale of the great carbuncle fired the imagination of the simple settlers to the highest pitch . . . and, notwithstanding their religion refused to admit the existence of the Indian demon, its guardian, they seem to have had little difficulty in crediting the reality of the jewel itself. At any rate, the belief that the mountain shut up precious mines has come down to our own day.[a]

The greatest romancer of this tale was Nathaniel Hawthorne, with his 1837 story "The Great Carbuncle: A Mystery of the White Mountains." It told the adventures of a "whimsical fraternity whose wits had been set agog by the Great Carbuncle":

Beneath the shelter of one hut, in the bright blaze of the same fire, sat this varied group of adventurers, all so intent upon a single object, that, of whatever else they began to speak, their closing words were sure to be illuminated with the Great Carbuncle. . . . They spoke of the innumerable attempts which had been made to reach the spot, and of the singular fatality which had hitherto withheld success from all adventurers, though it might seem so easy to follow to its source a light that overpowered the moon, and almost matched the sun. . . . But these tales were deemed unworthy of credit, all professing to believe that the search had been baffled by want of sagacity or perseverance . . . or such other causes as might naturally obstruct the passage to any given point among the intricacies of forest, valley, and mountain.[b]

Hawthorne's seekers ascend the mountain and find in their discovery of the stone the individual passions and human frailties which originally drove each on this quest. Each leaves the mountains better or worse, depending on the motives of his heart. Concludes Hawthorne:

Some few believe that this inestimable stone is blazing as of old, and say that they have caught its radiance, like a flash of summer lightning, far down the valley of the Saco. And be it owned that, many a mile from the Crystal Hills, I saw a wondrous light around their summits, and was lured, by the faith of poesy, to be the latest pilgrim of the GREAT CARBUNCLE.[c]

Most gold seekers set up sluices along the many brooks that drain the hilly township. Some more industrious souls tried their hand at diggings in the hope of striking it rich on the "mother lode" vein. None did.

However, by 1880 the local Plymouth Gold Mining Company was working a sixty-acre claim on a hillside near around Five Corners, a backwoods crossroads in the southwestern corner of the township. The company had reportedly one and a half million dollars of mining equipment and a hotel which, at that time, supposedly contained the largest ballroom in the state.

Soon another group, the Large Rooks Gold Mining Company, set up a large refining plant around a four-hundred-acre claim just two miles east. It wasn't long before the Rooks people announced their great strike.

From the *Evening Journal,* Boston, April 4, 1884:

A bar of gold dug from the soil of New England is a novelty, but a bar worth $2,891 was exhibited in the Journal office today by Mr. H. L. White, treasurer of the Rooks Mining Co., of Plymouth, Vt. In less than six months they have taken out $13,000 worth of gold at a cost of $5,000.

The Rooks officers then declared that their equipment could not keep up with the immensity of their discoveries. They razed the works and sent out a prospectus for new investors. After every investor had lined up and sunk his cash into the project, the money, the officers, the gold, all disappeared, leaving the shareholders 360-odd feet of empty mineshaft.

Today, weekend prospectors still wade the rivers to swish the alluvial sand in gold mining pans, and every so often someone goes home with the satisfaction of finding a fleck or two of the shiny yellow.

Vermont still leads the hill country in the profits from its bedrock, especially its granite. Cut for buildings, monuments, and tombstones, it goes to much of the nation and beyond.

Granite is common throughout the northeastern quarter of Vermont. Outcroppings appear among the hills east of the Green Mountain ridge and extend to cover over a third of New Hampshire and well into Maine. It is a rock that became an integral part of the region's nineteenth-century domestic architecture. Every brick house was sure to have doorsteps, window lintels, and perhaps corner quoins of rough gray granite.

During the nineteenth century, most granite for local use came from whatever deposits lay close by. Rocks were heavy and roads were poor, so it took a long time for granite quarrying to develop into a moneymaking business. Today, the main center of the industry is Millstone Hill, a modest 1,700-foot elevation in the town of Barre, near the state's center.

At first, this french-curve-shaped exposure of granite, some five by two miles in area, lying in the township's southeast corner, simply served as a convenient site for building materials and millstones to supply the bustling village growing up around the junction of two major stage roads through the Vermont hills.

As a town growing up around a busy crossroads, Barre, in the eyes of mid-nineteenth-century Vermonters, bade "fair to become a place of considerable business."[7] In addition to the usual tannery, grist and fulling mills, blacksmith shops, and shoe shops, it boasted an ironworks which took the raw materials smelted in furnaces near the local ore deposits and made mill machinery.

Yet the town saw its future in the smooth granite dome of Millstone Hill and the more precipitous cliff face by nearby Cobble Hill:

[Granite] is quarried from the rock by means of drilling and settling wedges fitted for the purpose, by which it is split to any length, thickness or depth required. This stone, when wrought by skillful workmen, is capable of receiving a smoothness nearly equal to marble; and a number of artists in the town are engaged in working it.[8]

Well before the Civil War, these artisans chiseled out "basements, or under-pinning, pilasters and caps for doors, caps and sills for windows, door steps, fence posts, aqueducts,"[9] and other cartable architectural accessories, as well as materials for the state capitol in nearby Montpelier and ten million cobblestones for Troy, New York.

When the Central Vermont Railroad was being laid out diagonally northwest across up to the north end of Lake Champlain, everyone assumed that the line would run through Barre. Original surveys called for it to follow the slow swings of the White River valley up from the Connecticut River, turn north up the Second Branch White River to pass through Williamstown Gulf into the west-running watershed at around nine hundred feet of elevation, and into Barre.

Politics, however, intervened. One of the Central Vermont's prime movers was also the governor, and he came from Northfield, just over the next ridge from Barre. When the Central Vermont's main line opened in 1849, its tracks ran through Northfield Gulf into Montpelier, bypassing the easier grade through Northfield Gulf and Barre.

Granite Quarry, Vermont, ca. 1890.

Sheldon and Slason's Marble Quarry, West Rutland, Vermont, 1861.

Barre continued to load its granite aboard wagons, and with great teams of oxen, haul it to the railhead at Montpelier, some seven miles away.

Barre finally came alive when a branch spur connected the town to the main line at Montpelier in 1875. The granite, however, still had to be hauled by teams down the 1,740-foot vertical descent from the "pits" atop Millstone Hill.

Despite this, the improved access to Barre's granite spread news of its wonderful qualities around the world. Wrote an 1890s historian:

Within comparatively few years it has become an immense business. The hills are noisy with the constant click of hammer and drill, the clang of machinery, and the sullen roar of blasts, and the quiet village has suddenly grown to be a busy town, with two railroads to bear away the crude or skillfully worked products of the quarries. In a single year a thousand Scotch families came to this place, bringing strong hands skilled in the workings of the Old World quarries to delve in those of the New, and a savor of Scotch highlands to the highlands of the New World.[10]

In the ten years between 1880 and 1890 Barre's population went from around 2,000 to almost 7,000.

The Scottish quarrymen faced a primitive life. Barre had no planned housing comparable to that of the mill towns; instead, the men inhabited "Stovepipe City," a cluster of shacks and tenements huddled around the quarries atop the granite dome of Millstone Hill. They spent their days hammering at the rock in exchange for subsistence food, low wages, and disease.

The average age of the men was just under thirty, and about half had families back in the British Isles. When their wives and children finally arrived, they usually were forced to live three families to a house.

Such conditions required that the men band together to support each other during injury and all-too-frequent epidemic illnesses. Worker complaints and the laborers' already established reliance on group cooperation produced a strong union movement. By the turn of the century, 90 percent of the work force was unionized. Most were part of either the Granite Cutters' National Union or the Quarry Workers' International Union of North America.

In 1889 a three-mile mountain railway, the Barre and Chelsea Railroad, opened, carrying the granite 1,740 feet down Millstone Hill. Around the same time steam-driven drills replaced the old hand techniques. They, however, also created clouds of fine granite dust. Men who started working around age eighteen died of silicosis in their mid-forties. The unions spent a great portion of their revenue supporting Stovepipe City's ever-growing number of widows and orphans.

By 1894, the original village of Barre, down in the valley, had been incorporated into a city, as stonemasons of other nationalities arrived from Europe and the Middle East to join the Scots. By 1910, its population was almost 13,000. About one half were northern Italian stonemasons. In addition to the Scots and Italians, there were groups from Sweden, Lebanon, Spain, and Ireland.

The town contained rows of long sheds where the men operated machine polishers to finish the stone. The dust in the closed sheds was worse than up in the open pits, with silicosis and tuberculosis even more common among the workers.

Strife between management and the unions plagued Barre for the first few decades of the twentieth century. The population repeatedly elected a mayor on the Socialist ticket, the companies broke up the unions' closed shops, and the rest of Vermont looked on in horror, viewing Barre as a Bolshevik powder keg.

Stability did not appear until around the time of World War II. Labor problems were resolved. Health threats disappeared. Suction vacuum cleaners became stan-

Stonecutters at a Barre, Vermont, shop.

dard equipment in all sheds. Later, flame and diamond cutters changed the style of quarry work, to be supplanted by modern electric machinery.

Today, Rock of Ages is the dominant name among the four granite companies that still work Millstone Hill.

The bustle of modern Barre reflects the good wages of the modern laborers combined with the devil-may-care attitude of the old Scotch roisterers. The encyclopedic *Vermont: A Guide to the Green Mountain State* in its 1968 edition tells us, in its entry on Barre:

Granite cutters are well paid for their work, which requires extreme skill, and is also hazardous. A free-spending pleasure-seeking people, stoneworkers are largely responsible for the vigor of Barre life. The swift circulation of money, the swarming streets and stores, the whole fast and lusty tempo that sets Barre apart from the rest of Vermont, is created by the hardworking, hard-playing stonecutters. . . . Darkness falling from the hills is defied by the lighted length of Main Street; cars and people moving ceaselessly under the blaze of neon signs; restaurants, shops,

and beer taverns bright and crowded; and the counterpoint of cash-register bells against the music of radio and jukebox.[11]   **Cemetery, Barre, Vermont.**

Yet Barre's real soul lies just up the road at Hope Cemetery. Here lie generations of stonecutters, beneath their own ornate monuments, carved for the day when the ills of their profession took away even their final breath.

There is no more beautiful cemetery in America.

Sandy River and Rangeley Lakes Railroad

One of Maine's most famous branch rail lines was the Sandy River and Rangeley Lakes Railroad. It was a narrow-gauge line, with the width of the trackage built closer together than a standard railroad's, to save on the cost of clearing, grading, and ballasting with gravel an otherwise wider roadbed. For some 120 miles of various branch trackage that was ultimately consolidated into the Sandy River and Rangeley Lakes Railroad, the distance between the rails was a Lilliputian two feet. The locomotives and cars hung well over the sides of the track.

This line began in 1879 with the opening of a modest run from the Maine Central trunk line at Farmington to Phillips, 18 miles and 74 trestles northwest up the Sandy River. Unlike many logging railroads laid out into the wilderness to be later taken up and relaid elsewhere when the timber had been exhausted, the Sandy River R.R. ostensibly was to be a permanent, profitable fixture.

The line never showed much of a profit, although one is unsure whether it was supposed to. The Maine Central line received a greater volume of business from the Sandy River line, as did the

logging companies and mills along its right-of-way. The region's little factories shipped out matches, spools, and dowels. In the height of the Victorian age, many a backcountry wood-turning shop did well in the croquet set trade. It seems that the Sandy River line was being run at a loss to bring profit to its users. Despite red-inked ledgers, branch lines appeared. There were the Franklin & Megantic, the Kingfield & Dead River, and the Phillips & Rangeley. By 1908, all had been consolidated into the one Sandy River and Rangeley Lakes Railroad.

Like its profits, its roadbed was sometimes shaky. One train fell

into a pond when the local beavers decided to add the trestling to
their dam. Houses along the route
were rated for their "hospitables"
by passengers and crew, who
sometimes found that snowdrifts
turned a one-hour, twenty-mile run
into a three-day expedition. Snow
shovels for clearing the track were
exactly that, wielded by the frozen
crew and passengers.

The not-too-wide stance between the tracks made the trains
somewhat unstable, with a tendency (as the locals put it) to "os-
cillate." The biggest problem was
water sloshing around in the
tenders, causing the train to plunk
over when the waves got too big.

*Phillips, Maine, just after 1900,
with two trains of the narrow-
gauge Sandy River & Rangeley
Lakes Railroad pulled up at the
station.*

Once this even happened with a
train parked at a standstill.

Train equipment alone was not
always the problem. Even today,
hunting season is not simply for
sportsmen. A deer in the freezer is
a big strain off the tight budget of
a hill-country family. Once a herd
of deer crossed in front of a slow-
moving train on the Sandy River
line. Without a second thought,
both the engineer and fireman
grabbed their rifles and jumped
from opposite sides of the loco-
motive cab to get off a shot. In a

minute, the pair was left staring at
each other across an empty track,
and at their train, now disappear-
ing around the bend with the
brakeman in full scuttle forward
over the tender.

The railroad lasted until 1935,
when trucking logs became easier
than transport by rail. It did outlast
many of its contemporary branch
lines, since for a long time it also
carried vacationers and sportsmen
into the wilderness vacationland of
the Rangeley Lakes. Today, a good
portion of its old rolling stock has
been preserved at the Phillips,
Maine, Rangeley Museum, and
some cars can still be ridden as
the Edaville Railroad in Carver,
Massachusetts.

9   *Rural Decline*

1860–1920

New England was only a few decades into the nineteenth century when the movement of its people to frontier lands turned from its northward direction into the nearby hills to westward expansion beyond the Alleghenies. Over the century, more and more hill families gave up their homesteads and followed the migration west. The effects of this declining population brought the New England uplands to its ebb in the last decades of the nineteenth century, producing social decay, intellectual degeneracy, and a sad malaise to an already precarious subsistence.

For most of us today, this is a forgotten chapter in New England's history, but in its time, it was a familiar story, told by researcher and novelist alike.

In 1917, Edith Wharton published *Summer*, the story of Charlotte Royall. Wharton's novel is the study of a decayed hill town, and the people who live in it. Charlotte is a Berkshire Hills girl who is seduced by a city visitor and finds herself pregnant.

The events take place in the fictitious village of North Dormer, a line of buildings along a

. . . grassy road that takes the name of street when it passes through North Dormer. The place lies high and in the open . . . a weather-beaten sunburnt village of the hills, abandoned of men, left apart by railway, trolley, telegraph, and all the forces that link life to life in modern communities. It had no shops, no theatres, no lectures, no "business block"; only a church that was opened every other Sunday if the state of the roads permitted.[1]

Yet even this village had some dignity when compared with the ramshackle settlement up on the "Mountain":

The first colonists are supposed to have been men who worked on the railway that was built forty or fifty years ago between Springfield and Nettleton. Some of them took to drink, or got into trouble with the police and went off — disappeared into the woods. A year or two later there was a report that they were living up on the Mountain. Then I suppose others joined them — and children were born. Now they say there are over a hundred people up there. They seem to be quite outside the jurisdiction of the valleys. No school, no church — and no sheriff ever goes up to see what they're about.[2]

This chapter of *Mountain New England* will tell the story of the fictitious communities of North Dormer and the Mountain. There were hundreds of real villages in the hills which could tell the same tale, but it would be unfair to single out for defamation a few individual towns; rather North Dormer will serve as an example of them all.

By the late nineteenth century, a bustling America had outmoded the old economies of the New England hills. The water-powered textile factories were undercut by coal-fired boilers and Australian wool. New England iron furnaces had been outmoded by the Bessemer plants in western Pennsylvania. Mineral strikes out west closed the New England mines. In southern New England, especially Connecticut, manufacturing cities arose around the production of specific products — Danbury's hats, Waterbury's brass, Bristol's clocks; in Massachusetts, the Berkshires had its paper manufacturing at Dalton and Woronoco, and whip manufacturing at Westfield. All these bankrupted the modest shop villages grown up in the hills around a waterpower site. For all the later publicity about New England's farm abandonment, actually the bankruptcy of the small village manufacturing concerns was much more complete. While farms still dot the hills, the shops and little mills are virtually extinct. Those that did survive existed because the railroad passed by.

Boy and his wagon, Bridgewater, Vermont, ca. 1900.

The railroad likewise brought competition. Western prairies supplied grain more cheaply than the Yankee farmers could raise it, and the old gristmills were abandoned around 1875. The local sawmills lasted another twenty-five years before also becoming curious relics of a past life.

In many cases, this destruction of the New England economy was a deliberate business practice, especially among the railroads. An 1890 writer tells:

The factories that under Protection, have sprung up throughout the whole North-East, have by their high wages drawn away the farmers' families from the agricultural districts, while a perfected railway system supplies these manufacturing centers with Western produce at price which defy local competition.[3]

The writer failed to point out that rail freight costs were rigged so that certain cargoes could be sent profitably only in one direction — raw produce to the east, and finished goods to the west. Items sent the "wrong" way incurred prohibitive tariffs.

The worst aspect of this changing economic picture was how it induced the rural youth to forsake their old homesteads. There was a common refrain in the late nineteenth century to the effect that "as soon as a boy could walk, he walked away from Maine."[4]

Before the 1870s, the emigration had mainly been westward, first over the Oregon Trail, then to the California gold fields. Others headed off to fight in the Civil War and afterward decided against returning home. Another human tide left for the prairie states in the decades after the Civil War. These migrations typically creamed off the villages' restless element, leaving the more steady population at home.

The sharpest decline began when the lure of the city beckoned. One contemporary observed that while in previous eras it took adventurous pioneers to set out for unknown places, this new wave of young men and women heading for the cities were simply leaving a bad place for something that could not possibly be any worse. There was no physical danger involved.

The reports of the high and steady wages to be earned in the shoe-shops and in the cotton and woolen mills made the young people even more restless than the reports from the gold-fields had made them, — the shops and the mills were so much nearer, — and many young women, as well as young men, went forth to try their fortune.[5]

Now both the bold, setting out to make their fortune in the world, and the complacent, happy to find refuge from the constant demands of farm life in the safe niche of a repetitive factory job, all left home. Between 1860 and 1900, two out of every five people born in Vermont had emigrated to other parts of the United States.

In areas farther south, Massachusetts and Connecticut, the percentage of emigration from the hill farms was greater, but the population remained within the state: "One of the most curious phases of the present condition of rural New England is that depression and decay are actually more obvious in the neighborhood of flourishing towns than in the remoter districts."[6]

The shorter the distance to the allure of city life, the easier it was to break the old ties. Today, while Vermont and New Hampshire have a more homogenous distribution of farms throughout their rural areas, the Massachusetts Berkshires are almost entirely reforested. Here virtually all the population left for the mills along the Hoosic, Housatonic, Westfield, Deerfield, and Connecticut rivers.

Edith Wharton's fictitious hamlet of North Dormer is such an outlying Berkshire town. It lay only a few hills over from the rail line which could quickly carry the villagers to Neddleton, the business center for the railroad and mills along the "Creston" river. Yet Charlotte Royall had made the few hours' journey only once, when the story begins, having been transported there along with the dozen other town youths by a visiting minister to hear a lecture on the Holy Land. While produce and information came in constant streams from the city to the country, the rural population seldom ventured beyond their own township, unless to leave for good.

The hill towns themselves copied the urban area pattern of abandoning homes not far outside the city to move into the city. Those who stayed in the hills typically moved away from their outlying farms into the village, leaving a countryside of empty fields, with the only signs of active habitation being the lonely sugar houses in their patches of rock maples. Before the wilderness reclaimed the empty lands, visitors found that outside a village, the township became "a labyrinth of roads, cut in all directions through the woods, wide enough for a city, but often not used once a day."[7]

All this population movement in the decades around the turn of the century created a nationally known image of New England's plight — the abandoned farms: fields of enveloping scrub, stonewalls running meaninglessly through stands of first-growth birch, large barns with their ridgepoles broken and crushed to twisted heaps by winter snows, and the old homesteads themselves, empty except for the winds.

The little old house — its wooden wall sun-bleached to a ghostly grey — stood in an orchard above the road. The garden palings had fallen, but the broken gate dangled between its posts, and the path to the house was marked by rose-bushes run wild and hanging their small pale blossoms above the crowding grasses. Slender pilasters and an intricate fan-light framed the opening where the door had hung; and the door itself lay rotting in the grass, with an old apple-tree fallen across it.

Inside, also, the wind and weather had blanched everything to the same wan silvery tint; the house was as dry and pure as the interior of a long-empty shell. But it must have been exceptionally well built, for the little rooms had kept something of their human aspect: the wooden mantels and their neat classic ornaments were in place, and the corners of one ceiling retained a light film of plaster tracery.[8]

Between 1880 and 1900, the national census found that 2,000,735 acres of Vermont, New Hampshire, and Maine had reverted from cleared land to wilderness, with 11,172 farms abandoned.[9]

All this emigration out of the hills, and the sad results it produced in what seemed the rock of America's character, created national concern. National magazines sent investigators into the hills for firsthand descriptions. Sociologists produced depressing studies of rural decay's psychological effects. State and federal agencies investigated the plight of the hills but concluded that abandonment was inevitable.

States published lists of farms for sale to encourage reoccupation. This produced little more than a number of lighthearted volumes carrying the reader through the back-to-nature experiences of city folk who had "adopted" abandoned farms.

Abandoned house in fields, Alstead Center, New Hampshire.

A few gifted writers, like Edith Wharton, penetrated into the core of this sad era with books like *Summer* and *Ethan Frome*. However, the real vision of what all this had done to the character of life in the hills came from the sociological studies and visitors' firsthand accounts. Even Wharton's fiction, however, could not generate the strength of belief to convey how really bad things had become for the rural hill villagers. It was a place lost in the past. One visitor to the hills in the 1910s wrote of finding ". . . raw, long-haired boys, gnarled men with quaintly trimmed beards, and faded women, the lines and expressions of whose faces brought up before one visions of olden times."[10]

Irving Bacheller (1859–1950) wrote of a visit to his now-empty homestead. Two local farmers stopped by, and one upbraided Bacheller for deserting the farm and letting it fall into its present degenerate state. The other farmer looked at the visitor and his own companion and observed, "Well, neighbor, I guess you are about right. If Irving Bacheller had stayed on the farm, I guess the farm would have looked better, but he would have looked worse."[11]

The old supports had died. Religion and education no longer had meaning or influence. In desperation, many ministers turned a blind eye to the sins of their congregations, in the hopes of retaining what little moral effect they could produce. Other churches adopted a blind rigidity, becoming "as immutable in [their] methods as in [their] doctrines . . . cold, unaggressive, self-righteous, and contemptible [contemptuous] of everything religious or anti-religious that [was] not part and parcel of [their] tradition."[12]

Sundays took on the old Puritan cast. The devout resurrected the old prohibitions against traveling, reading, working, or generally enjoying life on this day. One went only to church, and the more fanatical rode in closed-up carriages, lest they

The Ennui of a Farmer's Wife

Around 1920, a retired University of Vermont professor, William C. Kitchin, made a motor tour of New England, camping wherever he found himself when the sun set. From his travels in western Massachusetts:

I went into the farmhouse behind which was our camp to get some hot water this morning. A young mother, holding a six-months-old baby in her arms, was busily engaged in getting her own and the two older children's breakfast. The room was very clean and neat but the furniture looked scanty and cheap. . . .

"Here's my flu baby," she said. . . . "You see, sir, it was this way. Last March, my husband had the influenza, then, before he was

well, the two children came down. It was very hard. Next I took it. Had it not been for the neighbors, I don't know what would have become of us. I was so sick and, when at my worst, along comes this little fellow. That's why I call him my flu baby. They thought I wouldn't live, but I just couldn't die and leave my husband and my little ones; I just couldn't do it, and I didn't, you see. But my, we have had a hard time! . . . We are just getting on our feet once more."

Everything around me gave evidence that the getting on their feet had not yet advanced beyond a scarcely noticeable beginning. It was hard. In answer to her politely expressed inquiries about ourselves, I told her something of our motor-touring and of the

things we had seen. Then it was that I discovered what innately refined sensibilities this woman had, what a love of the best things in nature and life she possessed. And so little to satisfy this love!

"It must have been beautiful; how I should like to see things so pretty; it must be nice!" There was a soft cadence in her voice, a wistful longing in her eyes. Then she added brightly: "But the leaves are just beginning to turn, and really, sir, our autumn foliage here among the hills is just beautiful. When I have time, I go out there in the front yard and just look up at the hills; it is very, very pretty. How I love to look at them!"

My conscience smote me for having told this woman as much as I had of the beautiful things we had seen and thus awakened futile longings in her hungry heart.[a]

be seduced into beholding the beauties of nature. Fanaticism seems to have been the only positive reaction among the permanent population, who continually watched the departure of neighbors and town youth, and then lived out their lives among the crumbling remnants of what they left behind.

Defeatism was a highly contagious affliction, especially when a whole community had seen a half-century-long loss of prestige and population. By that time, the original self-pity had reconciled itself to complete indifference. "Things don't change in North Dormer," said Charlotte Royall; "people just get used to them."[13]

It became impossible to show the rural person any value in his or her surroundings. All of them had fallen under the spell of city life, poring over magazines which made their disparities even clearer. What little profits could be totaled at the end of the year often went for pianos, hanging lamps, picture albums, and other necessities of the proper Victorian parlor — all on the installment plan.

The women felt the disparity most. Sociologists may complain of the farmers' insensitivity to the surrounding wonders of nature, but the women stayed confined indoors, in a world where the only change since the days of their grandmothers had been the replacement of tallow candles with kerosene lamps. An 1895 report on these women said:

There are three meals a day to be prepared, dishes and milk things to be washed, and the house to be kept clean and in order, washing, ironing and sewing to be done, and often it is impossible to get help. After the necessary work of the day is done, they feel too tired to walk to a neighbor's.[14]

Instead, the women would sit down and look at ladies' magazines whose articles extolled the achievements of their peers and whose advertisements illustrated all the modern household conveniences. The hill country woman usually had neither achievements nor conveniences. Often, their physical and psychological ills found refuge in addiction to the quack medicines whose advertisements filled the back pages of these ladies' magazines. Suicides were not unusual.

The men drank, a mild vice compared to the others present. Food marketers in the cities complained that their rural suppliers were always trying to pull a fast one by "deaconing" their produce, "selling as fresh eggs that have been packed all winter, and taking it as a sort of personal affront that the men who stamp and guarantee their eggs can command a fancy price all the year."[15]

As early as 1869, the image of the hill country's moral decline brought out a comment about a sensationalist newspaper: "Whenever any peculiarly cruel case of desertion, bigamy, or child-murder occurs in any of the Middle, Western, or Southern States, the *World*, in chronicling the fact, couples with it the reflection: 'These are as bad as things which happen in Massachusetts.'"[16]

Social relations showed the most obvious evidence of how bad things had become. Said Charlotte Royall, "But anyway we all live in the same place, and when it's a place like North Dormer it's enough to make people hate each other just to have to walk down the same street every day."[17]

With little else happening in town, people spent their time discussing each other:

The neighbors take a good deal of interest in the young people's love affairs. They watch their goings and comings, and comment very freely. What they don't know they guess at. They take not a little pleasure in posting each other on new developments and imaginings, and in cracking jokes on the subject. . . . It is not often ill-natured, but is very apt to descend to meddling and unkindly gossip.[18]

"Woman marries husband's murderer." *One of Vermont's juicier stories is of East Montpelier's Laura Culter, seen here on the left, who had fallen in love with the hired hand Sherman Caswell, on the right, but later changed her mind and married someone else. When Caswell was told he would have to leave the farm, he instead took a rifle to the new bridegroom, killing him. Caswell then headed down the road to the capital city and turned himself in. Despite a life sentence, Laura again took a fancy to Caswell, marrying him in prison. Ultimately Caswell was paroled, and the pair lived happily ever after.* **(See Ralph Hill, ed.,** **Vermont Album: A Collection of Early Vermont Photographs,** *Brattleboro, 1974.)*

The older folks had plenty to discuss. For the lack of any other competing interests, sex dominated the minds of the youth. One sociologist addressing his peers at a meeting in 1916 stated:

As regards the relations between boys and girls, it would be idle for me to present here such statements [from interviews during a walking tour in 1911] as were given me, for they would be received with a shout of incredulity. . . . They are precisely what may be expected under the three conditions of lack of wholesome and innocent recreation, absence of religious influence and want of parental supervision. . . . What is more natural than that the boys should get together in the barn and while away the long winter evenings talking obscenity, telling filthy stories, recounting sex exploits, encouraging one another in vileness, perhaps indulging in unnatural practices?[19]

Charlotte Royall told how she sometimes envied the other girls, with "their long hours of inarticulate philandering with one of the few youths who still lingered in the village"; however, on specific contemplation of the available boys, "the fever dropped."[20] Despite the qualms of the Charlotte Royalls, illegitimacy had become so commonplace that many areas had, by common consent, established a standard amount to be paid by the young man to the girl's parents.[21] Charlotte Royall resolves the problem of her own pregnancy by marrying the aged lawyer who had taken her in as an infant. She does not love the man, but he loves her. For Charlotte's logical, unemotional mind, this is sufficient.

Lovecraft's Eldritch Villages

While Edith Wharton used the decayed hill community as the setting for a sociological examination of the people and their environment, and other writers invented fictional towns in order to avoid personal affront in their studies, one author, Howard Phillips Lovecraft (1890–1937), combined the mood of the degenerate countryside with accurate historical and topographical descriptions and made them the settings for tales of spectral horror. Lovecraft was a recluse from Providence, Rhode Island, who arguably wrote the best supernatural horror since Edgar Allan Poe. For generations, Lovecraft remained a cult figure, his books read to pieces by admirers. Today his name is slightly more familiar, but his style of horror is familiar to the modern moviegoer and to those who read modern novels about ghastly secrets coming forth to terrorize quiet communities.

Beyond the pure horror story, however, lies another aspect to Lovecraft's tales. The awful creatures that arise to terrorize the population are certainly Lovecraft's own, but the settings and the people of his stories are most definitely right out of the early twentieth-century New England hills. Laying horror and plot aside, the reader will find in Lovecraft's stories a superb evocation of the feel of life at that time in the New England hill country.

When a traveller in north central Massachusetts takes the wrong fork at the junction of the Aylesbury pike just beyond Dean's Corners he comes upon a lonely and curious country. The ground gets higher, and the brier-bordered stone walls press closer and closer against the ruts of the dusty, curving road. The trees of the frequent forest belts seem too large, and the wild weeds, brambles, and grasses attain a luxuriance not often found in settled regions. At the same time the planted fields appear singularly few and barren; while the sparsely scattered houses wear a surprisingly uniform aspect of age, squalor, and dilapidation. Without knowing why, one hesitates to ask directions from the gnarled, solitary figures spied now and then on crumbling doorsteps or on the sloping, rock-strown meadows. Those figures are so silent and furtive that one feels somehow confronted by forbidden things, with which it would be better to have nothing to do. When a rise in the road brings the mountains in view above the deep woods, the feeling of strange uneasiness is increased. The summits are too rounded and symmetrical to give a sense of comfort and naturalness. . . .

Gorges and ravines of problematical depth intersect the way, and the crude wooden bridges always seem of dubious safety. When the road dips again there are stretches of marshland that one instinctively dislikes, and indeed almost fears at evening. . . .

As the hills draw nearer, one heeds their wooded sides more than their stone-crowned tops. Those sides loom up so darkly and precipitously that one wishes they would keep their distance, but there is no road by which to escape them. Across a covered bridge one sees a small village huddled between the stream and the vertical slope of Round Mountain, and wonders at the cluster of rotting gambrel roofs bespeaking an earlier architectural period than that of the neighbouring region. It is not reassuring to see, on a closer glance, that most of the houses are deserted and falling to ruin, and that the broken-steepled church now harbours the one slovenly mercantile establishment of the hamlet. One dreads to trust the tenebrous tunnel of the bridge, yet there is no way to avoid it. Once across, it is hard to prevent the impression of a faint, malign odour about the village street, as of the massed mould and decay of centuries. It is always a relief to get clear of the place, and to follow the narrow road around the base of the hills and across the level country beyond till it rejoins the Aylesbury pike. Afterward one sometimes learns that one has been through Dunwich.[b]
— from "The Dunwich Horror"

When marriage did follow, the couple soon fell into the malaise of their parents. Wrote Clifton Johnson in his 1896 elegy on hill country life:

Caress and attentive courtesy and words of love are absent; nor is the man at all particular, as he was in the days of his courtship, to be neat in his dress or habits. If he is slovenly and dirty, and odorous of sweat and stale tobacco, the old time charm can hardly continue. Nor is the woman the same as before. She may be of flighty temper, or ailing, or untidy and a poor housekeeper; and now, in a house of her own, these qualities come out.[22]

A major event in the life of a rural youth was the Fourth of July celebration, with its parade of "Ancients and Horribles," floats, costumes, and other creations assembled from local materials. Here, for the 1898 parade, the bicycle-powered battleship Williamsville (Vermont) *is flanked by Lady Liberties.*

By the early twentieth century, the upland rural village had long since passed on its image of the typical New England community to the valley manufacturing towns. Its best qualities had been replanted elsewhere, and its remnant population looked at the world through dead eyes, living in hopeless defeat. The young who could not escape sometimes raged. Their elders stifled their own thoughts with alcohol and opiates.

Still there was some hope of a new dawn. Writer after writer, in examining the plight of New England's rural hills, found only one note of optimism. Immigrants, who had first come to the city factories, were slowly reclaiming the old Yankee farms. Irish, French Canadians, Poles, Swedes, and Italians found a life tilling the New England soil a better life than they had experienced at the mill or in their own homelands. Their arrival was not entirely welcome, and many old Yankees complained how these people (especially the Irish, who were the first real wave of New England immigrants) had begun to "creep out of the cities with [their] politics and [their] priest, and to usurp the sacred soil of the deacon and the preacher."[23]

Yet it was the very social cohesiveness and Roman Catholic unity which brought success to the new arrivals. Where Christian morals had long been forgotten, the Catholic church bound its members together in intellectual, social, and ethical compact. The seeds were not cast loosely, to be suffocated among the brambles, but rather together in groups, to flourish from their own strength of numbers and under the watchful care of their parish priest:

The truth is that the Old New England civilization and organization of society has here mostly come to an end. It has run its course, has completed its cycle, and we are beginning again with new and very different materials. We have already large portions of French Canadians and other foreigners, and it is plain that for a long time to come we shall have ... the civilization and the intellectual and social life which these people and the Roman Catholic Church will produce under the new conditions of life in New England.[24]

10 *Summer Boarders and Sportsmen*

 New England's tourism ultimately proved the salvation for much of the hill country. By the twentieth century it was the only reason why many areas had not reverted to unpopulated wilderness.

While the "industry" expanded greatly with the coming of the railroads through many parts of the hills after 1870, Americans had long sought out the hills' unspoiled wonders.

Observed an avid Manhattan angler in 1873:

When I was a mere lad travelers took stage or steamboat from New York for New Haven, the railroad to Hartford, a "stern-wheeler" up the Connecticut River to Springfield, stage to Northampton, and any available conveyance to indefinite regions beyond. I remember making the entire journey in an old rumbling parallelogram buttoned in hermetically by close glazed curtains, with a water-bucket slung under the axle behind. They were comparatively primitive times. Manufactories had not utilized every cubic foot of running water, and each wayside stream afforded sport for the angler.[1]

Wherever a stagecoach could penetrate the hills, there seems to have been tourists exploring the countryside. This proved especially true for the White Mountains region in New Hampshire and Maine.

The White Mountains, a mass of granite sculptured by the ages into mountains, cliffs, and narrow valleys, was considered an impenetrable barrier by colonial settlers. No routes could be found through, and all contact with settlements farther north was by way of the Connecticut River valley, or by following the Androscoggin far up into Maine and then turning west.

In 1771, a hunter followed the Saco River northward into the thickening hills. Ascending a rise at the end of the valley, he came out into a little meadow with a flat view northward. The first pass, or notch, through this sixty-mile-wide barrier had been discovered.

Within the next twenty years, explorers charted three other main passes. From west to east, there are Kinsman, Franconia, Crawford (the first-discovered notch), and Pinkham.

Crawford Notch, because it extends most directly from the Conway-Fryeburg interval with its easy connection down the Saco to coastal Maine, diagonally northwest to the settlements along the upper Connecticut River, proved to be the most important route in early years.

Settlers among the White Mountains encountered a rugged life. Unlike those of the other New England hill regions, the slopes here were much more precipitous and valleys more narrow. Unless upon the alpine barrens of the highest summits, a person saw little more than a constant foreground of dark forest and high crags. From "down at the bottoms of these defiles, the prevailing sense is one of shadows and gloom."[2]

The comforts of an easy life came quite late to the White Mountain settlers. As late as 1840, a traveler up Crawford Notch reported:

Here and there a log-house appeared in the midst of a clearing, its wood chimney, and mud-plastered sides, and windowless holes, looking cheerless enough. Generally speaking, there is too little neatness around log-houses to give the picturesque cottage air, so attractive to the traveller; and the squalid children crowding out of door to gaze at the passer-by, or rolling with the pigs in the mud and sand, make the tout ensemble of a new settler's habitation very repulsive.[3]

The chronicle of the region's domestic history at this time comprised a variety of catastrophes — avalanches, freezings to death, and maulings by wild creatures

Coaching party at Jaffrey Center, New Hampshire, Mount Monadnock in background, ca. 1890.

— which punctuated, and periodically terminated, local existence. In winter it took up to a cord of wood per day to stave off the blasting cold roaring down the notches.

The most fabled disaster was an avalanche sweeping away the Willey family in 1826. Their house stood low on the slopes in Crawford Notch. Great slides had scarred the steep ascents around them, and one night, in the words of a contemporary guidebook:

A very heavy one began on the mountain top, immediately above the house, and descended in a direct line towards it; the sweeping torrent, a river from the clouds, and a river full of trees, earth, stone and rocks, rushed to the house and marvellously divided within six feet from it [a great rock behind the house caused this division], and just behind it, and passed on either side, sweeping away the stable and horse, and completely encircling the dwelling, but leaving it untouched. At this time, probably towards midnight, (as the state of the beds and apparel, &c. showed that they had retired to rest,) the family issued from the house [heading for a "safe" location they had established earlier] and were swept away by the torrent. . . . A pole, with a board nailed across it, like a guide post, now indicates the spot where the bodies were found. Had the family remained in the house they would have been entirely safe. . . . Nine persons were destroyed by this catastrophe, and the story of their virtues and their fate is often told to the traveller by the scattered population of these mountain vallies, in a style of simple pathos and minuteness of detail, which has all the interest of truth and incident of romance in its recital. . . . The number of visitors to the White Mountains has been considerably increased, on account of the interest excited by these avalanches.[4]

The White Mountains, Ethan Allen Crawford, Crawford Notch, the story of the Willey slide — all became enticements drawing tourists north into the region. By the time of the Willey disaster, the mountains, a writer said,

have now become the resort of the idle wanderers who pursue pleasure even on their barren summits, or of the scientific enquirers, who explore their rocky sides with unbounded industry, who consider themselves happy, and their toils rewarded, if, perchance, they discover some quaint moss or obscure lichen, invisible to common observers and unknown to learned strollers.[5]

Scientists from New England colleges had been wandering the White Mountains since the 1780s, returning home with new discoveries and leaving their names on the landscape, as in Hitchcock Flume, Tuckerman Ravine, Boott Spur, and Bigelow Lawn.

The explorers and intrepid travelers of the first half of the nineteenth century came by stagecoach. It was a long haul over roads of soft sand and hard rock.

We were on our way through the white hills of New-Hampshire. It was toward sunset, in the month of July, after one of the hottest days of the hottest summer I ever knew. We were six inside, without reckoning bonnets, children, or bandboxes; covered with dust, out of humor with ourselves, the driver, the stage, the horses, the weather, and every thing else; and after a dead pull of eight mortal hours upon the stretch, part of the time through a loose gray sand, like powdered oatmeal, six inches deep, and the rest up hill, were just entering the Notch — a vast cool, shadowy gorge of the mountains, where it was evident enough a smart shower must have fallen within two or three hours at furthest, so thoroughly washed was the broad smooth high way, so noisy the birds, and so perfectly

Nathaniel Hawthorne's White Mountain Tales

The local folk were not the only ones to retell the Willey horror. In 1835, Nathaniel Hawthorne published "The Ambitious Guest," his melodramatic tale of a lodger who put up at the Willeys' that fateful night. The hero is a young man, filled with enthusiasm for fame: "As yet . . . I have done nothing. Were I to vanish from the earth to-morrow, none would know so much of me as you," he tells his hosts, chiding them for their contented life in this lonely valley. "But I cannot die till I have achieved my destiny. Then, let Death come! I shall have built my monument!" In the ensuing avalanche, he too is swept away, and his body is never found: "There were circumstances which led some to suppose that a stranger had been received into the cottage on this awful night, and had shared the catastrophe of all its inmates. Others denied that there were sufficient grounds for such a conjecture."

The homey Willey family passed into legend and the stranger to oblivion. Concludes Hawthorne, "Whose was the agony of that death moment?"[a]

Such maudlin Victorian shudders increased tourism even more, and by the 1850s, thousands were visiting the White Mountains each summer. By that time Hawthorne had also completed two other White Mountain tales: "The Great Carbuncle" (1837) and "The Great Stone Face" (1850), about the Old Man of the Mountains profile in Franconia Notch.

Edward Hitchcock (standing) and Edward Tuckerman (seated), early scientific explorers of the White Mountains. Hitchcock (1703–1864) was a geologist and president of Amherst College. Tuckerman (1817–1886) was a professor of botany at Amherst and man of letters.

transparent the overarching trees — peradventure, while we were watching the sky, and listening to the reverberations of distant thunder, or sweltering and sulking in the vast hollow, where the Willeys had perished so miserably but a short time before, wondering at the miraculous escape from the cottage they fled from, as they saw through the darkness of midnight the foundations of the great deep broken up! the mountains tumbling from their thrones and rushing together![6]

After coming out of the notch, they followed the road across flatter topography, and where there were tourists, there were people ready to provide lodging. Apparently everyone was not suitably impressed with White Mountain hostelry: ". . . and in fifteen minutes more found ourselves at Ethan Crawford's in the worst inn's worst room, that is, in the parlor of the White Mountain House, tired to death, and hungry as tigers, with our host, a man of six feet five, in a low crowned white hat, which he never took off, doing his best to make us *comfortable*, as he called it."[7] These tourists of 1837 had arrived at the lodging of the White Mountains' most fabled personality.

Ethan Allen Crawford (1792–1846) stood, by various estimates, above six feet five inches, and seemed almost as broad. He had come to the intervale west of Mount Washington as a child. His father, Abel, esteemed in his old age by all as the Veteran Pilot, was the first guide for "gentleman strangers,"[8] and had brought his wife and baby sons, Erastus and Ethan, to the region in the 1790s. He opened one of the first public houses for travelers when a turnpike through the notch was incorporated in 1803. It was a low structure, set in the side of a bank, with two stories underground.

For three hectic months each year, they received guests from all over the world, and spent the remaining nine months in utter snowbound solitude.

Ethan grew to manhood and assumed care of the inn; his appearance rivaled even Mount Washington for its fame:

Imagine such a man, with a rough, brown face, well tanned by exposure to sun and wind, but smiling benevolence upon you, putting on a fur hat, over which brush has never been drawn, with a coarse home-spun coat and pantaloons, a shirt-collar open at the neck, and stout cow-hide shoes, and you have a glimpse of our host and friend, Ethan A. Crawford.[9]

For all his fame, Ethan Crawford could not eke a decent profit from his inn. Other hostelries sprang up, debts weighted him down, and in 1846, he died, aged fifty-four.

Only a few years later, in 1851, the Atlantic and St. Lawrence Railway (now the Grand Trunk) opened its track northward from Portland, Maine, up the Androscoggin River:

Crossing that stream, it follows up its picturesque and romantic valley, bordered by the highest mountains in New England, till in its course . . . it reaches Gorham in New Hampshire, distant from the base of Mount Washington five miles only. From this point that celebrated mountain may be approached and ascended with more ease, in a shorter distance, and less time, than any other accessible quarter in the vicinity of the White Hills.[10]

Gorham lies at the northern outlet of Pinkham Notch, which passes up the eastern slopes of Mount Washington. In 1851, the year railroad construction reached Gorham, the Glen House hotel was built in Pinkham Notch at the base of Mount Washington.

Mount Washington and the Presidential Range from the Gorham House site.

A party atop Mount Washington, probably one of the first groups to come up in 1861 on the newly opened Carriage Road. As the party is sufficiently large to have required carriages and no animals are present (seen in other photographs of the same year), they probably came up the completed or mostly completed road. The roof of the Tip Top House was changed from flat to peaked in about 1861, dating this image no later than that summer. From a glass-plate stereo view, probably by Franklin White.

Contemporary resort directories spoke of a road then being laid out from the hotel all the way up to Mount Washington's summit. While only a bridle path at first, it took investors ten years of blasting away at the hillside with black powder to turn it into an eight-mile zigzag road wide enough for carriages to bring the laziest vacationer to the top of New England.

For a long time, the Carriage Road made the Glen House the most popular of the many White Mountain hotels springing up wherever competing railroads connected into the mountains. By 1873, it could accommodate 500 guests (at $4.50 per day), feed them in a dining room 100 by 45 feet, and entertain them in a parlor of the same size with a band hired for the season.

On the other side of Mount Washington — the western slopes which looked down upon the Crawfords' hostelries — railroads had yet to get within some thirty miles' distance, and the stage coaches through Crawford's Notch were still the main transportation.

The first railroad here was not a through line, but the famous Mount Washington Cog Railway, running from a base station at the edge of the valley right up the slope to the summit. The trains ascend an average of one foot up for every four feet of track in its three-and-one-half-mile journey.

The railway opened in 1869 after over ten years of promotion and construction under the efforts of Sylvester Marsh, a successful New Hampshire–born businessman. The world's first cog wheel railroad, it instantly became the Eighth Wonder of its day.

Base Station for the Mount Washington Railroad in the 1860s. Photograph by Benjamin Kilburn.

Small engines, their boilers angling downward from cab to front coupler in order to be level once the steep mountainside grades are encountered, push single passenger cars up the mountainside. Traction comes from a rack-and-pinion assembly in which the toothed drive-wheel under the engine cranks its way up along the cogged track set between the two rails. An 1875 guidebook informed the reader: "The cars are very comfortable, and the ascent is made in 90 minutes, during which time it is pleasant to think that, though these trains have been running for 5 years, not a single passenger has been injured."[11]

Since that time, there have been phenomenally few accidents, and the basic designs of engine and safety precautions have proved successful to the present day.

In 1875, the precursors to the Boston & Maine Railroad system completed a route up Crawford Notch, and the life it had once had in stagecoach days began to reemerge. The tracks worked their way evenly up the grade to the notch by means of a terrace cut into the slopes of the mountains. The views were magnificent, especially the glimpse of the lonely Willey House far down on the valley floor.

With the railroad through Crawford Notch, more hotels appeared in the valley west of Mount Washington — including the Crawford House, the Mount Washington Hotel at Bretton Woods, the Fabyan House.

Yet these were only just a few of the dozens of White Mountain hotels which appeared in every village or scenic prospect. For those unable to pay the $5.00 per day for a lavish hostelry, many hill farms that were easy to reach by railroad augmented their income by taking in summer boarders. This outside contact brought profit and social companionship and reintroduced a need for personal and domestic neatness:

It is easy to see in the large farm houses the effect of summer visitants for generation after generation. A wing has been added here and there, and that which was once merely a farm has taken on the aspect of a magnified country place, dear to the hearts of those who have there found their sweethearts, or find bracing air in such environment for their children. The simple friendships fostered in the hills are among our dearest recollections.[12]

Looking south down Crawford Notch, New Hampshire, from the summit of Mount Willard. The line of the railroad can be seen partway up the valley slope to the right. Photograph ca. 1890 by C. P. Hubbard.

An old farmstead now taking summer boarders, near Salisbury, Connecticut, ca. 1880s. Photograph by R. S. DeLamater.

For the hill farmers themselves, the contact with their boarders turned the whole into an extended family, with the accompanying responsibilities.

Aunt Mary [the proprietor] assumes a motherly direction over all her charges. They are not merely boarders. They are her own family, and she privately warns them of the snares set. The two high school girls are her special anxiety lest any cynical city youth should make an impression upon them. The two school teachers, however, who have imbibed modern notions, Aunt Mary feels are old enough to take care of themselves, and her sympathies are on the side of the bachelors in that case. . . . It is safe to tell Aunt Mary what is on your mind. Not only so, but it is not safe to do anything else.[13]

Some virtually abandoned villages, like Paris Hill, Maine; Alstead, Canaan Street, and Park Hill, New Hampshire; Landgrove and Grafton, Vermont, were bought up and restored into living museums by summer people.

The tourists often came for extended periods. Some spent a week or so, others "did the season," which for many hotels was really only the months of July and August. Mother, children, and servants appear in hotel registers, signing in for the summer. The husband came up for a couple of weeks in August, when city business slowed. Those who did the season were typically not at a loss for cash.

For the affluent, especially the youth, repeated summers at the mountain houses were a dreamy joy of new acquaintances and renewed friendships, and sometimes romances.

Those who came with more limited budgets, the "must see" tour consisted of ascending Mount Washington either by the carriage road or railway, a night at the summit hotel, and a descent down the other side, with a return to one's own lodgings by stagecoach or train around through Crawford Notch. Next, if time permitted, came a visit to Franconia Notch.

The resort hotels themselves provided much entertainment — croquet, bowling, and, later, golf gave the summer visitors something to do while they absorbed the magnificent vistas that everywhere met their eyes.

There was much nostalgic evocation of the pre-1850s era of White Mountains ambiance, with coaching parties setting out to tour the backwoods villages. Lunch would be at some rustic inn. There would be stops to view the many falls, brooks, vistas, and rock profiles. Local folk established themselves at various scenic must-sees, like the Pool in Franconia Notch, a circle of water more than a hundred feet in diameter, surrounded by high cliffs. Here the Philosopher of the Pool took up his station: "For many summers an eccentric rural philosopher has lived here, in a rude boat, amusing visitors with his quaint speculations and original cosmologies."[14]

Spare moments were apparently spent in prowling the immediate area of one's resort for rocky outcroppings that might in any way vaguely resemble a familiar profile. Those doubting the discovery bordered on heresy. Said an 1888 guidebook, itemizing the sights around the North Conway intervale:

The White-Horse Ledge is about 960 ft. high, and derives its names from the fancied resemblance of a light colored spot on its front to a white horse dashing up the cliff. New-comers at N. Conway are seldom allowed to rest until they have seen, acknowledged, and complimented the equine form of this amorphous spot.[15]

Some of the tourists took hikes on well-laid-out paths through the hills. A recommended route for the young and hardy was the walk down from Mount Washington's summit.

The Philosopher of the Pool, Franconia Notch, New Hampshire. "This Stygian pool is surrounded by cliffs 150 ft. high, whose deep shadows add to its weirdness and gloom. For many summers an eccentric rural philosopher has lived here, in a rude boat, amusing visitors with his quaint speculations and original cosmogonies," said the author of **The White Mountains: a Handbook for Travelers** *(Boston, 1888).*

Those inclined toward less strenuous forays up the mountainsides went on ponies or burros, which were preferred over horses. Trails were sometimes quite steep, and narrowed along cliff edges. Riders preferred low mounts, where their feet hung near the ground. Such steeds gave some comfort in the thought that, if the animal stumbled, the rider could quickly step off during the early stage of the poor creature's tumbling descent down some chasm. In actual practice, riding was often safer than walking. The initiate tramper all too often became enamored of some grand vista and tripped over the thick roots exposed across the path.

Until the 1890s, White Mountain tourist business depended on hotel advertising, thick regional guidebooks, and classic texts such as Thomas Starr King's *The White Hills: Their Legends, Landscape and Poetry* (1859) and Samuel Adams Drake's *The Heart of the White Mountains: Their Legend and Scenery* (1881). These volumes served as vivid armchair tours, both for the city dweller in his easy chair before the fireplace, and the sore-footed vacationer in a wicker chair on the hotel veranda.

Around the turn of the century, railroads, especially the Boston & Maine and Maine Central systems, actively promoted the region's attractions.

The White Mountains now reached their heyday. Summer villas appeared on the lower slopes. Towns just north of the major range boomed. Bethlehem was the biggest. Its Maplewood Hotel rivaled the Crawford House and the Fabyan House with accommodations for 400 guests (the great Glen House had burned and been replaced with a smaller structure). Standing on a plateau, about 1,500 feet in altitude, the Maplewood offers a majestic panorama for the whole White Mountains:

When the village has received its full quota of two thousand summer-guests, and the long two-mile plank walk, rising and dipping by the roadside, becomes the favorite promenade of bevies of gaily-dressed city-people, and the tennis-courts and ball-grounds are in full play, and merry driving parties are setting out for the neighboring rural roads, the Bethlehem presents a charming sight, and justifies the admiration of its many devotees.[16]

So touted a Boston & Maine Railroad vacationers' booklet.

The most magnificent of all the resort hotels opened for the season in 1902: the Mount Washington Hotel at Bretton Woods. Accommodating 550 guests, it is a Spanish Renaissance extravaganza. Where its competitors were good New England inns on an enlarged scale, it has all the exuberance of its New York origins. Five stories of rooms, octagonal towers, inside swimming pool, smart shops, ticker tape, broker's office, ballrooms, and verandas offering the most magnificent views of sunset against Mount Washington all made it the high style.

The White Mountains' grand era lasted as long as the railroads dominated travel, emptying the most affluent neighborhoods of Pittsburgh, Philadelphia, New York City, and Boston onto the station platforms of resort communities. When the automobile began to spread vacationers into a more homogenous distribution throughout the New England hills, the 1897 prediction of a railroad's tourism promoter finally came to pass:

As the traveller approaches the mountains by this route of the Boston & Maine, he soon realizes that in these elevated sections all localities are lavishly endowed with characteristics that render them eligible as summer resorts; and that he need not encamp nor abide within the very shadow of the mountain-sides and peaks in order to find a satisfactory sojourning place for his vacation season. Scattered all along within the New Hampshire limits are delightful rural, farming, and inland neighborhoods, seemingly especially designed for the resting and recreation of overworn humanity; and these places appeal as strongly in their attractiveness for the wanderer through these qualifications, as do the upheavals and wilds and glens of the mountain situations by their impressive features and belongings.[17]

From the 1920s onward, the grand hotels slowly faded to the more modest tourist court. Today, only a handful still open their doors to guests. As these grand old ladies of architecture passed one after the other into oblivion, their registers, to the very last season, showed the names of now-elderly men and women who had come back every summer of their lives. They still dressed in black tie, or jewels and furs, for the weekly bingo game in the music room, dined at the same table which they had occupied for sometimes seventy or eighty summers, smiled discreetly at the newlyweds, and watched the sunset from the high veranda, in dazed surprise that the mountain hotels' twilight should precede their own.

By the 1870s, a sportsman in Maine had to venture halfway to Canada before escaping "to regions untainted by the odor of lavender or cologne, where 'parasols' never venture."[18] Even the fabled remote Moosehead Lake, with its four hundred miles of shoreline, had by then been thrown open to the genteel vacationers by railroads, bemoaned this writer, and the sounds of the night creatures were now replaced by piano recitals, the silent birch canoes by tooting lake steamers.

Amateur huntsmen abounded in the proximity of these resorts, and woe betide the unwary hiker during open season. Commented a resident living a few miles from Moosehead's northern shore:

As soon as the law is off on deer there's the darndest rush of sports in here that ever you see, all wantin' to hunt, and so excited they don't know what they're doin'. They gather around the borders of the clearings waiting for the deer to come out to feed, and if they get sight of anything movin' they take for granted that it's game and shoot in a hurry. So in the late evening or early morning, when the light is dim, if you get anywhere near 'em, they most likely plunk you.[19]

Hunting season came in the fall. It began a few weeks after cold weather had killed off the last of the summer's mass of black flies and lasted to around the first heavy snow, about a month.

Other hunters took railroads, steamers, stages, and canoes farther into the north woods. While big-city sportsmen's clubs were buying up abandoned farms to consolidate them into preserves in the lower states, Maine's open wilderness was so vast that it could swallow with little effort the estimated 10,000 out-of-staters who came annually by 1900.

They shoot and tramp and swing the axe, swap experiences with their guides or comrades, listen to their weird tales about the Spectre moose whose giant form is always seen in the woods every year, but never by the city sportsman; smoke around their camp-fires by night and loaf in the silent cathedrals of the woods by day, and finally emerge, bronzed, unkempt, but supremely satisfied with themselves and the world.[20]

Some actually hunted, but for many of the male crowd (as today) the lure of the woods included smoking, card playing, drinking, and most certainly excluded wiping their feet on the mat, watching their language, or bathing.

The getaway types patronized the many organized camps set along lakeshores.

The White Mountains from Bethlehem, New Hampshire. Photograph ca. 1900–1910, by Henry G. Peabody.

Ethan Allen Crawford

Ethan Crawford was a rugged mountain man, who could take city-dwellers up a mountain with the worst weather outside the Antarctic and bring them back unscathed. He once carried a lady on his shoulder two miles down from Mount Washington. He was the most sought-after guide for climbs to the summit. He blazed a trail up to timberline which by 1819 could be used by horses. In 1840, the whole journey could be made on horseback. No one feared for their safety with Ethan as guide.

However, reading between the lines lauding his wilderness expertise, one quickly discovers a less

"The Notch of the White Mountains (Crawford Notch)," by Thomas Cole, 1839. (National Gallery of Art, Washington, D.C.; Andrew W. Mellon Fund.)

obvious strength — Ethan's ability to withstand the formidable onslaughts of his guests.

Request from him a favor to yourself or your friends and see how readily and cheerfully he moves to do it. Follow up your questions and demands; ask things which you know he cannot obtain for you without great inconvenience to himself or household; nay more, worry his dogs, over-ride his horses, leave open his garden gate, dirty his parlor, and he is still the same imperturbably good-natured Ethan A. Crawford.[b]

He was a showman who would have made P. T. Barnum proud. One set of attractions for the non-climbers was the "two-and-forty pounder cannon" and "bugle" Crawford sounded to echo off the cliffs. In actuality, visitors found "the first a mounted horse-pistol, the second, a sort of tin pipe with

a funnel-sloped mouth, and the third, a magnificent reverberation among the mountains. You'd thought a whole park of artillery, with half a hundred bugles, were all sounding and playing together!"[c]

Every visitor shuddered at the prospect of the great bears in the woods, which, unless protecting their cubs, would usually have to be chased, cornered, and periodically stabbed before they would attack a man. In 1830, Crawford took to keeping a tame bear to delight his guests. Woe betide, however, any wild bears discovered wandering on the loose when tourists were about. It immediately suffered the danger of becoming grist for a good press release:

We had descended two thirds perhaps of the mountain, and were in the depth of the forest, when

Crawford, who was in advance, sprung out of the path, and, as it seemed to me, fell headlong over a fallen tree. As he said not a word, I started toward him, the others of the party being several rods behind us, supposing him to have fallen; but what was my horror, to find him grappling a huge bear, who was tugging with all his strength to escape from the firm hold which Crawford's two hands had upon his hair. The contest lasted hardly long enough for me to cry "a bear, a bear," for Bruin, turning suddenly upon one side, threw his antagonist upon his back [i.e., threw Crawford to the ground], and made off hastily to the woods.

The bear, it seems, was asleep behind the log, when Crawford, with his usual impetuosity and fearlessness, and without at all calculating upon the risks of the adventure had flung himself upon him, and when I came up, had nearly drawn his knife, to cut his throat. We laughed heartily at our adventure, and it served as a topic to introduce many stories, during the evenings, of our host's encounters with the wild animals of the mountains.[d]

Here, some dozen log cabins, each holding four or five beds, were connected by a plank walk to a large common dining room.

The true hunters set out into the wilderness with pack and guide. The hunting trip became an annual experience of the freedom of the woods. They set up camp in some logged clearing; at night the fire cast weird shadows among the surrounding forests. Just behind the bedrolls, opposite the fire, a canvas tarp made a wall to reflect the heat back at the sleeping hunters. Far above, stars shone clear against the black.

At morning, only coffee and the early hunt shook off the chill. All in all, these expeditions were more a surrender to nature than a conquest of it by the firearm.

The many logging paths crisscrossing the Maine forests allowed easy travel through this spongy landscape. The game included deer, ruffed grouse, foxes, with an occasional bear and moose. The last, however, were soon in short supply.

During the Victorian age, wilderness life was considered anathema for the proper lady, who always carried civilization, in the form of considerable luggage, wherever she ventured:

There is nothing more absurd and unreasonable than the growling which some men make about the quantity of ladies' baggage. When you have ladies in charge, take every luxury they may require. It is as easy to take care of ten trunks as two, and the secret of pleasant travel is to avoid as far as possible all that can be called "roughing it," by having in the luggage every possible comfort.[21]

Thus remarked a gentleman-sportsman on a trip through northern New Hampshire in the early 1870s. This would all change by the turn of the century.

Since the railroads profited by transporting both the sportsman and his needs, they soon turned to promoting the Maine wilderness as they had the White Mountains. Parlor cars ran direct from Boston to Moosehead Lake. Logging railways bought cars to distribute hunters and fishermen into the most pristine tracts.

By the turn of the century the state of Maine began regulating this growing industry. Anyone not a Maine resident was obliged to hire a licensed guide. Strict hunting seasons for certain game were enforced.

With the railroad virtually the only mode of transportation in and out of the backwoods hunting areas, a handful of game wardens stationed at the state's half-dozen major railroad junctions could keep track of kills taken out of state.

When a train from the north came in, they climbed aboard, and passed down the cars yelling out, "Identify your game!" It must have taken great reserve when entering the smoking car to hear, for the thousandth time, its occupants yell out in unison, "Poker!"

By the 1910s the hunter could check his game in a special baggage car, where it was automatically registered and stored for the whole journey home. Accounts are vague as to exactly where the hunter stowed his dead animals before this system came into use.

While hunting received the greatest attention during the nineteenth century, the state and railway promoters soon realized that by 1900, for every one hunter there were three fishermen who "scatter over a far wider territory, stay longer, and, in the aggregate, leave more cold cash with the thrifty residents."[22]

Unlike the huntsman, the fisherman could exist in closer contact with the summer folk. His hours alternated with their revelries. The noisy boats of happy vacationers occupied the waters by daylight, and as the dusk brought them to shore to prepare for dinner and dance, they were replaced on the waters by a few silent figures quietly fishing.

A Deaf-mute Guide in the White Mountains

William B. Swett (1824–ca. 1880) was a deaf-mute carpenter who in 1865 went to work for the Profile House hotel in Franconia Notch. He quickly took to the mountains and became a guide. The curiosity — a mountain guide with such afflictions — however, is today secondary to the many wonderful descriptions of his White Mountain experiences. In one account, he, like many who venture up the mountain trails, sometimes found the strange and often terrible atmospheric phenomenon of the heights even more majestic than the mountains themselves. From his *Adventures of a Deaf Mute*:

The most remarkable sight I had ever witnessed, occurred one afternoon this season [1866]. The clouds were gathering, and slowly descending, and there was every appearance of a rain-storm, when I determined to venture up the Mountain, to see whether it was clear at the top. I hurried up as fast as I could, and having made the ascent, passing through a dense cloud on my way, I was rewarded by a singular sight. Below me, and shutting off all other view, was, apparently, a thick field of cotton, almost tempting me to jump into its soft folds. I learned, afterward, that soon after my departure from the hotel it commenced raining heavily, and the people there thought I was in a

William B. Swett, deaf-mute guide and White Mountain adventurer.

bad plight for venturing on the Mountain at such an improper time. They did not appreciate my love of adventure, and my desire to experience the sensation of being above a storm-cloud. I had often read of persons standing on top of a mountain while there was a storm raging below them, and I now felt quite elated at my good fortune in witnessing a similar scene.

Very soon the cotton-cloud changed to a bright red color, as if on fire, caught from the sun, which was shining brightly above. The scene now became sublime, beyond my ability to describe. I was reminded of the Israelites fleeing from Egypt, guided by a pillar of fire by night. For many miles around, this magnificent sight met my eye. Soon, however, I noticed that the cloud was rising, which

made me feel quite uneasy, for fear that I should get a thorough soaking, which would render me quite uncomfortable, and perhaps place me in a dangerous plight from the cold and wet, and there was no chance for escape; so I had to content myself by waiting its approach. I saw no lightning, nor did I feel any jar from the thunder, in which I was somewhat disappointed. As the cloud arose, I was agreeably surprised to find that it did not rain at all, but there was a thick mist or cloud rising fast, and in a few minutes it had passed above my head, slowly uniting, until it appeared like a great white cloth or sheet spread over many miles around. The whole Mountain range came into full view, in all its grandeur and majesty.

I was riveted to the spot in amazement at this unexpected scene, and I can hardly find words to portray the beautiful spectacle. The rising of a mammoth curtain in a mammoth theater, might give some idea of what I beheld coming into view: a grand panorama of splendid and varied landscape. Mount Washington, thirty miles away, revealed itself in mighty grandeur, with all its surrounding minor hills. But the descending sun warned me not to tarry, but to hasten down while yet there was daylight enough to guide my steps. I found most of the path very wet and muddy, but reached the hotel without harm.[e]

Dawn however, is the angler's true hour. And with joy he rises as the last partiers are finally going to bed. From the seat of his canoe he watches the coming of first light: "If you have never seen mountains wake out of the darkness when the morning is yet far off, you have something to see in this world yet."[23]

While fishing season traditionally was the month of June in Maine (the ice did not go out until May), fishermen were soon in abundance during the whole warm season. After 1900, the resorts found that many women now joined their male counterparts in this contemplative sport, adding a second sex to the adage "No

Camp in the Rangeley Lakes region, Maine. Photograph by Charles A. Farrar, 1870s.

"A typical lean-to," in a Maine camp, ca. 1902.

man is in perfect condition to enjoy scenery unless he has a fly-rod in his hand and a fly-book in his pocket."[24]

Men and women also came solely to tramp the wilderness without rod or gun. Others took canoe voyages. Many were avid nature photographers, stalking their game with a Kodak, "... absolutely dangerous animals are subject to this snap-shot process of hunting. There is no amateur photographer quite as proud as is he who has captured on plate or film the picture of a startled deer or defiant moose, or perhaps some suddenly surprised bear."[25]

Cover of a 1916 Maine guide directory issued by the Maine Central Railroad.

Brass band on Echo Lake, Franconia Notch, ca. 1860s. For the entertainment of guests at the Profile House, a band would row out on the lake in the evening and play, to be accompanied by echoes off the surrounding cliffs. Photography by Benjamin Kilburn.

A lady fisher on Sunday River, Bethel, Maine, around 1906.

Activities around the dock of Mt. Kineo House, Moosehead Lake, Maine, ca. 1910.

With all this new interest in the wilderness, more and more development was seen along the larger wilderness lakes. Great resort hotels in the White Mountains style appeared at Moosehead, Rangeley, Belgrade, Sebago, and other Maine waters.

Moosehead, still the last point of civilization before the vast wilderness, boasted the Mt. Kineo House. Set halfway up the forty-mile lake, at the base of an eight-hundred-foot flint cliff where Indians once came to gather material for their weapons, the grand resort had a golf course, carriage drives, specially prepared bicycle paths, and boat races. It could be reached only by a steamer up the lake, and from the water it resembled the Isle of Capri with pine trees and moose. Naphtha-powered launches and crack speedboats occupied the docks, where nearby, canoes lay pulled up along the marshy shore. Wall Street magnates in their smart golf outfits and powerboaters in their blue and whites stood side by side with the red flannel of lanky Yankee locals and massively oversized Indians fitting out along the shore for expeditions down the Allagash.

Ultimately the automobile changed the character of the Maine tourist economy, as it had done in the rest of New England. The hunting and fishing camps continued, but the big hotel trains became less frequent as the big hotels gave way to the roadside inns. This change took a while longer in Maine because of the greater problems involved in laying down good roads through the vast tract of Maine's north woods. The backwoods hunting and fishing camps continued to flourish, but the old great hotels — the Kineo House, the Poland Springs Hotel, the Rangeley Lakes House — lost their trade as trains, like the Maine Central's *Vacation Flyer*, stopped running. Instead, the auto brought more transient vacationers, willing to spend a few days at various stops. Few visitors came for the season by the 1930s; more and more were taking the motor tour. That will be the story for a later chapter.

11 Twentieth-Century Improvements and the Depression: The 1920s and 1930s

 The first decades of the twentieth century had continued the economic and social trends begun in the late nineteenth century: farm abandonment, growing resorts, a steady woolen industry, and the survival of various holdout local manufacturing. The larger changes in hill-country life occurred in the 1920s and 1930s, as modern inventions, like the telephone, electricity, and the automobile, spread into the rural uplands.

Farm abandonment still continued at a rapid rate. Of the farms existing in 1900, by 1930 the number had fallen by half in New Hampshire, by one third in Maine, and by one quarter in Vermont.[1] Few were migrating west anymore; the steady stream was now to New England's industrial cities.

For the farmer, one positive aspect of this growth in urban population was the city families' constant need for fresh local produce, such as milk and eggs.

Pasteurization created the milk trains in the last years of the nineteenth century, and by the turn of the century, they stopped at every hamlet depot in southwestern Maine and lower New Hampshire on their way to the industrial cities around Boston. By 1930, all of Vermont and portions of Canada were supplying the southern New England market.

Dairy farming, however, tied the farmer down because of twice-daily milkings. Bad roads also limited dairy farming to farms lying close to rail depots. An agricultural expert wrote in 1905:

Four miles of hilly road is an undisputed limit for the average farmer short-handed as to labor. Otherwise the time for drawing milk in to the train from the farm, being drawn away from active, creative farming, eats up the profits. There are those who would set the limit in New Hampshire, with drifting roads and irregularly inclined planes for highways, as two and a half miles.[2]

By the 1920s, milk tankers made daily circuits through their regions, allowing the milk-producing regions to expand. The age of the motor car had come to the hills.

Telephones, electricity, and automobiles now became necessary parts of rural life. Electricity brought to long winter nights light and, later, the radio. The telephone brought the instant companionship of one's neighbors.

Until the production of the inexpensive Model T, few farmers could afford automobiles. By 1930, however, almost three in four farms had a Model T "flivver" to haul produce, the family, or calves, pull stumps, or, by removing a tire and replacing it with a pulley, power sawmills, lift grain, or whatever:

Not long ago, on one of our stage cruises "up the State" [in the Berkshires] we encountered a brand-new automobile driven by a native under the guidance of a professional instructor. It was an incongruous spectacle, almost anachronistic. Here was a middle-aged farmer, arrayed in his field motley, sitting at the wheel of a very up-to-date car of ample proportions. He was steering a wobbly course; his jaw was set; his eyes protruded. Our stage took to the bushes to let the car go by on the narrow road.[3]

The Model T allowed the farmer to truck his own produce to the railhead, and also to bring his family into town each weekend. "Farmers owning automobiles and living within a ten-mile radius of any town of size, consider themselves as living in town," wrote a reporter for an agricultural paper in 1910.[4]

The telephone lines first appeared along the old turnpikes around the turn of the century. Villages had community "party lines." Neighbors could now not only talk with each other to learn what was going on, but it was also perfectly acceptable to pick up a telephone receiver and listen in one everyone else's conversations. The party line provided much the same entertainment as our modern television soap operas, with their ever-changing parade of characters, plots, and events.

Electricity followed a few decades later. In 1930, only half the New England farms (a few more in southern New England and a few less in northern New England) were wired.[5] The radio brought entertainment and instant contact with

Richford, Vermont, November, 1927. The greatest hazard of living in the narrow valleys of the northern hills is floods, which can come in two ways. Winter snows can be suddenly melted by a prolonged warm rain in midspring, or a similar rain can become total runoff if it falls onto already frozen or saturated ground in early winter. In the first few days of November of 1927, the latter happened, inundating major portions of Vermont and New Hampshire. Montpelier homes had flood water to their second-story windows. A short distance down the Winooski River, at Waterbury, Vermont, the torrent skipped out of the old riverbed and carved a new channel down the main street. In Vermont, fifty-five lives were lost. Most of today's reservoir and flood control dams in both states are products of the lessons learned in the 1927 horror.

world events. At evening the glow of its vacuum tubes replaced the flickerings of the hearth now that central heating had arrived.

The telephone and radio saved the sanity of the farm wives. It is said that first the telephone and then the radio each reduced by half the number of women committing suicide up in the rural hills.[6]

In the 1920s and 1930s, the Depression, coupled with disastrous floods, devastated many of the valley mills and much of the intervale lands. Throughout the hills, shops closed from water damage or the failing economy.

Some manufacturing weathered the depression, although most industries experienced hard times, and those which lasted to the mid-nineteenth century were sometimes only remnants of more widespread ones.

The one industrial standby to weather the changing economy of the twentieth century was the woolen mills. While the manufacture of cotton and synthetic textiles had begun moving out of New England in the early twentieth century, the woolen industry remained a staple New England business to almost the mid-twentieth century, this despite the fact that the sheepherding that supplied this wool had long ago left New England for the west, Australia, and elsewhere in the world.

The production of woolens peaked around 1920 and after that slowly fell away, as innovations in synthetic material (especially rayon, which cost one third the price of wool) created a lagging market. Other factors reducing the need for warm woolens were the use of central heating in homes and enclosed automobiles.

Despite the lessened demand, many mills went into three shifts to counteract the lower selling prices with higher production. World War II buoyed up the demand, but afterwards, especially during the late forties and early fifties, the mills began closing. By 1962, 60 percent of the country's textile jobs were gone, and many of the remaining woolen mills had by then relocated in the American South.[7]

The Depression hit the manufacturing villages harder than it hit the rural areas. The farmers were quite used to living hand to mouth, and at least they could raise their own staples.

Efforts to alleviate the Depression's effects on the jobless families, however, were stronger in the factory towns. While many of the laborers were old Yankees down from the hills, they had also been joined by immigrants, especially Poles, Czechs, Russians, and some Scandinavians. This ethnic unity in many villages greatly facilitated public aid. Unlike the farmers spread out through the hills, the workers lived in a compact community where one office could easily distribute food, clothing, and other staples. The tight social and religious makeup of these immigrant populations also made it easy to identify those in need. People looked after each other, and the wife whose husband still had a job made sure that her children were always inviting different friends to stay for dinner. The social club became an aid society, and the parish priest was not above using whatever weight his office allowed to tithe the few with any largess that were not willing to help the needy. Much the same occurred with the village Protestant groups. However, up in the rural sections, the Congregational and Baptist ministers found that the geo-

Tower of the Hillsborough, New Hampshire, woolen mill, built 1865.

Snowflake Bentley

Wilson Alwyn "Snowflake" Bentley (1865–1931), of Jericho, Vermont, was a wonderful example of Yankee ingenuity still alive and kicking in the twentieth century.

His forte was picking up individual snowflakes with a splinter of wood, laying them on a chalkboard, and photographing them. He amassed a collection of almost 6,000 images. His volume *Snow Crystals*, first published in 1931, is a visual classification of the varieties of hexagonal patterns, plus oddities, in which flakes form.

Bentley received only local education and lived most of his life in his hometown. Yet his expertise in atmospheric phenomena made him a sought-after consultant to the U.S. Weather Bureau and encyclopedias. He seemed to have also been something of a court of last resort for researchers in the Smithsonian Institution. If they couldn't figure it out, up it went to Bentley to solve.

One problem the Washington, D.C., scientists couldn't solve was how to establish the size of raindrops. They could catch one or two on a slide and then bring them in and measure their volume, but how does one measure a great number of them to find large and small and average sizes?

Bentley gave them the answer. He simply filled a large tray with flour and put it out in the rain. Each droplet hitting the tray formed into a small ball of dough. He then brought the tray inside and put it to bake in an oven. The balls hardened, allowing Bentley to sort them easily by size. Determining their original water content was done by comparing them to balls he had previously made by using an eyedropper to drip measured amounts of water onto the flour tray. It was kitchen chemistry at it simplest and most subtle.

During his lifetime, Bentley sold prints from his snowflake book. They still turn up in antique stores and are quickly bought by those who recognize them as what they are.

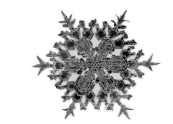

graphical and social isolation of the farms made it much harder for them to keep an eye on the needs of their parishes.

There was, however, something of a reverse flow back onto the farms by those who had nowhere else to go:

When times are hard and manufacturers are flat and the mills in the industrial states around us are shut down, and the newspapers are talking about bankruptcies and breadlines, the Vermont family, exactly as rich and exactly as poor as it ever was, remarks with a kindliness tinged with pride, "Well, we'd better ask Lem's folks to stay for a spell, till times get better. I guess it's pretty hard sledding for them."[8]

Many came for a while, or sent their children. Some, especially members of factory-village ethnic groups, moved out of their mill houses to work farms in the lands surrounding the town. They did not stray far, as there was always a desire to stay in contact with their ethnic community. The land often went for a song, and, with the spread of suburbia a few generations later, these fields turned the descendants into quite successful real estate dealers.

There were a few classic examples of urbanites fleeing the metropolis, never to return. As city careers fell apart, a few brought their families back to what they considered the solidity of their childhood rural lives. Here they rebuilt their sense of reality. While some ultimately returned to the metropolis, in others, the disillusionment had been so overpowering that they never again ventured into a city for the rest of their lives.

In some ways this one generation's return to their upland homesteads spurred the economic resurgence of a generation later. Their children, growing up in the early to mid-twentieth century, felt ties to the land which they would not have possessed had their parents stayed in the city. Many, as they grew up, made use of the highways of post–World War II America to revisit their homesteads, sometimes parceling out a piece of the old farm for a summer cottage. Later, A-frames appeared. In all, it brought a more homogeneous spread of summer folk into the hills, creating a cash flow which did not directly depend on the existence of any nearby resorts.

"Beaver Meadow," by Paul Sample, 1939. (Hood Museum of Art, Dartmouth College, Hanover, New Hampshire. Gift of Paul Sample, Class of 1920.)

12 *The Touring Car in the Landscape*

 The growing auto age brought more than farm families and milk tankers to the rural lanes. The vacationers in their "touring cars" soon became a regular facet of hill country traffic.

The auto tourist came slowly at first. The state highway departments, established around the turn of the century, concentrated on extending roads into the hills for farmers trucking their produce to the rail depot. The motoring tourist had yet to be recognized as an economic force.

The southern New England states acted earlier than their northern neighbors. In 1912, Maine's legislature finally abandoned its constitutional restrictions on state debt. With this, observed one humorist, the laws were "so amended that highways were given place with rebellion, invasion and war as justification for incurring debt."[1] Two million dollars in road bonds created smooth avenues of gravel or macadam sparsely distributed among the spongy mire.

Nine miles beyond Bethel [Maine] we entered the defile leading up to Grafton Notch; our good state road came to an end, and a dirt mountain road, bad at best but now made much worse from the heavy rain of the night before, made our going not only difficult but, in places, positively dangerous. For ten long, weary miles, we crept along up to the summit of the pass and then down the slope to the other side, the car skidding and slipping from one margin of the narrow road to the other, often threatening to go beyond control and take a leap into the ravine, the brink of which was sometimes alarmingly near the side of the road. The country was wild and desolate, scarcely a human habitation in the entire ten miles, — plenty of unspoiled nature most surely.[2]

The automobile manufacturers, especially those whose vehicles could actually withstand the rocks and mires of country byways, were the first to promote auto touring.

One company, the White Automobile Company of Cleveland, began in 1907 to issue guides to three recommended routes for owners of their steam-driven buggies. Route Number One was New York City to Pittsfield, Massachusetts; Number

Two was New York City to Gettysburg and the Shenandoah; and Number Three was New York City to Boston.

East Proctor, Vermont, 1913.

Even these "main routes" left much to be desired when they struck out into the country. The New York to Boston route followed the old upper path of colonial days, which took it through the hills of central Massachusetts. "Between Springfield and Worcester, there are several stretches of bad going and, in some spots, the country is very desolate, no human habitation being in sight."[3] The directions kept the vehicle as close to any extant trolley lines, with many a "left at the horse trough," "continue past the war memorial," and warnings about dangerous rail crossings.

The first real auto tour promoted for getting people into the New England hill country was "The Ideal Tour," the 1907 brainchild of a Waterbury, Connecticut, hotel owner. He teamed up with a number of grand resort owners to lay out a tour which guaranteed "A FIRST-CLASS HOTEL AT THE END OF EACH DAY'S RUN."[4] The route led the New York vacationer up to Waterbury, then over to the Berkshire Valley to Pittsfield, and on to Manchester, Vermont. From there the tour cut over the Green

Mountains to Newport, New Hampshire, then north up central New Hampshire through Franconia Notch, down again through Crawford Notch, over to Portland, Maine, down the coast to Boston, and finally returned along the upper post road to New York City:

The autumn makes an especial appeal to many persons, and in constantly increasing numbers. In September and October, the gorgeous foliage of the hills and mountains, in their garb of red and golden brown, mingling here and there the darker hues of the evergreen, is a never to be forgotten picture. While the crisp cool days of fall with the bracing air . . . add zest to the joy of motoring amid such an unrivalled setting. The evening lends an added charm, as one forsakes the broad piazza for the cheerful warmth of the open fire to discuss the incidents of the day's journey.[5]

The tour attempted to keep the vacationing motorist coming to the old established resorts which had risen to prominence in the days of railroad travel — like Manchester's Equinox House, the Crawford House and Mount Washington House, Poland Springs House, and Portsmouth's Wentworth-by-the-Sea. In effect, it comprised a series of stays in New England's poshest hotels, interspersed by expeditions through dusty roads and covered bridges. The northern hotels along the route soon extended their usual July-first-to-September-thirtieth season by a few weeks at each end to accommodate the motoring crowd.

The Ideal Tour proved an instant success. True, such short seasons required exorbitant rates, making many of the mountain hotels among the most expensive in the world; but in those days, anyone who owned a motor car could afford such costly fare.

As more and more people took the tour, local towns improved their sections of the route. New editions of *The Ideal Tour* appeared with annual updates. The cover of *The Ideal Tour*'s 1914 issue showed an open motor car following a smooth road winding beside a stream down an autumn valley. Mountains rise in the background, and on an outcrop on the foreground stand a man and woman in Puritan garb. They look down with wonder (Priscilla) and pride (John) upon this vehicular marvel.

The automobile seemed a perfect way to enjoy New England's diversity:

New England has become the favorite touring section of America, for nowhere else can there be found such a variety of scenery contained within a comparatively small area, so much good or so many places of historic interest. For generations isolated New England resorts were famous, but with the coming of the motor car the entire region has become one vast resort from the rocky cliffs of the Naugatuck Valley to the White Mountains' highest peak.[6]

Spin-off tours followed. The New England Hotel Association promoted its "New England Tour." There were "The Real Tour" and "The Real Tour to the Berkshires," among many. All the tours were promoted by the larger hotels in their attempt to keep motorists coming to the established resorts.

Auto touring's first geographical shifts came with the construction of roads especially designed for vacation traffic. The first, and instantly most famous, was the Mohawk Trail. Before highway construction began in 1912, this famous historical route had been a quiet lane along the Deerfield River, tracing its source west out of the Connecticut River valley and swinging north with the river at the high Hoosac Range. No real road passable by autos ascended the divide.

On September first, 1914, two years and $345,000 later, the new Mohawk Trail

Highway opened. Immediately, a rush of enthusiastic motorists arrived. "The route, originally blazed in savage vengeance and hatred, has now become one of the most popular and beautiful roads of the country," wrote an authority on turnpikes in 1919.[7]

The road, sixty-three miles from the Connecticut River to the New York line, contained scenic vistas unsurpassed by any other location in America accessible by automobile.

Accessible sometimes became a gray term. In the 1910s and 1920s, a drive up the Mohawk Trail lent as much neighborhood prestige to the family car as a "This Car Climbed Mount Washington" bumper sticker does today.

To drive up the winding valley was an idyllic experience, but there were hills to climb at each end of the trail. Many of the early promoted auto tours, such as The Ideal Tour, gained popularity in part from guiding the autoist through the mountain passes, and relatively level notches, relieving the early cars of any taxing grades. Only Crawford Notch had any great slope, and there the guides planned the route so that the slope was taken downhill. The Mohawk Trail took the car straight up and over.

A tour of the Mohawk Trail from the east began from Greenfield and the Hotel Weldon, then a popular resort hotel. The first hurdle was the ascent of Shelburne Mountain onto the highland peneplain. The original highway up out of the Connecticut Valley was a steep, direct route, later rerouted into a more gradual diagonal along the face of the slope. A weekend view of the slope from below showed two lines of cars, both facing downhill. The Model T's reverse gear, it seems, had more torque that its first gear forward; also, when the car was pointed up a steep incline, gas from the tank could not flow to the engine. Many took the hill in reverse.

At Shelburne summit, the radiator took on water and the engine cooled while the folks enjoyed the vista from the first of many "tearooms" that soon dotted the trail. Commercialism and history soon were bed partners, as every antique structure became a historical shrine. Proprietors of every roadside stand were ready to

Cover to **Beautiful Mohawk Trail,** *one of the early guides to this then-new auto tour.*

describe whatever history they could lay their hands upon while vending felt Mohawk Trail pennants and miniature birchbark canoes.

At Shelburne, the Sweetheart Inn became a noon stop. Here the tourists bought their "Maple Sweethearts," the maple-sugar candy which soon joined the felt pennants and baby canoes in the roadside stands. Shelburne's other main attraction was an abandoned five-span trolley bridge across the Deerfield River, which, in 1929, the town's Women's Association began decorating with flowers.

From Shelburne, the road followed the river past outlook turnoffs and little hamlets to Charlemont, passing by the old sycamore beneath which once slept, almost two hundred years ago, the first white settlers in the valley.

Nearby, since 1932, stands the worst historical absurdity of the trip. In the intervale just west of the village, at the confluence of the Cold River with the Deerfield stands a bronze Indian, facing east, with his hands outstretched. The inscription reads: "Hail to the Sunrise / In Memory of the / Mohawk Indian." One wonders at what the peaceful Pocumtucks and other Connecticut River tribes would have to say about a memorial upon their land to a tribe which brought only fear and death, especially one depicted facing their homeland with hands spread wide, ready to fill them with pillage.

Once past this statue, the Trail leaves the Deerfield River to ascend the heights along a side valley. The road follows the gradual arc of the Cold River up to the height of land. This became the most spectacular portion of the trip — the most awe-inspiring stretch of eastern wilderness then accessible by automobile. The section became nationally famous as "The Curve of Beauty." The stream seems to follow a wide spiral down from the heights; the bed itself is wide and boulder-strewn. On each side dense forest rises abruptly to an impressive height.

Gradually the valley gets narrower and steeper, with the stream and road being completely shaded by vegetation. Finally the peneplain is reached, and the auto emerges into relatively flat upland surroundings. At the crest is the little village of Florida, and just beyond is the next grand stop of the journey: Whitcomb Summit, some 2,010 feet in elevation, with its outlook down upon the seeming wilderness of the meandering Deerfield Valley.

From here the road continues over the Hoosac plateau to its western slope. The vista at Western Summit (2,020 feet in elevation) is a complete change from the forests of the eastern view. One now sees an impressive blend of industry and pastorale: North Adams and its mills far down the slope. Beyond is Williamstown, to the north lies a dotting of Vermont farms. Not far west, Mount Greylock rises to curve off the valley.

Invigorated, the travelers head for their last emotional experience of the Trail. Heading down the steep switchback of the western Hoosac slope, passengers come to Hairpin Turn and its view of the thousand-foot drop to the valley floor they will probably make if the brakes fail. It is that last surprise dip when you finally think the rollercoaster ride is about to end.

The Mohawk Trail tour became so popular by the 1920s that those without a car, or who were hesitant about driving the Trail, could take scheduled bus tours running from Boston to New York. There was of course the train, but much of the grandeur was lost by the Hoosac Tunnel.

"I would prefer a bus over the Mohawk Trail far above the tunnel, thus seeing some of the loveliest views in America instead of being pulled through a hole in the ground under them," commented one travel writer.[8]

It took six days by bus from Boston, over the Mohawk Trail to the Hudson, to New York, and then back north by the Fall River Line and bus:

Hair Pin Turn

The Gray Line limousine "Berkshire," is the nearest approach to perfection which has ever been reached in a passenger-carrying vehicle of any kind. The interior is finished in solid mahogany with compartments for umbrellas and golf sticks. It has the finest of leather upholstery, and the deepest and most comfortable of cushions. It is lighted by electricity for the evening. It has a locked baggage compartment where bags and suit cases may be carried and not exposed to the weather or the view of the public.[9]

The price, with accommodations and two days in either New York or Boston, was forty dollars. The exact luxury of the "teakettle" bus depicted in the advertising brochure is left to personal remembrances. However, it must have been a sturdy item in order to pull its passengers over the steep slopes and still be featured in company brochures printed a decade later.

While Massachusetts had underwritten the cost of the Mohawk Trail on its own, the Federal Aid Road Act of 1916, with its 50 percent payment of any state highway improvements, spurred much activity and increased motor traffic.

Other special routes appeared. Another famous road through the hill country was the Theodore Roosevelt International Highway. Laid out in 1919, it ran from Portland, Maine, to Portland, Oregon. It followed present-day Route 302 from Maine, through Crawford Notch, then onto routes 10 and 18 to Saint Johnsbury. From there it followed Route 2 to Montpelier, Burlington, and over the northern end of Lake Champlain. Although promoted as a tourist route, it never caught on as a through highway, and some of its Vermont stretches were not paved until the 1930s.

By the 1920s more and more cars, buses, and vacationers were setting out to see the glories of the White Mountains, Berkshires, Bar Harbor, and Cape Cod. The Model T Ford began appearing in every garage, making Sunday drives in the country and summer vacations an established facet of American life.

The states began planning their highways in earnest now. Development was greatest in New England's three southern states, with Vermont's roads the worst of the northern three. In all, however, New England fared well in overall comparison to the rest of the nation, allowing promoters to tout the qualities of "New Hampshire's splendid gravel highways or the thousands of miles of smooth tarvia which criss-cross Massachusetts end to end."[10]

Exact definitions, however, often proved important, as one 1924 motorist warned: "All roads in Maine are good in the sense of being dry from the middle of June to the middle of July, in the average year."[11] The standard promise of any advertised route was that it was "hard and dustless."

Tourists also needed direction and warning signs. New Hampshire's first efforts consisted of erecting throughout the state a wonderfully worded advisory: "25 mi. outside of thickly/settled sections, 15 mi./inside therof."[12] Maine put up road signs near its borders listing various safety tips and ended with the warning "Don't Make Ruts."

As roads multiplied and the old signposts at the crossroads proved ineffective, states adopted a plan of painting colored bands around telephone poles to show the way. Every road was either red, yellow, white, or blue, with a few grays or striped combinations for special thoroughfares. Inevitably a lot of identically colored roads crossed and made things worse than the old signposts. By the mid-1920s numbered routes replaced the colored bands.

Sooner or later, however, people got lost, and the Yankee farmer made acquaintance with the city slicker in his newfangled machine, the kind that kept scaring cows and horses. The ensuing conversation quickly became an old chestnut.

Motorist: "Where does this road go?"
Farmer: "Don't go nowhere. Been in the same place since I was born."

Such brevity was probably more merciful than when the isolated farmer actually tried to give directions, as recounted by Wallace Nutting in one of his up-country photographic tours, who was informed:

The best way to Ware is the first left hand road after you pass a right hand road. That is, you do not take the narrow road into the woods but the first wide left hand road. You go down over the hill until you come to the school house and you take the middle road there. When you come to a bridge you do not cross it but keep straight ahead on this side of the river, and then you had better inquire again.[13]

Halfway through these directions Nutting found himself even more bewildered:

By this time the road is springy and rocky and narrow. You hear an inquiry, "What would you do if you met a car?" Anybody who imagines that there is not mystery and variety, romance and heroism, to be had on an exploring trip does not understand hill roads and human nature.

After about eight miles we seem to be on familiar ground and find ourselves at a corner where we diverged. This is comforting because we are on the right road now, only we are going in the wrong direction *and have been for three miles!*[14]

There is something in the motorist psyche that keeps one driving forward ten miles, rather than turning around and retracing one mile. Getting lost became the Sunday adventure, and such expeditions required both a highly developed sense of direction and a new set of rules for survival: "No matter how small the roadside stand may be, if it is neatly painted and bright with well-kept flower beds around it, the meal will be good. If it is painted only so-so, and is decorated with tin candy-bar and soft-drink signs, flee as from the pestilence."[15]

Others advised that anyone entering a "tearoom" should abide by an established number of dirty menus, soiled linen, or flies, which, if exceeded, should signal a continued search for lunch.

The best country meals were from a picnic basket, on a side road, by some shaded brook. Wrote Wallace Nutting, in one of his many comments promoting getting out into the country by motor car, "This is your little world for the time being. . . .

"For you is all this beauty, unrecorded by others, unappreciated by the rushing crowd, the murmur of whose passage is dully heard in the distance."[16]

Contemporary writers found this to be more the ideal than the actual, noting that motorists were "too often on their way to places perhaps better avoided"[17] for the indulgence in such pastoral delights.

Roadside attractions sprang up in droves during the late 1920s. Every geological freak, every vague profile, now had an admission charge, and painted billboards

Picnickers along Highway 12A, Hanover, New Hampshire, August, 1941. Photograph by Jack Delano.

Benjamin Talmadge House, 1775, Litchfield, Connecticut

Mount Monadnock, New Hampshire

Store, North Leverett, Massachusetts

Leyden, Massachusetts

Berkshire dawn, Massachusetts

Gondola lift at Mount Mansfield, Stowe, Vermont

Farm in the valley, winter, Halifax, Vermont

One-room schoolhouse, Hill, New Hampshire

Woolen mill,
Bridgewater, Vermont

Hubbard's Brook, Granville, Massachusetts

announcing it for miles in every direction. Anything too big to be hidden behind the admissions booth was surrounded by rough-bark "trading post" souvenir stands and motor camps. Wallace Nutting complained:

It might be said with a show of probability that automobiles would better the American citizen by taking him out of doors. With the tendency, however, to closed cars, which are now in quite general demand, it may be questioned whether one may not as well remain at home as to get into a nearly air tight box and begin to smoke. Indeed, there is danger under these circumstances that the American will degenerate into a rather poor sort of jerked meat.[18]

While they may not have stopped to enjoy nature all that much, the motorists penetrated farther into the hills, and for longer stays. Country inns joined with boardinghouses to accommodate the new business. Again came the warnings:

There are very numerous summer inns in smaller towns and in the country where poor service and high charges prevail and the traveller will have to be on his guard or he will pass an uncomfortable night when he happens to put up at one of them. He will find them unheated on chilly nights, the hot water faucets may fail to function, the bathrooms (if any) are antiquated and uncomfortable, the meal service is often not very inviting and, to crown it all, the prices are quite up to the standard of the best hotels.[19]

Roadside lodgings were at first something to endure, rather than enjoy. Drivers off the beaten track in the 1920s were advised to ignore advertisements in the rural areas and simply approach the village's banker or physician for his suggestions.

A new element in the motoring landscape became the tourists' cabins, the first of which reputedly appeared at Whitcomb Summit not long after the opening of the Mohawk Trail highway. These roadside cabins' standard accommodations — one chair, an old bed, and plumbing and heating which was more ornamental than operational — varied little from the old country inns, their individual-lodging nature proved compatible with the closed-car privacy travel psyche bemoaned by Nutting.

Forest Lake Inn and filling station, Winchester, New Hampshire, ca. 1920s, from a postcard.

Ultimately, commercialism and demands for modernization changed the character of the hilly landscape. The old farms now wore neat appearances as they became the summer homes of gentlemen farmers, then called "agriculturists":

One can tell at a glance whether a farm is real, in the sense of being a self-sustaining enterprise, or whether it is owned by a summer resident. Increasingly our Eastern farms are going into the hands of those who play with them rather than live by them. This is well for the neighboring farmer in that it furnishes him with lucrative odd jobs . . . it has been wittily said that the difference between an agriculturist and a farmer is, that the one puts his money into the land while the other takes his money out.[20]

For the people buying old houses in the hills, modernization became the word, with bay windows inserted, ells demolished, old fireplaces removed — all the domestic renovations which today support our current restoration industry. What the rich city people did, the local population often followed, typically with even less finesse than their more affluent neighbors. Complained Wallace Nutting, who spent a lifetime admiring old houses and old furniture: "An important underlying and generally unnoticed tendency is the abhorrence by the thoughtless city man and the thoughtless country dweller, and his wife, of anything old. If the dwelling is old it is not repaired but abandoned for a new one not nearly so good."[21]

In the decades before World War II, affluent summer folk discovered and bought up much of Grafton, Vermont, as they did in many other villages. What sets Grafton off from the rest is that all power lines in the village are underground, giving a full Currier & Ives feeling to the hillside community.

Before (top) and after (bottom) "renovation" of a New England homestead from the 1916 book **New Homes under Old Roofs.** *"The house is ours as we will, — but there is little object in making homely use of it at all unless we engage in both renovation and modernization. . . . While we are aware that this business of reclaiming farmhouses has its friendly opponents, and even at times its disheartening results, it nevertheless seems to be growing as an established art," says the introduction. If you ever want to do in an architectural historian, just give him a copy of this book and watch him keel over in apoplexy.*

Most through routes had been well modernized by the end of the 1930s, and here too, came a lament for what had been lost:

Instead of a poetic world of narrow winding roads and friendly faces, we find broad highways built for speed and more speed, — as if speed had anything in common with mountain scenery. Speed is just what we go to the mountains to

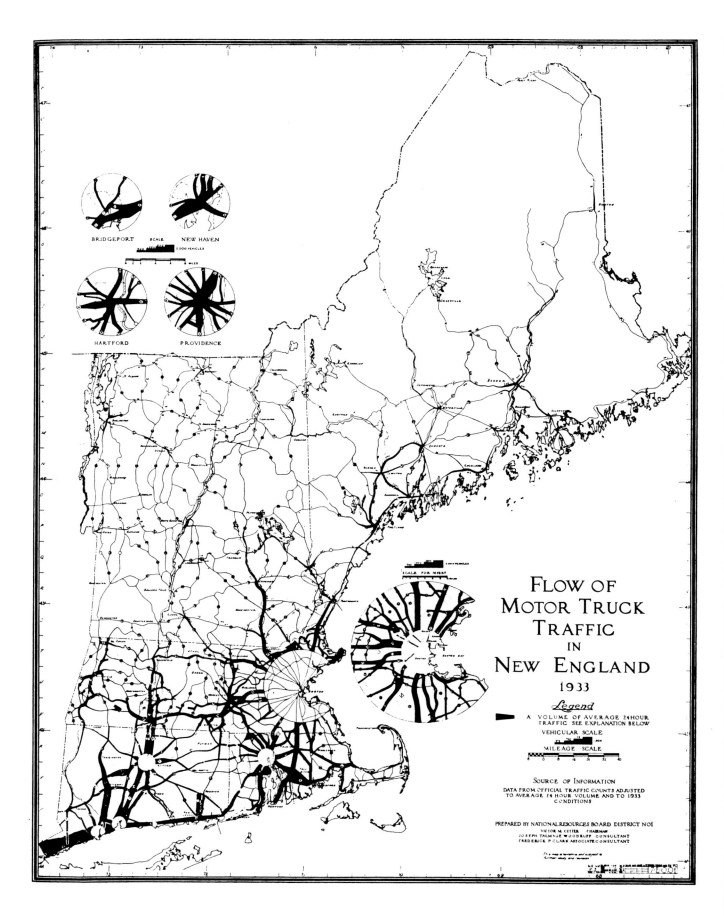

FLOW OF
MOTOR TRUCK
TRAFFIC
IN
NEW ENGLAND
1933

Legend

A VOLUME OF AVERAGE 24 HOUR
TRAFFIC SEE EXPLANATION BELOW

VEHICULAR SCALE

MILEAGE SCALE

SOURCE OF INFORMATION
DATA FROM OFFICIAL TRAFFIC COUNTS ADJUSTED
TO AVERAGE 24 HOUR VOLUME AND TO 1933
CONDITIONS

PREPARED BY NATIONAL RESOURCES BOARD DISTRICT NO.1
VICTOR M. CUTTER   CHAIRMAN
JOSEPH TALMAGE WOODRUFF CONSULTANT
FREDERICK P CLARK ASSOCIATE CONSULTANT

BRIDGEPORT   NEW HAVEN

HARTFORD   PROVIDENCE

escape. Yet an ambitious highway department thinks mainly in terms of getting there, and its straightened roads bring to the land of inspiration the very people who do not belong there. . . . Somewhere to go, I suspect, is all the highlands of New Hampshire mean to them.[22]

The greatest lament of pre–World War II motorists was the gradual extinction of the old covered bridges:

They whisper still of the dear old horse-and-buggy days, and they must have been astonished when the first toddling motors drove more swiftly over them. . . . They are voices out of the past, sudden reminders of times less filled with noise and confusion, relics of a day never to come again. But down they go in the throb of the present, and in their place rise short suspension bridges of iron and steel; beautiful, it is true, but with none of the picturesqueness of these memorials.[23]

The New England hills had arrived into the mid-twentieth century. In some places, traffic problems made it appear as if "the Sunday driver is trying to find out how many cars can be placed end to end on each road."[24]

Up in the remote hills, however, the roads lay quiet and empty; the exodus of a hundred years left a

ghostly silence. . . . For there are long, long miles when you encounter no other motorists, and New England people have a way of remaining out of sight. You do not see them even at their windows or on their porches. They are mysteriously hidden . . . in the hamlets and villages they keep to themselves, strangely invisible . . . the shops were vacant as we ambled by, and so were the cottages, as far as we could see.[25]

Even today, no matter how far suburbia and tourism penetrates, it seems assured that farther up in the hills, somewhere, the old aura survives. The old farms and little villages still beautify landscape.

There, up in the heights of the ancient peneplains, one still feels the old New England: "There is a calm and aloofness of physical atmosphere, a sense of being on top of the world."[26]

13 *New England Outdoors: Hiking and Skiing*

In the mid-1930s, at the depths of the Depression, the federal government made Vermont an offer. If the state spent a half million dollars in federal loans to buy up a right-of-way along the crest of the Green Mountains, Washington would spend $18,000,000 to build the "Green Mountain Parkway." It would be a skyline drive, like the one on Virginia's Shenandoahs, running the length of Vermont. Despite the promises of jobs and future tourism, Vermonters recoiled in horror and defeated the idea in a 1936 referendum, and Washington abandoned the project.

Instead of an alpine superhighway, only a footpath winds along the Green Mountain heights — the famous Long Trail. Begun in 1911 and finally cleared to the Canadian line in 1930, it takes the hiker through a wilderness of valley streams, summit outlooks, abandoned cellar holes, beaver ponds, scolding chipmunks, dripping leaves, and the most wonderful sense of being in the total realm of nature, where man is only a passing visitor.

The hikers, with backpacks, shorts, sturdy boots, and solid legs, have become an important part of today's image of the New England hills. Their existence is an affirmation that there is beautiful wilderness still to be enjoyed, and their active lobbying, publicity, and legal actions are a promise that wilderness will remain.

In New England, hiking as an organized activity was first prominent in the White Mountains, where the trails cut out of the forest by the Crawfords and others had, by the late nineteenth century, been codified in various guidebooks.

These have always been New England's glamour hikes, for the White Mountains' alpine routes offer the eerie joy of walking in the strange landscape above timberline. The breezes make rushing moans, and the cautious measure their steps by the distance from available shelter, for there is nothing between you and unexpected storms of Arctic intensity.

Nathaniel Hawthorne, in his story "The Great Carbuncle," describes best the sensation of ascending above the timberline. His characters set out from the Crawford Notch side of the range, toiling up the forested slope, until

Frontispiece by Beatrice Stevens for Odell Shepard, Harvest of a Quiet Eye *(Boston, 1927),* **which gives accounts of walking the rural uplands of Connecticut.**

they reached the upper verge of the forest, and were now to pursue a more adventurous course. The innumerable trunks and heavy foliage of the trees had hitherto shut in their thoughts, which now shrank affrighted from the region of wind, and cloud, and naked rocks, and desolate sunshine, that rose immeasurably above them. They gazed back at the obscure wilderness which they had traversed, and longed to be buried again in its depths, rather than trust themselves to so vast and visible a solitude.[1]

In 1907, the famous Appalachian Mountain Club, a Boston-based group organized in 1876 for the promotion of hiking and the preservation of the wilderness, published their first *Guide to Paths in the White Mountains* and began to assume responsibility for maintenance of the trails. They also erected a series of huts and lean-tos, allowing the hiker to travel light.

Some huts also offered meals. Student members of the A.M.C. toted in the provisions. While the huts make hiking through the White Mountains more enjoyable, it is rather disconcerting for the vacationing hiker lifting his feet with sweaty care up the sloping path, to hear a polite "Coming through, please!" from back down the trail. Before you can even stop to turn, a figure briskly passes you with a shopping cart's worth of canned soup tied to his pack frame. He is gone over the next rise before the awe subsides, along with your Thoreauvean self-image.

The activities of the Appalachian Mountain Club in the first few decades of the twentieth century reflect the booming public enthusiasm for "tramping," as it was then called. The interest in hiking accompanied a national concern over scenic preservation. The White Mountain National Forest began with federal purchases of land in 1911. New Hampshire, operating jointly with the Society for the Preservation of New Hampshire Forests (organized 1901), bought Crawford Notch the same year the federal government began purchasing forest. The state and the Society later collaborated in acquiring Franconia Notch and other locations.

Where New Hampshire has the barren heights of its Presidential Range, and Vermont its alpine zone of Mount Mansfield, Maine's famous "above timberline" is Mount Katahdin, known by the Indians as "Ketté-Adene," "greatest mountain."

Katahdin, Kttdn, Kttadn, Ktaadn (the various spellings of this name include other, vowelless combinations as well), lies at the northeast terminus of the gradually descending, sixty-mile-wide range of hills that stretches from the White Mountains to central Maine. Here, amid low hills, lakes, and wilderness, rises the granite mass of Mount Katahdin, almost a mile high.

It is a range unto itself, an eight-mile-long plateau, irregularly sculpted by glaciers and weather, rising 4,200 feet out of the surrounding countryside. Its highest point is Baxter Peak, the first place in the United States touched by morning sunlight.

The Indians considered Katahdin to be the realm of gods, where simple humans had no right to venture. Clouds precipitating out of the winds rising over the great monolith often shrouded its upper portions.

Thoreau, in his "Maine Woods," tells of his climb in 1846. The rest of his party had abandoned the ascent about halfway up, and he struck on alone, finally reaching the flat tableland at 4,200 feet:

The mountain seemed a vast aggregation of loose rocks, as if some time it had rained rocks, and they lay as they fell on the mountain sides, nowhere fairly at rest, but leaning on each other, all rocking-stones, with cavities between, but scarcely any soil or smoother shelf....

At length I entered within the skirts of the cloud which seemed forever drifting over the summit, and yet would never be gone, but was generated out of that pure air as fast as it flowed away....

Occasionally, when the windy columns broke in to me, I caught sight of a dark, damp crag to the right or left, the mist driving ceaselessly between it and me.... It was vast, Titanic, and such as man never inhabits. Some part of the beholder, even some vital part, seems to escape through the loose grating of his ribs as he ascends. He is more lone than you can imagine....

The tops of mountains are among the unfinished parts of the globe, whither it is a slight insult to the gods to climb and pry into their secrets, and try their effect on our humanity.[2]

Thoreau abandoned his climb, and retreated. Today, with the knowledge that many have gone before, a multitude of hikers track over, in the words of a mid-nineteenth-century adventurer, Theodore Winthrop, "the best mountain in the wildest wild to be had on this side of the continent."[3]

After the retreat of the great Continental Ice Sheet, a number of glaciers still hung off the sides of the Katahdin uplift, gouging out horseshoe-shaped cirques,

thousands of feet high. Some slopes are beautiful precipices of pink granite, showing eternal sunset hues. In one location two cirques formed on either side of a ridge, gradually cutting back until only a ridge called the Knife Edge remains to separate the two. Today, it is a challenge of nerve to cross this mile-long double-sided cliff, only a yard wide in places. There is an exuberant relief in having made the crossing, though, in the words of one early-nineteenth-century hiker, "It is certainly not a place for giddy heads, nor for steady ones, for that matter, in the face of a blow."[4]

Hiking was not entirely confined to the high hills in this new enthusiasm for the open air. Many people who felt the vagabond spirit simply rode the trolley out to the end of the line and set out on foot into the rural districts:

One does not need to worry over where he will sup and sleep on the excursions. It is part of the game not to know, except from day to day, just where camp will be pitched. There are good enough inns along the road, and always a farmhouse or two where they like to turn an honest extra dollar by keeping a respectable stranger overnight.[5]

The real purist headed for the far backwoods hills, getting to the start of their hike by arranging a ride on the "mail stages" which ran from the valley rail depots up into the remote villages. Sometimes they were still the old horse-drawn surreys, while others were solid little tin lizzies:

It is not rapid transit, to be sure, not even in a motor car, for stops to deliver mail and to discharge errands are frequent, nor is it a luxurious mode of travel, with your feet tucked in among the mail sacks and express packages, but it is withal an inexpensive and delightful way in which to explore the "back country."[6]

The drivers themselves were usually local people who contracted with the government to carry the mails, and as such, were wonderful guides and sources of information on everything in view. It was like riding with the stagecoach driver of old, wrote one hiker, yet with one improvement: "Thanks to the rigid requirements of the postal service he is less given to drink than many of his predecessors."[7]

It was not a want for places to hike that made tramping a problem for its advocates in the early twentieth century; it was one of not being recognized as a hiker by the local population. Casual wear, or the sporting-goods hiking outfits of today, was then nonexistent. Early photos show hikers attired in ensembles resembling either the uniform Teddy Roosevelt wore in his dash up San Juan Hill, or the outfit of a bank teller, who, on the way home, loosened his tie and slipped off for the woods: "Men, when they do their first climbing, usually wear coats or carry them along. Some of them wear vests. A few cling to a boiled shirt and detachable collar. These attributes of civilized life are discarded in the reverse of the order named."[8]

Experienced hikers preferred the well-worn business suit. As a result, farmers and hostelers had trouble distinguishing between the tramper in his shabby once-Sunday best and the tramp in much the same attire (except that the latter's outfit had made an intermediary stop with the Salvation Army). It took a few decades before a recognizable hiking outfit came into vogue, finally separating the vacationers from the vagrants.

Gradually, increased motor traffic made roadside walking less attractive. One Vermonter complained that the early autos' ripping exhaust noises and the drivers' custom of tooting their horns around every turn gave once-quiet country lanes "all the sound effects of hell on a holiday."[9]

Hikers began to understand and envy Thoreau's boast of his ability to meander Concord without coming in sight of "civilization": "It requires considerable skill in crossing a country to avoid the houses and too cultivated parts. . . . I can easily walk ten, fifteen, twenty, any number of miles, commencing at my own door, without going by any house, without crossing a road except where the fox and mink do."[10]

Hikers began looking toward trails which might not promise great vistas, as in the White Mountains, Katahdin, or the high peaks of the Green Mountains, but simply returned one to the genteel bowers of Mother Nature. One favorite locale for this was the southern section of Vermont's Long Trail. Here, by the mid-1920s, man had all but abandoned the highlands:

Today, save for an occasional sporting camp . . . and the inn at Kelly Stand, there is not an occupied habitation of any kind over a distance of fully fifteen miles . . . not only has the farmer gone, but the big modern steam mills, with their attendant villages of hands' houses, have had their heyday, and are now, for the most part, falling into squalid ruin. For nearly a score of years the forests have been free of the shriek of saw and whistle . . . and the only man-employing industry is found in the annual autumn fern-pickers' camps, where the graceful fronds are gathered by the million for the florists' markets of the cities.[11]

Vermont's Long Trail (about 260 miles) distinguishes itself as one of the first sizable hiking paths geared not so much toward the ascent and descent of mountains as toward extended wilderness journeys. Although towns lie not far away in the valleys to the east and west, one can even today walk for weeks on end, encountering only a few mountain roads and trail huts. One can relive the world of the early foresters, although not so much its dangers as its insanities: porcupines which eat your boots for their salt sweat, raccoons adept at unbuckling packs, and lovelorn screech owls whose noctural screams lead one to demonstrate that it is possible to get up and run while still zipped into a sleeping bag.

NIGHT

Much of the Long Trail today lies within the bounds of the Green Mountain National Forest, which was formally proclaimed in 1932 out of the first federal land acquisitions in 1929. Much of the land had been well logged, and hikers first

Published by the
APPALACHIAN MOUNTAIN CLUB
5 JOY STREET   BOSTON
1934

found not so much the original shadowy forests of spruce as a scrub of cherry, poplar, ash, and raspberry, "a cover which let in the sun and shut out the air."[12] It created a humid climate, just right for insects, and early-twentieth-century hikers waited for the early fall.

In 1921, a Massachusetts hiking enthusiast suggested a longer edition of the Long Trail, one which would run the whole Appalachian Range from Maine to Georgia. By 1930, the Appalachian Trail had been marked out along stretches of existing trails — Katahdin, the White Mountains, the Dartmouth Outing Club paths, and the Long Trail. In 1938 the federal government took the project under its wing and passed laws for the trail's protection.

Governmental aid to wilderness activities surged in the Depression years. While the Green Mountain Parkway never gave jobs to the unemployed, projects such as the Civil Conservation Corps took youths to camps in state and national forests. Here they cleared trails which form the basis for most of New England's shorter hiking paths.

Today the blue or white painted circles that dot so many forest trees mark out the thousands of miles of New England paths. While most are inevitably up some hill, few lead to any great vistas. Instead, they promise feelings of physical satis-faction and mental calm: "Your transition from a mole to a lark requires time. At the beginning there is only a steady plodding, distinguishable from any lowland forest tramp largely by the fact that it is all laboriously uphill. Even the mountain that is your objective has vanished. You take the trail on faith."[13]

While New England's summer wilderness activities gradually developed out of early hiking trails, its winter sports grew in a rush during the 1930s, bringing the New England hills its latest economic transformation.

Scandinavian émigrés had organized New Hampshire's first ski club in 1872. But except for a few hearty souls, such as members of the Appalachian Mountain Club, it was as much a Nordic curiosity as saunas.

Skiing, in those days, meant a cross-country push on rudimentary downhill skis. Thus, it combined the worst of both forms of skiing, heavy equipment with no thrill of the downhill rush. Winter enthusiasts preferred sledding or snowshoeing.

The first changes in winter sports came around 1910, when Dartmouth College organized its Outing Club, and held a winter carnival, which was immediately copied by virtually every northern New England male college that heard how many coeds took the train up to Hanover for the event. National magazines quickly picked up on this wholesome emergence from hibernation, and soon everyone was taking a second look at the winter white outside.

With most skiing then simply a shuffling up and down slopes in the manner of snowshoeing, the more adventurous of those bitten by the winter bug took to the ski jump. Intrepid souls slid down a hundred-foot-plus ramp, lofted into the air, and, in the words of Fred H. Harris, who as an undergraduate had founded the Dartmouth Outing Club, "the jumper, provided he alights with his skis together and at the correct angle, simply glides on, at terrific speed, until, with a perfectly executed telemark swing, he brings himself to a halt in a whirl of snow."[14]

Jumping quickly became a popular spectator sport, promising a variety of possi-ble entertainments. Correctly executed, the jump had the aesthetic beauty of a high dive and the speed of a drag race. A single error, however, turned the scene into one reminiscent of the condemned man descending through the trapdoor at a public hanging, as the crowd marveled at the acrobatic positions a human body can assume during its trajectory between the lip of a ski jump and the point of snowy impact.

Such requirements of derring-do at the jump, and the heavy equipment for regular skiing, made it an unattractive activity for most people during the 1910s and 1920s.

However, the students of many college outing clubs gradually developed a love for downhill skiing. They trekked up slopes for hours at a time for the few minutes' run back down. The slopes ranged from a backyard hill to the almost vertical face of Tuckerman Ravine, a glacial cirque in the side of Mount Washington. This half-bowl-shaped geological oddity drops off almost perpendicularly in a headwall which gradually decreases in pitch to a flat runout. The wonderful characteristic of Tuckerman's Ravine is the way in which its shaded slopes offer snow until Memorial Day. Those with the expert ability to avoid the exposed patches can even make runs on the Fourth of July. Today Tuckerman's is the ideal place for spring skiing (avalanches make it hazardous in winter), when the snows have melted off the other ski areas. A visit in April or May will reckon up the image of skiing circa 1920.

The scene along the ascending trail at Tuckerman's resembles those old pictures of gold seekers filing up some Alaskan pass leading to the Yukon gold fields. Instead of picks, shovels, and supplies, these hikers carry skis strapped to their backs.

The only modernization of the scene comes from the sound of police bullhorns echoing off the cirque's walls as Forest Service rangers attempt to herd the ascending skiers away from the sections set off for the descending skiers, rocketing down in various states of control from their launch-points around the lip of the bowl.

The presence of the Rangers is not simply for traffic control. States the Forest Service:

Skiers assume certain responsibilities for their own welfare when skiing on Mt. Washington. Never ski alone. Injured skiers must be carried out and down to

T. H. Wood, class of 1919, of the Dartmouth Outing Club, then the college's best jumper, going for a record distance.

The bowl of Tuckerman Ravine, New Hampshire, as seen from Pinkham Notch.

shelter which takes several hours from time of injury to arrival at Pinkham Notch. A minimum of two and sometimes three 6-man teams are required to carry a victim down the mountain. If injury is serious, the patrolman will accompany the victim. It is the responsibility of the injured person's friends to return first aid equipment to its original location within 48 hours of use.[15]

The sight of a skier being carried off the field of battle laid across his skis has thankfully lessened since the earlier days of rudimentary "bearclaw" bindings, and even more rudimentary technique.

In the late 1920s, ski fever hit after the Winter Olympics in Europe in anticipation of the upcoming 1932 Winter Games at Lake Placid, New York. Every child rummaged in the garage for old barrel staves and set off for the sledding hill. The owner of a White Mountain inn even imported an Austrian ski instructor in 1928. New England vocabulary acquired a set of phrases like *Telemark, gelendensprung,* and *schuss.*

Still, however, enthusiasts spent 95 percent of their time practicing their uphill hiking and 5 percent (at most) with their skis pointed in a relatively downhill direction. A really good day on the slopes meant a half hour of actual skiing. The big breakthrough to change all this was imported in 1933, from Canada.

In that year, a local ski entrepreneur in Woodstock, Vermont, stretched a circle of cable around a pulley at the base of a slope and the back wheel of a Model T at the top. America's first rope-tow ski lift was born. No matter that the slack rope snaked back and forth over the ground, ready to ensnarl the skis, or did not have any safety stops (so any panicky novice who did not let go in time suffered the possibility of becoming incorporated into the automotive structure), it worked. A few minutes' contortion in holding onto the rope meant 95 percent skiing, and 5 percent lift time each day.

Purists immediately decried the innovation. How could anyone appreciate the joy of a downhill glide without having stomped or herringboned every inch of the way to the top of the run? Everyone else went out and bought skis.

Tows, rope and otherwise, soon appeared throughout the hills. "One brief decade has seen the evolution of winter sports from what was long considered a fad into a huge industry," wrote a Boston columnist in 1940.[16] By that time one could leaf through a seventy-two-page *Skiers Guide to New England,* which described the region's ski towns: forty-nine in New Hampshire, thirty-one in Vermont, thirteen in Massachusetts, and twelve in Maine.

Rope tows were the most common, but there were a few that utilized more sophisticated equipment. Vermont's Mount Mansfield and New Hampshire's Belknap Mountain by Lake Winnepesaukee had chair lifts. Up in the White Mountains, there was system of "kiddie cars" on tracks up Mount Cranmore in North Conway, and Franconia Notch's Cannon Mountain had a state-built gondola system. Both could carry warm-weather tourists as well as winter skiers.

As skiing became increasingly popular, more ski areas opened. Sometimes doing this consisted of simply clearing the trees from a north- or east-facing slope and hauling an old jalopy to the top for running the tow. Sometimes a little Madison Avenue touch was needed to draw interest, as when Mount Pisgah in southern Vermont was rebaptized as Mount Snow. Nobody missed it: there are still two other Mount Pisgahs left in the state.

Since few people actually knew how to ski with any real competence, the attraction of many slopes became their instructors. The sport had a Tyrolean mystique in those days, so the best resorts imported Austrian ski instructors. At first it

took a bit of doing to lure them over. The Nazi Anschluss soon changed matters, and the hills of New England and New York welcomed the many German, Austrian, and (sometimes) Italian ski instructors who were among those declared undesirable by the Third Reich. In his day, the Austrian instructor Hannes Schneider was the most famous Jewish émigré to the New England hills. Today in Stowe, Vermont, the Trapp family, of *Sound of Music* fame, most epitomizes this group, both Jew and gentile, that exchanged Alps for northern Appalachians.

Despite the proximity of the hills for the Yankee rural population, it was the city people who first embraced skiing in a big way. In the winter of 1931–1932, the Boston & Maine Railroad began running a "snow train" out of the North Station in Boston up to Conway, New Hampshire, and back each Sunday. The first run filled three cars with 197 people. By 1940 the Boston Snow Train carried some 3,000 skiers. Trains then ran every Sunday out of New York, and frequently from Albany, Hartford, and Springfield, Massachusetts.

When New York City's first snow train pulled into Pittsfield, Massachusetts, headed for the rope tow at Bosquet's ski run on February 10, 1935, the five hundred avid New Yorkers found themselves outnumbered two to one by all the Berkshire people who came down to the station to see what a skier looked like.

Within a few years New York and Philadelphia were running weekend snow trains that left on Friday evenings, returning on Sunday nights. Major ski areas sprang up wherever good slopes lay near the railroads' main lines.

The trip itself became quite a show: "The idea of embarking with a swarm of skiers, speaking any language, or several, and dressed in any color, or several, and having any one or more different attitudes towards the adventure they have set out upon, is all a bit different, I dare say, from any other kind of journey."[17]

The only way to envision the high adventure of a snow train is to be trapped on a train being ripped apart by college students returning to campus after their team's victory over a football rival. The railroads provided a special baggage car that rented and repaired equipment, and the rest of the train consisted of a string of beat-up cars scavenged out of the storage yard.

Overnight, certain hills became famous throughout America, and never again would the New England winter bring its lonely isolation: "The greatest boon that skiing has brought to Vermont isn't the new winter visitors or the income from entertaining them, but the improved morale of our own people in a season which heretofore was regarded as a depressing one."[18]

This is not to say that the Yankees passed up the monetary opportunity. They happily rented out their spare rooms, or transformed the old drafty barn into an old drafty ski dorm. They opened restaurants, ski shops, and were known to modify their Yankee twang into rather unusual dialectal equivalents of an Austrian accent.

The New York crowd has always been a strong influence on New England skiing, and their voiced approval has rocketed some slopes, including Vermont's Mount Mansfield and the nearby village of Stowe, to international fame.

The village of Stowe lies at the foot of the 3,000-plus-foot Worcester Range to the east, which parallels the Green Mountain range a half dozen miles west. The town sits in the valley intervale of the Waterbury River, where its West Branch meanders back up to drain the side valley leading up to Mount Mansfield and Smugglers Notch. The town's main street follows the wanderings of the Waterbury stream through the flat intervale, giving a sense of discovery to the driver rounding the curve into town.

The eastern slopes of Mount Mansfield hold good snow from December to April, about the longest natural skiing season of any New England resort. It also lies only a dozen miles up the valley from the Central Vermont Railroad's main line.

Stowe was always something of a resort town. Its summer folk had settled the village into a neat, compact community long before the skiers arrived. As early as 1861, the town historian observed:

The village constantly has a busy, bustling, lively appearance, and when, for some three or four months in summer, from three to five hundred strangers are thrown into it, with all the means of show and parade they bring with them, of fine apparel, fine carriages, and fine horses ... this village has quite the appearance of a considerable watering-place and has been called by some of the public journals, the "Saratoga of Vermont."[19]

Cover of a 1941 brochure listing 60 Massachusetts towns with ski trails.

MOUNT MANSFIELD
STOWE, VT.

Stowe, Vermont, ca. 1920s, from a postcard.

Later, Stowe kept its outside contacts by an electric trolley that connected the town with the main line of the Central Vermont Railroad in nearby Waterbury.

In the early auto age, Stowe again remained important, as the idyllic Currier and Ives village that one always stopped in on the motor tour through Smugglers Notch.

Stowe, said one Vermont writer, "is what we like to think of as a typical Vermont town, with a preponderance of white, story-and-half houses connected with barns by a series of sheds, and having the advantage of a million-dollar-view, as the whole majestic length of Mansfield is spread out across the valley, like a backdrop for the town."[20]

It has remained the archetypal image of a New England ski village, a nestling community of white churches, old houses, and inns tucked under the mountain's shadow — today surrounded on every road out of town by ski shops, motels, gas stations, fast food chains, hot-tub dealerships, and "Irish pubs" advertising guitar-singalong "happy hours."

In the 1920s, the village promoters began putting on a winter carnival, the main event of which, at first, consisted of snaking a line of well-populated tobaggans down the snow-covered main street behind a wildly swerving speeding car.

The fame of Mount Mansfield's slopes grew for the next few decades, attracting skiers and skier-businessmen. In 1940, the Mount Mansfield Lift, Inc., a group of New York investors, opened a chair lift up the mountain. They had leased the right

to the area from the state for a yearly fee plus 10 percent of any gross annual revenue over $40,000. It was then the world's longest chair lift.

The renown of its slopes was helped by Lowell Thomas's being one of the lift company directors. He made many of his weekly broadcasts from Stowe, unabashedly enthusiastic. High society soon moved into town, and a 1941 issue of *Harper's Bazaar* showed sporty debs and matrons in the latest ski wear against the backdrop of Mansfield and Stowe. It was hard for the place not to catch on after that.

When the Trapp family escaped to America, they spent a few years looking before settling down on a ridge that spurs out from the Mansfield range, with the high mountains at their backs, and before them, the village of Stowe nestled far below in the valley.

By the 1950s, Saks Fifth Avenue had a Stowe branch, Interstate 89 was following the route of the Central Vermont Railroad across the state, and the A-frame was soon to begin appearing on the dirt roads through the woods. Mount Mansfield and the surrounding slopes became an internationally rated ski resort, and Stowe made *Playboy* magazine's Number One rating for eastern winter resort nightlife.

Today, the downhill skiing has become a highly sophisticated and lucrative industry (it is interesting to note the parallel development in using space-age plastics and graphites in the fabrication of both ski equipment and après-ski orthopedic devices). Equipment has been improved for safety, ease of skiing, and keeping warm in the ever-lengthening lift lines.

Looking toward Mount Mansfield and Smugglers Notch from the Stowe road.

Many have turned away from the groomed slopes to embrace the quiet joys of cross-country skiing. While not offering the suicidal joy of tucking oneself down flat and tracking straight to the bottom, cross-country skiing provides a more Thoreauvean experience of nature in the winter. Old roads into the forest become one's private solitary domain. One is never so much a silent master of the wilderness as when one glides on soundlessly to startle a deer or other forest creature nibbling at a limb of dried apples at the remains of some long-abandoned farmyard.

The popularity of cross-country skiing, if it grows, promises a new age for the New England hills, one in which the cozy snowbound inn surrounded by quiet hills holds as much attraction for the winter visitor as do the well-groomed ski slopes, disseminating these visitors over the landscape in much the same way that the automobile spread the tourist industry out from the great mountain hotels.

In any case, the three-season hiker and the skier have spread a wider, more stable base for the tourist economy in the New England hills. Even the old bugbear of dry winters, with resulting snowless ski slopes, has been gradually defeated with ever-more-sophisticated snowmaking equipment. While it has, at times, caused the urbanization of some once-rural villages, it has also created a large and vocal population, natives and visitors alike, determined to preserve the New England hills' best before it is forever lost.

Edward Martin Taber's sketch of "Winter Costume at Stowe," 1889.

14   *The Hills Today*

The hills today are gradually returning to wilderness. More and more summer and winter people may be buying old homes or constructing new ones, but the forests are enveloping the land. The patchwork of hill farms, replaced by the wide bare expanse of sheep pasture, has, in most places, disappeared.

A person combing the hillsides to find the lookoff from which a nineteenth-century photographer took a panoramic vista of a valley settlement today finds the view obstructed by trees, trees, and more trees. The once-stark, denuded landscape is now timbered.

The people of the hills, however, are still the old familiar in modern cover. Where once the lady writer of the village was Harriet Beecher Stowe of Litchfield, Connecticut, accumulating memories as the minister's daughter for her *Poganuc People,* the local author a century later has become Grace Metalious, with her chronicle of life in a small New Hampshire milltown somewhere east of White River Junction, a community she named Peyton Place. While the works differ in their reading audiences, each gives a deep sociological insight into the life of the New England hill-country town. What makes them doubly intriguing is that each could have been written in the other's era. Harriet Beecher Stowe could have been writing about the 1930s and 1940s, and one could find all Grace Metalious's characters acting much the same way in the 1840s. The books are simply the two sides to the same coin.

Likewise the back-to-the-land "counterculture" of the 1970s, when much of city and suburban youth moved upland to establish communes, has strong overtones of the multifarious religious fervor of the early nineteenth century. The hills, woods, and remote farms are once again chosen for the spiritual rebirth of their tenants. Once again, hard manual labor and good solid logic are mixed with a bit of permissive morality.

The best sketch of this latest, current influx of new sociological forces comes from Lisa Alther's *Kinflicks,* partially set in the Northeast Kingdom town of Stark's Bog, a typical amalgam of past and present:

The town proper consisted of one road, which came from St. Johnsbury and led to a border crossing into Quebec. Where the road passed through town, it was lined with a feed store, a hardware store, a hotel where the hunters stayed in the fall, an IGA grocery store, a gun shop, a taxidermy parlor, a funeral home, a farm equipment franchise, and a snow machine showroom called Sno Cat City. All these were housed in buildings from the early 1800's with colonial cornices and returns and doorways, which were pleasing in their simplicity. Pleasing to everyone but the Stark's Boggers, who were sick to death of them and had done their best to tear them down or cover them over with fluorescent plastic and neon tubing and plate glass and gleaming chrome. Each businessman yearned to raze the clapboard and beam structure on his premises and erect a molded plastic- and aluminum-sided showroom in its place. Sno Cat City, for instance, owned by Ira Bliss IV, had a huge orange mountain lion springing out from its facade; it being summer, row after row of gleaming yellow Honda trail bikes sat out in front. Likewise the goal of each Stark's Bog householder was to knock down or sell the despised frame colonial his family had infested for centuries, and throw up a prefab ranch house that would be airtight, with everything working properly.[1]

The Stark's Boggers of today are the people still struggling to cope with life in the hills. For them the chatter of talk on the CB radio has replaced the party-line conversations. The snowmobile is not merely an expensive toy, but a means of defying winter and its enforced isolation. Hunting, like a woodpile, is less a pastime than a way of filling the larder for winter and stretching that modest factory wage.

Mist and wood smoke, West Branch North River valley, Adamsville, Massachusetts.

Upland life still retains overtones of the old "Age of Homespun," yet in a more modern way. The hill farmer working his family acreage will arise early, see to the cattle, then go off for his job in the mill. Evenings will be spent on other farm chores. The wife becomes the farm manager and, if there are no able children, assumes the role of hired hand.

Along a frozen swampy dirt road, hung on a contour halfway up a late February hillside, the ruts carry through the barnyard of a struggling farm. In the fields, a flock of crows pick at the stubble gradually reappearing out of the lessening snow-cover. In the muddy right-of-way between back door and barn, the farmer and his wife make ready to fertilize the snowy fields before spring thaw turns them to mire. On the downhill side, by the shed next to the house, the husband is flat on his back changing the tractor's oil, all bloody knuckles from the frozen crankcase bolts. On the uphill side, by the barn, the wife pushes a wheelbarrow, wheeling the various loads of manure into a ready pile.

Such people did not prove a receptive audience for the philosophical utterings of those back-to-the-landers who ultimately set out to proselytize their neighbors:

The time had come, we decided, to involve ourselves with The People. We had kept to ourselves for too long, allowing a mythology to spring up among the Stark's Boggers: The Soybean People were Communists, lesbians, draft dodgers, atheists, food stamp recipients. Our seclusion had been necessary to get the Free Farmlet going. But now the sparse stunted produce from our overgrown garden was in jars and trays of sand in the musty dirt cellar. Wood for the cabin and for the sugar shack was cut and split and stacked. It was time to descend into Stark's Bog and mix and mingle with the folk with whom we had cast our lot. It was time to win over their heads and their hearts to The Revolution![2]

Today, as the two camps make contact, the exchange of ideas is not so one-sided. Those "hippies" who have developed a serious love for the "simplicity" of rural life ultimately find themselves at the feed store, weighing their townsmen's various advice about seed, tractors, and planting times. Conversely, this newest wave of hill-country settlers have effected a modest revitalization of the rural communities. Old fields are again planted. The newcomers' social consciousness ultimately channels itself into volunteer town welfare activities, helping to improve the life of the more struggling citizens. They have entered local politics, and found their own sense of personal independence not too disparate from that of those born and raised in the hills. Pay your bills and mind your own business. Today, Vermont is about the only state in the Union which prohibits prosecution for secluded skinny-dipping. Independence and personal freedom still reign.

When we turn to a look at the economic character of the New England hill country today, we see that one of the best ways of breaking the region into separate sections is to see the kinds of communities in which one finds the larger shopping areas, with the nationally known supermarkets and chain stores. Categorized in this way, the New England hill country falls roughly into three regions: south, middle, and north. In the southernmost region, it is the factory and mill towns which contain the active business centers. In a middle region, agricultural towns, with their grain towers and rail sidings, are where the larger stores serve the local population. Farthest north, the upper region concentrates its metropolises around resort areas and wood-product mills.

It is not sociology or economics, however, that conveys the true feel of the New England hill country of today. It is rather the back roads and country lanes which

Underhill Range of the Green Mountains, from the Trapp Family Lodge, Stowe, Vermont.

can lead you through three hundred years of historical landscapes, to places you never dreamed still existed.

You follow a road along a valley stream; on each side, the wooded slopes edge close and high. Ahead, the narrow valley widens to a modest intervale. The road abruptly swings perpendicular to the ever-rushing brook, crosses a bridge and passes, on the left, two white worn churches; on the right is a small empty common, more a grassy meadow. The road curves around two sides of the common, again heading upstream, passes a wooden porched store, an old schoolhouse turned post office, a few dwellings, and reenters the shaded glen.

Farther upstream, a larger intervale shows active dairy farming. A deepcut stream meanders through, marked by the cows that line its banks. Glacial deposits periodically undulate the valley floor, giving the smooth grazing grass the look of a well-planned golf course. The farmhouses here are quite substantial, in contrast to the make-do aspect of their hillside neighbors.

At the edge of the intervale, on a flat shelf of land above the flood plain, the glacial kame terrace, the village is a single street of houses and stores.

If there are falls, an old factory or little antiquated shop buildings line the waterside, their back windows looking directly down onto the rushing stream. Where there are insufficient flats to hold the millhand population, streets cut across the ravine's slope, with front doors facing the chimneys of the next street. The town buildings here will be a Victorian melange of gingerbread, western fronts, towers, and porches, all a stark contrast to the Greek Revival of the hilltop centers.

If you turn up a side valley to follow a brook back up the heights, you see that the homes are the one-and-a-half-story design of the early nineteenth century. Any larger Federalist structures are sure to have their long line of sheds connecting to the cow barn. This allows both the farmer and the rats to escape the winter blasts when moving between the house and the sheltered livestock.

Halfway up to the heights, a side road makes a dirt track across the contour of the slope. The old brown unpainted story-and-a-half homes face down the hillside. Behind, above, the pasture rises steeply. In front, the little porch overlooks the dirt shelf of a road. There is no lawn or yard, only mud and vehicle tracks against the skirts of the house. The wagons of old have been replaced by four-wheel-drive vehicles and cars in various stages of disassembly. Between the posts that hold up the porch roof hangs the white of the family wash, in the precarious vicinity of the surrounding mire.

Up at the crest of the heights, the ridge is sometimes simply forest, broken only by a wide field of stacked lumber, high cones of sawdust, and the bustle of trucks hauling in logs to the sawmill. Here only a line of old oaks and a decaying cemetery marks an old hill town.

If life has not abandoned the hilltops, clear pastures roll down each side, giving panoramas of the valley far below. The old village centers, their white church, signposts, and geometric green (denoting an earlier era of optimistic town planning) occasionally survive, though often descended to the south or lee of the true heights.

Plain, empty, and silent, these remnants of a forgotten hope have an astringent beauty found nowhere else in the world.

Site List

This is a somewhat subjective list of sites, locating both places that are not listed in the commonly available guidebooks and those that are and serve as excellent examples of themes in the text. In short, it is a personal selection of what the author considers to be interesting and fascinating places in the New England hills that might otherwise escape the knowledge of a person simply relying on the standard (though excellent) regional guidebooks. Likewise, many additional locations have not been included here, simply because they are so well covered in the readily available guides. Finally, no list can ever be complete. I extend my apologies to those whose favorite locales have been omitted, and invite suggestions for additional sites.

The sites are listed by general geographical location, identified by township, and by village within the township if necessary. To help in locating each community within the state, abbreviations are given after each town name to allow a quick scan to find the general placement within the upland region of that state — northeastern, southeastern, northwestern, and southwestern Maine, Vermont, and New Hampshire, and the eastern and western highlands (Berkshires) of Massachusetts. The divisions used will become readily apparent to the map user in search of nearby locations. All township names used are shown on the official state tourism maps available from each state's department of transportation or department of tourism, although they may not appear on ordinary road maps.

Please note: those places identified as charging admission may be open in season and are subject to varying fees and hours. The reader should check current tourist literature.

Connecticut

(All in Litchfield Hills area.)

Canaan. Housatonic Rail Road Company. Canaan Union Station. Excursion train, runs south to Cornwall Bridge. Views of fields with glacial erratics. Passes active limestone industry.

Limestone Quarry. *Lower Road, 1 mile east of Route 7, south side.*

Glacial kames. *Against hillside, North Canaan, off Route 44.*

Cornwall. Covered bridge. *Cornwall Hollow.*

Dark Entry Ravine, section of Appalachian Trail. *Up hill, east side of Cornwall Bridge center.*

Cathedral Pine. Mast pines, full growth white pines. *From junction routes 4 and 125, go west on Route 4, then first left (south) onto Pine Street to end, then left (east) onto Valley Road, then left (east) onto Essex Hill Road and go short distance to Appalachian Trail crossing marker, with pines on left (north).*

Goshen. Old ridgeline village.

Kent. Kent Falls. *At state park, Route 7, north of center.*

Lakeville. Old Pocketknife Factory Building, now a restaurant. *Holley Place.*

Litchfield. White Memorial Foundation. Nature center, museum, and hiking area in regrown farmland. *2 miles west of center on Route 202, left side.*

Opulent hill town. Mansion houses along streets leading from center.

Tapping Reeve Law School.

New Preston. Ravine shop village.

Old Mill. *Main Avenue below Lake Waramaug dam.*

Norfolk. Summer-boarder village of the 1890s. Mansions.

Dennis Hill State Park. Panoramic view. *From center, go 2 miles south on Route 272 to park entrance on left (east).*

Haystack Mountain Stone Tower. Panoramic view. *From center, go 1 mile north on Route 272 to state park entrance on left (west); ½ mile hike to summit.*

Riverton. Hitchcock Chair Factory and Museum. Old New England woodworking industry.

Sharon. Northeast Audubon Center. Nature museum, sanctuary. Beavers, river otters, series of regrown fields. *Route 4.*

Washington. American Indian Archaeological Institute. Museum. *Off Route 199 south of center.*

Maine

Albany. (SW) Bumpus Mine. World-famous rockhounding locale. *East side approximately 1 mile south of where routes 5 and 35 join after coming south from Bethel.*

Augusta. (SE) Fort Western (1754). Museum. *Bowman Street. Admission.*

Maine State Museum. Excellent collection of artifacts and state industry displays. *State of Maine Cultural Building, next to State House, Sewall Street.*

Bethel. (SW) Street of nineteenth-century homes and stores. Twenty-seven buildings (1813–1906). *Broad Street in village.*

Bowdoin College Grant East. (NE) Hermitage Preserve. Tract of white pine. *On paper company road, approximately 6 miles northwest of Katahdin Iron Works, along bluff, north side of river at Appalachian Trail crossing.*

Gulf Hagas. Scenic 3-mile gorge. *Continue north from Hermitage Preserve along Appalachian Trail, then west up West Branch Pleasant River.*

Byron. (NW) Swift River gold region. *From village, Route 17, take side road northeast for approximately 1¼ miles to bridge over East Branch Swift River. Park and hike (or drive on trail) downstream to gold area, spanning ½ mile to 1 mile from bridge.*

Coos Canyon. Scenic locale at Byron village.

Carrabassett Valley. (NW) Glacial cirque. *On Crocker Mountain, accessible along Appalachian Trail.*

Chesterville. (SW) Glacial esker. *From village, take Ridge Road south approximately 3 miles. Esker between ponds.*

Chesuncook. (NE) Old lumbering settlement. *Accessible only by water, north end of Chesuncook Lake by West Branch Penobscot River.*

Concord Township. (NW) Bingham glacial esker. Almost 100′ high. *From Bingham, take Route 16 south 2 miles.*

Corinth. (SW) Nineteenth-century rural hamlet. *West Corinth. From junction routes 11, 15, and 43 at East Corinth, go south on Route 15 for approximately 1½ miles, then turn left (west) onto West Corinth Road to village at crossroads.*

Dexter. (NE) Gristmill (1818). Local historical society museum. *In village near junction routes 7 and 23. Admission.*

Dover-Foxcroft. (NE) Blacksmith shop (1863). Museum. *From center, go north on Route 153, then left (west) onto Chandler Road.*

Fryeburg. (SW) Covered bridge (1857). *From village, go east on Route 302 approximately 5 miles to East Fryeburg. Turn left (north) onto Hemlock Bridge Road to bridge by Kezar Pond.*

Grafton. (SW) Grafton Notch State Park. Scenic natural sites, all a short walk from auto route: Moose Cave Gorge, Mother Walker Falls, Gorge, Screw Auger Falls Gorge. *Along Route 26. Consult roadside signs.*

Greenville. (NE) Moosehead region museum. Eveleth-Crafts Sheridan Historical Home. *Pritham Avenue in village.*

Lake steamer *Katahdin* (1914). Museum. *In village. Admission.*

Scott Paper Company lumbering tours. *Summer only. Inquire ahead at (207) 695-2241.*

Guilford. (NE) Covered bridge. (1857). *In village.*

Harrison. (SW) Up-and-down sawmill. Barrows-Scribner Mill (1846). *From village, go south on Route 35, turn left (east) onto Carsley Road and continue past Maple Ridge Airport. At end of Carsley Road, turn right (south) onto Maple Ridge Road, then take first left (east) onto road to mill on Crooked River.*

Hastings (Batchelders Grant). (SW) Evans Notch. Scenic locale. *In White Mountain National Forest, Route 113.*

Houghton. (NW) Height of land, scenic vista from ridge. *Route 17, approximately 5 miles north of Houghton village.*

Katahdin Iron Works. (NE) Restored iron furnaces. *From Brownsville Junction, take Route 11 north approximately 5 miles to road left (northwest) to state park.*

Kingfield. (NW) Exhibition of photographs by Chansonetta Stanley Emmons, nineteenth- and early twentieth-century genre photographer. *Historical Society Museum, High Street.*

Lebanon. (SW) Nineteenth-century village. *West Lebanon. From South Lebanon, go north on routes 11 and 202 approximately 1 mile, then turn left (northwest) onto West Lebanon Road; continue approximately 3 miles to village.*

Joseph Hardison gristmill (1774). *From routes 11 and 202 at East Lebanon, turn south onto Little River Road to mill by hamlet of Lebanon.*

Limington. (SW) Academy building (1854). *Route 117 in village.*

Livermore. (SW) Working nineteenth-century farm, town buildings, Norlands Living History Center, schoolhouse, church. *From village, go east on Route 108. At bend in road to south, turn left (north) onto Norlands Road. Admission.*

Millinocket. (NE) Great Northern Paper Company logging tours. *Mid to late summer only. Call (207) 723-5131, extension 1274.*

Region. Nineteenth-century logging camp. *Accessible only by water. Township 1, Range 9 WELS (West of East Line), Ambajejus Island, Ambajejus Lake, West Branch Penobscot River, near road to Baxter State Park.*

Monmouth. (SW) Museum of Rural Maine History. Group of houses, stores, and shops, depicting nineteenth-century life. *Route 132 in village.*

Mount Katahdin. (NE) Alpine and glacially formed scenery. Great Basin, glacial cirque, Knife Edge, intersection of two cirques. Sheepbacks. *Consult hiking guidebooks.*

Traveler Mountain. Lava-rock volcano-formed mountain. *Northeast corner of Baxter State Park. Consult hiking guidebooks.*

Moxie Gore. (NW) Moxie Falls. High waterfall. *From The Forks, Route 201, turn east onto road to Moxie Lake, go 2½ miles to side road left (north) leading to falls.*

Newburgh. (NE) Preserved nineteenth-century general store (1839, closed to business 1910, unchanged since). *Jabez Knowlton Store, Newburgh Center, routes 9 and 202.*

Newfield. (SW) Restored nineteenth-century village. Willowbrook, 27 buildings. *Admission.*

Classic rambling sawmill. *West Newfield, junction routes 11 and 110.*

New Gloucester. (SW) Sabbathday Lake Shaker Village. *Route 26. Admission.*

New Portland. (NW) Wire suspension bridge (1842). *From junction routes 27 and 146, go east on Route 146 ¼ mile, then turn left (north) onto Wire Bridge Road.*

Newry. (SW) Step Falls Preserve. Scenic waterfalls. *Route 26, just south of Grafton Notch State Park.*

Covered bridge (1872). *From village, go south on routes 2, 5, and 26 to North Bethel. Turn right (west) onto Sunday River Road, continue past turnoff to ski area.*

Norridgewock. (NE) Site of Fr. Rale's Indian village. *From junction routes 8 and 2, turn northwest onto Winding Hill Road along southwest side of Kennebec River. Follow road to location at meadows at mouth of Sandy River.*

Museum of Indian and Rale Artifacts. *In village.*

Old Town. (NE) Penobscot Indian community.

Onawa. (NE) Paper-region village. High trestle railroad and a half-dozen homes in the midst of paper-company land.

Orono. (NE) University of Maine Anthropological Museum. Indian artifacts. *Stevens Hall, University of Maine campus.*

Oxford. (SW) Glacial esker. *Drive south from village along east side of Thompson Lake, bear left (east) at V in road. Esker divides ponds on left (north).*

Patten. (NE) Lumberman's Museum. Extensive collection, lumber camp. *In village along Route 159 west. Admission.*

Phillips. (NW) Sandy River & Rangeley Lakes Railroad. Museum and rides. *Admission.*

Pittston. (SE) Arnold Expedition Historical Museum. *Route 27, south of village. Admission.*

Poland. (SW) Remains of Poland Spring resort. Gigantic main building burned. Railroad station, chapel, and other buildings remain. *Route 26, south of Poland.*

Porter. (SW) Covered bridge (1876). *Just east of Route 160, bridge over Ossipee River.*

Rangeley. (NW) Scenic village.

Cascade Stream Gorge. Scenic locale. *From Rangeley, go 3 miles south on Route 4 to southern corner of lake. Park at trail head left (east), opposite South Shore Drive (first road right around lake), hike east up Cascade Stream approximately ½ mile.*

Rumford. (SW) Planned factory housing (ca. 1900). *Strathglass Park, in village.*

Impressive commercial and public buildings (ca. 1900). *In village.*

Shapleigh. (SW) Old Schoolhouse. *North Shapleigh. Route 11 north from Shapleigh, about 5 miles.*

Solon. (NW) Caratunk Falls. Thirty-six-foot waterfall in Kennebec River. *West off Route 201, north end of village.*

Stow. (SW) Scenic drive through Cold River valley. *Route 113.*

Unity. (SE) Maine Tribal Unity Museum. Indian artifacts. *From village, go south on routes 9 and 202 ¼ mile, then left (east) on Quaker Hill Road to museum on campus of Unity College.*

Waterford. (SW) Nineteenth-century village.

Weld. (NW) Scenic panorama. *Center Hill Picnic Area, Mount Blue State Park. Small fee.*

West Paris. (SW) Mineral museum. *Perham's Maine Mineral Store. Junction routes 26 and 219.*

Paris Hill. Old hilltop "shire" village.

Winslow. (SE) Fort Halifax. 1754 blockhouse, one of the region's last colonial-era fortifications, used by Benedict Arnold's expedition. *From center, go south 1 mile on Route 201. Admission.*

Massachusetts

(Western Highlands [Berkshires]; Eastern Highlands [east of Connecticut River])

Adams (and Neighboring Towns). (WH) Mount Greylock Reservation. Auto route to summit, hiking trails (Hopper Brook is a favorite). *Consult hiking guides.*

Ashfield. (WH) Spruce Corner Schoolhouse. *From junction routes 112 and 116, go west on Route 116 approximately 2 miles to bridge across small stream. Schoolhouse on left side (west) of stream at left (south) curve in road.*

Barre. (EH) Eastern highlands "shire" town.

Balanced Rock. *From town green, take Route 122 (West Street), then left (south) onto old Hardwick Road to Rockingstone Park.*

Bernardston. (WH) Feed mill powered by belts connected to turbine at nearby waterfall.

Blandford. (WH) Sanderson Falls. Scenic gorge and waterfalls. *Chester-Blandford State Forest. From Chester, go east on Route 20 to state forest signs and picnic area. Turn right (south) onto Sanderson Brook Road.*

Buckland. (WH) Hillside village. Old town buildings.

Charlemont. (WH) Buttonwood tree under which original settler slept (1743). Ravaged trunk. *By Warner House, Route 2, in village.*

Old schoolhouse (1765). *Route 2, East Charlemont.*

Chesterfield. (WH) Chesterfield Gorge. Narrow channel cut in geologically recent times when glacier dammed original watercourse. *From Chesterfield, go west on Route 9 to bridge at West Chesterfield. Turn left (south) onto River Road, then left to gorge at signs.*

Freestone abutments to 1739 bridge on Boston-Albany post road. *At head of gorge.*

Colrain. (WH) Covered bridge (1866). *Lyonsville Road, off Route 112.*

Old factory village, *Lyonsville.*

Old mill and dam. *From Route 112 at Griswoldville, go west on Adamsville Road to where road leaves intervale and begins up stream valley. Old buildings on left (southwest) just beyond intersection with Lyonsville Road.*

Christian Hill Church. Small old hilltop hamlet church, restored. *From Route 112 at Griswoldville, go west on Adamsville Road. Follow road across bridge over river at edge of intervale, take third right (north) after bridge onto Clark Road. Continue uphill to church left (west) at crest.*

Conway. (WH) Covered bridges.

Florida. (WH) Whitcomb Summit. Scenic outlook from heights along Mohawk Trail. *Route 2.*

Original section of Mohawk Trail Indian path, now a hiking trail. *From Whitcomb Summit, take Route 2, go east to Drury post office just before overhead warning signs spanning road — "Steep Hill — Curves Next 2 Miles — Prepare to Stop" — take left (north, post office side) on side road about 20 feet before sign. Continue on this road to end of pavement with side road right, road ascending rise ahead. Scenic vista across field on left. Indian trail ascends hill into woods at right.*

Gilbertville. (EH) Old factory mill buildings. *Route 32 south from village along stream to west.*

Granville. (WH) Granville State Forest. Mountain streams. *From Route 57 at West Granville, go west a short distance, then turn south onto West Hartland Road to park entrance. Another approach is from County Route 20 in Hartland, descending to north end of Barkhamsted Reservoir. Take road north along stream, park at end of pavement at state line and hike up dirt road along stream.*

Toy drum factory (established 1854). *South of village right (west) off Route 189.*

Hardwick. (EH) Old one-room schoolhouse. *From village, go north on Route 32A approximately 3½ miles to school on right (east) (approximately 100 yards south of Thresher Road).*

Heath. (WH) Old hill village.

Hinsdale. (WH) Scenic village.

Fieldstone clerestory-roof mill, unused. *Along Route 8 northwest of village, corner Housatonic Street and Hinsdale Road just before Dalton town line.*

Lanesborough. (WH) Balance Rock. *From Route 7 at Lanesborough-Pittsfield town line, go north to north end of Pontoosuc Lake. Turn left (west) onto Bowl Hill Road, continue on road as it curves left (south), pass store, then turn right (west) onto Balance Rock Road, follow road around curve left (south), cross small stream, then take right (west) through gate into park just after stream. Follow paved road to parking lot at end. Rock is right (north) in woods at beginning of parking lot.*

Leverett. (EH) Woodworking mills and water-powered sawmill. *Along North Leverett Road (river road) east from North Leverett.*

Moores Corners. Remnants of a stream-valley factory shop village. *Continue east on North Leverett Road to right (south) onto unpaved Dudleyville Road and bridge over stream with shop and mill buildings.*

Pioneer Valley Charcoal Works. Operating charcoal kilns. *From North Leverett, go east on North Leverett Road, then right (south) onto Coke Kiln Road, then left after crossing stream.*

Leyden. (WH) Hill hamlet. Scenic view of village from woods south and east.

Hill Farm. Classic hilltop farm silhouetted along ridgeline. *Looking east from County Road south of village.*

Monroe. (WH) Scenic views of Deerfield River gorge. *At Monroe Bridge and along River Road from Monroe Bridge to Zoar.*

Mount Washington. (WH) Bash Bish Falls. Scenic locale, state park.

New Marlboro. (WH) Hilltop green with 1755 tavern.

Old whip factory. *Southfield.*

Rocking Stone. Forty tons, still rocks. *Four-tenths mile southwest of Southfield, just outside state forest property.*

Campbell Falls. State park. *Off Connecticut Route 272 at Connecticut-Massachusetts state line.*

New Salem. (EH) Scenic village. Now on side road after the main thoroughfare that once ran through the center to the east was discontinued because of Quabbin Reservoir land condemnation. No stores or traffic; just homes, churches, schools, and town buildings. *Follow signs off Route 202.*

Bear's Den Gorge. One hundred feet deep. *From North New Salem (off Route 202), go west on Neilson Road to signs.*

North Adams. (WH) Hairpin turn. Scenic outlooks. *Route 2, Mohawk Trail.*

Hoosac Tunnel Museum.

Site of Fort Massachuset.

Western Summit. Scenic vista and hang glider launch site. *Overlooking Hoosac Valley from heights along Mohawk Trail, Route 2.*

Peru. (WH) Hilltop hamlet along old stage route. *Present Route 143.*

Petersham. (EH) Restored hill village.

> Fisher Museum. Exhibits depicting New England land use and regrowth. *Harvard Forest, Route 32 north of village, approximately 3 miles south of junction routes 2 and 32.*

Princeton. (EH) Wachusett Meadows. Upland meadows, large sugar maples, Audubon Society Forest. *Go west from village on Route 62 for approximately ½ mile, then turn left (south) onto Goodnow Road to sanctuary parking area. Maps available. Admission.*

> Redemption Rock. Where Mary Rowlandson was ransomed from her Indian captors in 1676. *Route 140, just before Westminster town line. Roadside sign.*

Rowe. (WH) Artifacts of Fort Pelham. Historical Society museum. *In village.*

> Shop factory building. *In village, Pond Road by lake.*

> Prospect Brook. Scenic outlook.

Royalston. (EH) Old summer boarders' hill town.

> Doane Falls. *Royalston Falls State Reservation, Route 68.*

Russell. (WH) Woronoco Mills. Valley ravine factory village, Strathmore papermaking. *Off Route 20.*

Savoy. (WH) Balanced Rocks, Tannery Falls. *Savoy Mountain State Forest. From Savoy village, go east on routes 8A and 116 approximately ½ mile, then turn left (north) onto Center Road (with sign for Savoy State Forest). Go approximately 3 miles and turn left (west) at junction onto Adams Road, then after a short distance go right (north) onto New State Road. Go approximately 1½ miles, then turn right (east) onto unpaved Tannery Road. At approximately ¾ mile, road turns abruptly left (north). Continue straight up mountain on unpaved road (by foot or partway by auto in season) to large glacial erratic, or turn left (north) on Tannery Road and continue to parking lot, then hike short distance north upstream to falls.*

Shelburne. (WH) Salmon Falls glacial potholes. *Shelburne Falls, near Bridge of Flowers.*

Shutesbury. (EH) A few town buildings scattered around a green set on a high plateau.

South Carver. (SE corner of Massachusetts) Edaville Railroad. Rolling stock from Sandy River & Rangeley Lakes narrow-gauge railroad. *Admission.*

Townsend. (EH) Spaulding Gristmill. *Off Route 119, at east end of lake, Townsend Harbor.*

Ware. (EH) Scenic vista of uplands drowned by Quabbin Reservoir. *Route 9 west to Quabbin Dam, right (north) on Quabbin Hill road to signs for Quabbin Hill Tower.*

Wendell. (EH) A crossroads hamlet.

West Brookfield. (EH) Brookfield Plantation site. *From village, go east on Route 9 a short distance to road up hill. Site along top of hill and fields to south.*

Westfield. (WH) Westfield Athenaeum. Indian and colonial artifacts. *Elm and Court streets at green. Free.*

Westhampton. (WH) Rocking Stone, at 1,400-foot level. *Two miles northwest of village.*

Williamstown. (WH) 1753 pioneer's house reconstruction. Built in 1953, using mid-eighteenth-century tools and materials. *On green, Main Street, junction routes 7 and 2.*

> Sand Springs. Thermal spring. *From Main Street, go north on Route 7 approximately 2 miles, then right (east) onto Sand Spring Road. Go ¼ mile to spring on left.*

Windsor. (WH) Old woodworking mill. *East Windsor village, old Route 9, near Windsor-Cummington town line.*

> Windsor Jambs Gorge. *Boundary Brook, Windsor State Forest, along River Road, which runs south from routes 8A and 116 just east of Savoy and north from Route 9 just west of West Cummington.*

Worthington. (WH) Old Stagecoach Tavern. *Worthington Corners, junction routes 112 and 143.*

> Cleared upland farming land, reminiscent of early nineteenth-century vista. *Worthington Corners. Old North Road, Route 143.*

> Old factory shop. Healy Wood Products, Inc., "Saw and Plane Handles, since 1847." *West Chesterfield, Route 143 east side of Westfield River.*

Zoar. (WH) Soapstone deposit, worked by Indians. *At serpentine in river.*

New Hampshire

(Most covered bridges are not listed, as they are clearly marked on many state maps.)

Acworth. (SW) Hill village. Scenic hilltop hamlet.

> Intervale hamlet. *South Acworth, mill by timber bridge.*

Albany. (NE) Lovejoy Marsh Wildlife Preserve. Beaver dams, esker. *From village, go southwest on Route 16 to preserve on right (west).*

Alstead. (SW) Stone mill buildings, Early factory shops. *Along Route 123 at village and upstream eastward.*

> Chase's Woodworking Mill. *East Alstead, Route 123 at Lake Warren outlet.*

Amherst. (SE) Ponemah Bog Audubon Preserve. Glacial kettle holes. *Route 101A, approximately 2 miles east of junction routes 101 and 101A.*

Ashland. (NE) Active papermill town.

Bartlett. (NE) Glacial erratic perched on four boulders. *Route 302, 1 mile west of station.*

> Heritage New Hampshire. Museum. Extensively detailed dioramas of New England history. *Village of Glen, Route 16, north of junction with Route 302. Admission.*

Bennington. (SW) Papermill village.

Berlin. (NE) Old industrial town. Paper manufacturing, shoes, rubber goods.

Bretton Woods. (NE) The Bretton Arms resort hotel.

Glacial potholes. *Upper Ammonoosuc Falls.*

Bristol. (SE) Profile Falls. Scenic locale. *Go south from village on Route 3A approximately 2 miles to bridge over Swift River. Falls downstream on left (east) a few hundred feet.*

Canaan. (NW) Victorian summer colony village. *Canaan Street.*

Canterbury. (SE) Shaker Village. *Follow signs from Loudon, Route 106. Admission.*

Charlestown. (SW) Old Fort No. 4. Reconstruction of a 1744 colonial fort built during the French and Indian Wars. *Route 4, 1 mile north of center.*

Claremont. (SW) Wooden railroad bridge. *Route 103 east along Sugar River.*

Colebrook. (NE) Beaver Brook Falls. Spectacular at times of high water. *Route 145 approximately 2 miles north of village. Roadside sign.*

Contoocook. (WE) Wooden railroad bridge.

Conway. (NE) Conway Scenic Railroad. *North Conway.*

Dixville Notch. (NE) The Balsams resort hotel.

Dixville Notch. Scenic locale.

Dorchester. (NW) Secluded hamlet of old town buildings around triangular green. *Just off Route 118.*

Effingham Post Office. (SE) Once-important farming community. Academy building. *West from village, Route 153, on Hobbs Road, on right (northeast).*

Schoolhouse, ornate town hall. *Center Effingham.*

Enfield. (NW) Old Schoolhouse Museum. *Lockhaven Village.*

Errol. (NE) Scenic view, from bluff overlooking bend in Androscoggin River. *Route 16 at state picnic area approximately 3 miles south of village.*

Franconia. (NE) Iron furnace. *Along west side of stream in village just south of junction routes 18 and 117.*

Franconia College. Old resort hotel.

Franconia Notch. (NE) Cannon Mountain Aerial Tramway.

The Flume.

The Old Man of the Mountains.

The Basin. Twenty-foot-diameter glacial pothole.

Old Franconia Notch stagecoach. *At Flume parking lot.*

Franklin. (NE) Daniel Webster Birthplace House reconstruction. Museum. *From village, go southwest on Route 127 approximately 2 miles, then follow signs. Admission.*

Gilmanton. (SE) Old Academy Building. Still in use as town school. *Route 107 in village.*

Goffstown. (SE) Rocking Stone. *Shirley Hill.*

Grafton. (SW) Intervale with meandering Smith River. Classical glacial geology. *Route 4.*

Ruggles Mine. Great complex of mica and pegmatite diggings. *From Route 4, Grafton Center, turn southeast and follow signs. Admission.*

Greenville. (SW) Railroad trestle, 104 feet high, 700 feet long. Highest in New England.

Groton. (NW) Glacial potholes. Stream gorge. *From village, take partly graveled Sculptured Rocks Road west along Cockermouth River to scenic locale near picnic area.*

Hancock. (SW) Opulent village.

Hanover. (NW) Dartmouth College Museum. Exhibits of northern New England history.

Montshire Museum of Science. Nature exhibits. *Lyme Road, Hanover Center.*

Harrisville. (SW) Preserved textile factory village.

Haverhill. (NW) Mill. *Route 25 at Pike village.*

Lime kilns (restored ca. 1930s). *From Center Haverhill, go east on Route 116 approximately ½ mile. Bear right (south) at fork onto Lime Kiln Road, follow signs for Lime Kiln Camp.*

Hebron. (NW) Scenic village.

Hillsboro. (SW) Textile factory town. *Mills by bridge Route 149, south of junction with Route 9.*

Wooden railroad bridge. Has shed-roofed sidewalk on west side. *West of Route 149 bridge.*

Hill village. *Route 149 northwest to Hillsboro Center.*

Quaking Bog. *Fox State Forest. From Hillsboro at junction routes 149 and 202, go north on Center Road approximately 1 mile (museum, administration building, and hiking maps are farther north on Center Road), then turn right (east) onto Whitney Road, then left (north) onto Bog Road. Go approximately ½ mile, and on left (west) in forest is mud pond with floating vegetation around its rim.*

Franklin Pierce Homestead. Restored to depict affluent family home ca. 1810–1840. *By junction routes 9 and 31. Admission.*

Holderness. (NE) Squam Lakes Science Center. Nature exhibits, steam-powered sawmill, nineteenth-century buildings. *Near village, Route 113.*

Hopkinton. (SE) Smith Pond Bog. Glacial kettle hole. *From junction of Route 103 with routes 9 and 202, go south on routes 9 and 202 ½ mile to pond on left (south).*

Jaffrey. (SW) Mount Monadnock. Glacial phenomena, sheepbacks, glacial scour.

Monadnock Ecocenter. Nature exhibits. *Monadnock State Reservation.*

Scenic Village. *Jaffrey Center.*

Laconia. (SE) Colonial boundary marker (1652), Endicott Rock. *In streambed, Route 3 northeast of Weirs Beach bridge.*

Lancaster. (NE) Scenic panorama. *Weeks State Park, Route 3 south of village, auto route to observation tower atop Mt. Prospect.*

Lempster. (SW) Old one-room schoolhouse, Turnpike Tavern, and meetinghouse. *Lempster village.*

Lincoln. (NE) The Basin. Glacial potholes. *Franconia Notch.*

Railroad Equipment and rides. *Clark's Trading Post, Route 3. Admission.*

Lisbon. (NW) Stone charcoal-burner kiln (ca. 1860s). *From junction Route 117 with routes 10 and 302, go north on routes 10 and 302 approximately 2 miles to kiln on left (west), historical marker.*

Madison. (NW) Glacial erratic, one of world's largest, 83′ × 37′ × 23′. *Madison Boulder State Reservation, road west off Route 113, 2 miles north of village.*

Manchester. (SE) Currier Gallery of Art. New England landscape paintings and other works of art. *192 Orange Street.*

Milford. (SE) Purgatory Gorge and Cave.

Milton. (SE) New Hampshire Farm Museum. *Route 16 in village. Admission.*

Mt. Vernon. (SE) Hilltop village, once a bustling nineteenth-century resort.

Purgatory Gorge. Scenic waterfalls, glacial potholes. *From village, go west on partially unpaved Purgatory Road approximately 3 miles to Purgatory Brook.*

Newport. (SW) Rocking Stone.

North Conway. (NE) Wide intervale.

Conway Scenic Railway.

Ossipee. (NE) Ossipee Mountains ring dike. Circular mountain range.

Heath Pond. Quaking bog. *From Center Ossipee, go east on Route 25 approximately 2 miles to marker on right (south).*

Esker and white pine stand. *Pine River Esker. From junction routes 16 and 28, go south on Route 16 approximately 2½ miles to old fish hatchery on left (east). Esker just east of hatchery.*

Peterborough. (SW) Auto route to summit of Pack Monadnock Mountain. *Miller State Park, park entrance on Route 101 at Peterborough-Temple town line.*

Pinkham Notch. (NE) Mount Washington Auto Road, Appalachian Mountain Club, Glen Ellis Falls. *All accessible from Route 16.*

Shelburne. (NE) Shelburne Birches. Beautiful stand of white birch trees. *Route 2 west of village.*

Springfield. (SW) Royal Arch Cave. Hillside cavern, scenic outlook on Sunapee Lake 2 miles to south. *In Gile State Forest.*

Stoddard. (SW) Wooden clerestory shop mill. Three stories, quite beautiful. *On Abbott Brook at outlet of Cold Spring Lake, south side of Route 123 west of village, halfway between village and junction routes 10 and 123 in Marlow.*

Stark. (NE) Scenic locale. Church (1853) and covered bridge (ca. 1850s, rebuilt 1949). *In village just off Route 10.*

Stratford. (NE) Old lumbering village.

Suncook. (SE) China mill.

Washington. (SW) Scenic village.

White Mountain National Forest. (NE) Mount Washington Cog Railway. *West side from Route 302.*

Wilton. (SE) Frank J. Moors Sawmill. *From junction routes 31 and 101, go west on Route 101 for approximately 1 mile; mill on left (south) across river by dam and wooden bridge.*

Hill village. *Wilton Center.*

Frye's water-powered woodworking shop.

Woodstock. (NE) Glacial potholes. *Lost River, Agassiz Basin.*

Mummies. Glacial potholes. *North Woodstock.*

Balance Rock. *From junction routes 3 and 112, go north on Route 3 approximately ⅔ mile to old Alpine Hotel and golf links on left (west) (just before Woodstock-Lincoln town line), hike along edge of links across bridge and follow north side of Pondfield Brook approximately 1½ miles to rock and Bell's Cascade.*

Vermont

Barnet. (NE) Old mill. *On road up Peacham Hollow Brook valley (Barnet–East Peacham road), 1 mile west of Barnet Center.*

Barre. (NE) Granite industry.

Rock of Ages Craftsman Center. Quarry tours. Museum.

Rock of Ages Quarry Railroad Ride. *Admission.*

Bennington. (SW) Bennington Museum. Revolutionary War artifacts. *West Main Street.*

Braintree. (NW) Rocking Stone. *Braintree Hill, ½ mile northwest of Braintree Center.*

Bridgewater. (WE) Old Woolen Mill (begun 1825). *Vermont Native Industries, in village.*

Wooden framework dam. *Just upstream from mill.*

Brookfield. (NE) Classic example of a shop village. Millpond, dam, mill, dirt main street down a small ravine.

Floating Bridge. *Across lake at top of village street.*

Brookline. (SE) Round brick schoolhouse (1822), built by a former English highway robber.

Brownington. (NE) Hill village. Congregational church and Old Stone House School (1822). *On crest of hill, northwest of center.*

Buel's Gore. (NW) Appalachian gap. *Route 17 road through Green Mountains.*

Burke. (NE) Burke Mountain Auto Road, 3,267′ summit. *Darling State Park. From Route 114 at East Burke, go east on road to Burke Mountain Ski Area and park entrance on left at curve. Admission.*

Cabot. (NE) Cabot Farmers' Cooperative Creamery. Cheese-making tours.

Calais. (NE) Kent Tavern Museum (1837). Stagecoach tavern, lumbermill. *Kent's Corner.*

Gospel Hollow Church, Pekin. Lovely wooden church in an otherwise deserted little valley, now used as Calais town hall.

Cambridge. (NW) Smugglers Notch. Scenic natural locale. *South on Route 108. Closed in winter.*

Chelsea. (NE) Beautiful valley town. *Good view from hillside up lane west side opposite junction Route 113.*

Hillside hamlet. Chelsea West Hill. *From village, go south on Route 110 3 miles right (west) onto side valley road to East Randolph. After 1 mile turn right (north) onto Meadow Brook Road, continue for approximately 3 miles, bearing left to Chelsea West Hill.*

Chester. (SE) Valley town with row of ornate Victorian houses.

Chester Depot. Village of fieldstone houses.

Clarendon. (SW) Clarendon Gorge. *From junction routes 7 and 103, go east on Route 7 2 miles to signs for Long Trail. Park and hike south on Long Trail 500 feet to suspension bridge over Clarendon Gorge.*

Mineral Springs Hotel (1834). *Clarendon Springs.*

Kingsley's Gristmill. Multistoried. *East Clarendon. From Clarendon village, go east under Route 7 and follow along north side of river, then take first right (south) to East Clarendon covered bridge, cross river, park, and hike a short distance east along south side of river to best view of mill on north side of river.*

Craftsbury. (NE) Hill town. *Craftsbury Common.*

Danville. (NE) Stoddard Swamp cedar bog. Twelve acres, over 10,000 years old. *From Danville, take road south to Harvey, continue south approximately 1 mile, then take side road west approximately 1½ miles to swamp on left (south) by head of lake on right (north).*

Derby. (NE) Black Island Hemlock Forest. Ancient hemlocks over 2′ across base. *Accessible only by boat, in Lake Memphremagog, just south of U.S.–Canada line.*

East Montpelier. (NE) Gristmill. *North Montpelier.*

Glover. (NE) Runaway Pond. *At picnic area, Route 16 south of village.*

Goshen. (NW) Mount Horrid Cliff. View across Champlain Valley. *Route 73 at Brandon Gap (Long Trail crossing), park north side, left uphill and follow sign for steep ½-mile trail to outlook east.*

Grafton. (SE) Restored village. All power lines in the village have been put underground. Idyllic.

Granville. (NW) Charcoal kilns. *Route 100, Lower Granville.*

Moss Glen Falls. Scenic locale. *West side Granville Gulf, Route 100.*

Greensboro. (NE) Rocking Stone, 40′ × 30′ × 20′ high, still rocks. *In north part of town.*

Groton. (NE) Rocker Mills. Sawmill complex in operation since ca. 1800. *Route 232 at outlet to pond.*

Halifax. (SE) Halifax Gorge. *Route 112, approximately 1 mile north of Vermont-Massachusetts line.*

Hardwick. (NE) Early settlement along the Bayley-Hazen military road. *Hardwick Street; from Route 16 at East Hardwick take road north to Caspian Lake.*

"Street" is row of old colonial houses along the route.

Hartford. (WE) Quechee Gorge. Scenic locale. *Route 4 at state park.*

Hartland. (SE) Turnpike crossing. Taverns and inn buildings hemmed in close to intersection to attract the nineteenth-century stagecoach trade.

Gristmill. *Hartland Four Corners, Route 12.*

Jamaica. (NE) Balance Rock.

Jericho. (NW) Old gristmill, now craft shop. *Route 15.*

Johnson. (NW) Johnson Woolen Mills. Still-active woolen mill.

Killington. (SE) Gondola ride. Scenic vista, 4,241′. *Mount Killington Ski Area.*

Lowell. (NE) Balance Rock. *Beside Route 100 north.*

Manchester. (SW) Mount Equinox Skyline Drive. Auto road to Taconic's highest peak, 3,835′. *From Route 7. Admission.*

Marlboro. (SE) Luman Nelson Museum of New England Wildlife. *Route 9 near village.*

Montpelier. (NW) The Vermont Museum. *Pavilion Building, 109 State Street.*

Moretown. (NW) Scenic village on a high plateau. *Moretown Common.*

Morrisville. (NE) Railroad town. Commercial village, late nineteenth-century architecture.

Mount Holly. (SW) Crowley Cheese Factory. Tours. *Healdville.*

Newfane. (SE) Old hill village moved down to the flats. Beautiful village green and surrounding buildings.

Newfane Hill. Original settlement site.

Northfield. (NW) Glacial cut gorge. *Route 12.*

Old Woolen Mill.

Orwell. (SW) Gristmill.

Peacham. (NE) Nineteenth-century hill village, moved slightly downhill.

Pittsford. (SW) New England Maple Museum. *Route 7.*

Ice Caves. *On mountain slope 1 mile east-southeast of Grangerville.*

Plymouth. (SE) Plymouth Cheese Corporation. Tours.

Gold-panning streams. *Pinney Hollow Brook, parallels Route 101A from Plymouth Union to stream source near Bridgewater town line. Broad Brook: from Bridgewater Corners, stream parallels Route 101A south, then take left (straight south) where Route 101A turns right (west) and continue along side road to Five Corners. Panning along length of both streams. Take a plastic-wrapped magnet to remove heavy magnetite particles in order to get to any gold on the pan's bottom.*

President Coolidge Homestead. Home preserved as it was in 1923 when Coolidge was sworn in as President here. Also farm museum. *In village, Route 100A.*

Pownal. (SW) Snow Cave. *North Pownal.*

Proctor. (SW) Glacial pothole, 100′ above Otter Creek streambed. *Route 3, 1 mile south of village, east wall.*

Vermont marble exhibit. *Route 3. Admission.*

Putney. (SE) Green Mountain Spinnery. Makes wool yarn from local fleece. *Tours.*

Randolph. (SE) Italianate railroad station. *Depot Square.*

Hill Village. Still has the old air of uncommercial opulence in village, now occupied by Vermont Technical College. *Randolph Center.*

View of a hill hamlet. Lone church of Braintree Center. *At Randolph Center, drive north on Ridge Road to Brookfield. Stop where Route 66 turns right (east). Look west toward next range of hills for church.*

Reading. (SE) Hammondsville old settlement. Cellar holes of a village where a great map company began. *From Hammondsville village Route 106, take graveled side road west across and up along Bailey Brook, take second right (approximately 2 miles from Route 106) uphill approximately 1½ miles, bearing left at fork onto dirt road to settlement site with historical markers.*

Valley ravine shop village. *South Reading.*

Indian captivity stones. Placed in 1799 to commemorate birth in 1754 of Elizabeth Johnson, whose parents were then captives of the Abenaki, being marched to Canada. *Go south on Route 106 almost to Cavendish-Reading town line, pass side road to right (west). Slate markers are on left (northeast) just before bridge over Knapp Brook.*

Readsboro. (SW) Stagecoach Inn (1783). *Heartwellville.*

Old sawmill. *Readsboro Falls. From Readsboro, go north on Route 100 approximately 3 miles to Readsboro Falls. Sawmill in gorge left (southwest) at side road descending across stream.*

Richmond. (NW) Huntington Gorge. Scenic locale, glacial potholes. *From Route 2 at Jonesville, go south across Winooski River bridge, bear right (west), then take first left (south) after crossing Huntington River bridge. Gorge short distance on left (east).*

Rochester. (SW) Scenic auto route. *Route 73 west from Talcville.*

Rockingham. (SE) Rockingham Meeting House (1787). Steepleless church of the post-Revolutionary era of frontier settlement.

Royalton. (SE) Valley town.

Scenic vista. *Looking down on village from I-89 northbound.*

Academy Building, now a community center. *In village.*

Ryegate. (NE) Granite industry finishing sheds. *South Ryegate.*

Ryegate Corner. Upland farming area, village street in open fields on high sloping hillside plateau.

Saint Johnsbury. (NE) Fairbanks Museum. Exhibits of northern New England natural history and archaeology. *83 Main Street.*

Maple Grove Maple Museum. Museum and factory. *167 Portland Street.*

Sherburne. (SE) Climax Forest. Giant trees in an ancient forest. *Gifford Woods State Park, Route 100 just north of junction with Route 4.*

Springfield. (SE) Active ravine manufacturing town.

Eureka Schoolhouse (1758, relocated 1968), also wooden covered bridge. *Route 11, ½ mile west of Route 5 junction.*

Crown Point Military Road. Trail leading off up side of hill. *Route 5, .7 mile north of Route 11 bridge, west side, near marker.*

Stowe. (NW) Ski town.

Mount Mansfield Auto Toll Road. Drive to 4,000′ elevation. *Route 108 approximately 1½ miles southeast of ski area.*

Gondola ride to summit from ski area. *Admission.*

Strafford. (SE) Intervale village, surrounded by classic examples of glacially caused landscaping.

Elizabeth Copper Mine. Buildings, mine, and smelter. *From Route 132 at South Strafford, where Route 132 turns northeast to cross river, take road that parallels south side of river and follow road uphill to mine works on left.*

Townshend. (WE) Scenic village. Covered bridge.

Troy. (NE) Big Falls. Scenic locale. *From North Troy, go east on Route 105 across river, then follow side road right (south) along east side of Missisquoi River to falls on right (west).*

Tunbridge. (SE) Village set along a valley kame terrace. Old mill, covered bridge at village.

Glacially deposited landscape. *Along Route 110 south of village.*

Vershire. (NE) Ely Copper Mine. Rubbled site of a mining village. *From Route 113 at West Fairlee, take road west toward South Vershire, go approximately 2 miles to open area on right (north).*

Waitsfield. (NW) Old hill village center. *Waitsfield Common, approximately 1½ miles on road running due east from Waitsfield village on Route 100.*

Wallingford. (SW) Scenic, and still active, manufacturing village.

Ice bed. Snow throughout year. *From Route 7 at South Wallingford, cross bridge and go north on road on east side of Otter Creek. Continue approximately 2 miles to White Rocks Picnic Area. Ice beds area is approximately 1 mile east on blue-blazed forest road, beginning approximately ¼ mile below parking area. Consult* Day Hiker's Guide to Vermont *for trail directions.*

Wardsboro. (SW) Old Stagecoach Inn.

Washington. (NE) Scenic hamlet. Meetinghouses and old hotel on green.

Scenic farming valley. *Route 110 south toward Chelsea.*

Waterbury. (NW) Glacially deposited landscape. *Looking west from Route 100.*

Weathersfield. (SE) Crown Point Military Road. Rutted trail leading diagonally up hillside. *From Perkinsville, continue on Route 106 north ½ mile to paved road right (east), which leads around south side of pond past private camping area on left, follow road around curve to right (south), continue past dirt road left (east) up side valley to Weathersfield Center, cross stream that parallels previously mentioned dirt road. Stop car and park at stream, as road ahead curves right. Look at edge of road in woods on left (east) for rut, which angles up into forest.*

Crown Point Military Road 10-mile milestone (1759). *From junction routes 106 and 131, go east ¼ mile on Route 131, turn right (south) onto Town Road 34 just before river, continue approximately 500 feet past gateposts. Marker at edge of woods about 50 feet from roadway.*

Crown Point Military Road 12-mile milestone (1759). *From junction routes 106 and 131, go .7 mile east on Route 131 to village of Amsden (store), turn left (north) onto road connecting to Route 106, go .2 mile. Stone on west side along road about 15 feet beyond house driveway.*

Vermont Soapstone Company. *Route 106, Perkinsville.*

Westfield. (NE) Hazen's Notch. Scenic natural locale. *Route 58. Unpaved, closed in winter.*

Westmore. (NE) Lake Willoughby and cliffs. Scenic natural locale, long finger lake with two cliff-faced mountains rising on both sides to edge part of its shores. *Route 5A.*

Weston. (SE) Water-powered mills. Commercially used. *In village along Route 100.*

Whitingham. (SW) Water-powered woodworking mill. *Route 100 at outlet of Sadawga Lake.*

Williamstown. (NE) Williamstown Gulf. Glacially cut gorge. *Route 14 south of village.*

Scenic view. *Along I-89.*

Windham. (SE) Remote hill hamlet.

Windsor. (SE) American Precision Museum. Collection of tools and machinery reflecting Yankee ingenuity. *Main Street. Admission.*

Mount Ascutney Auto Road. Paved road to 3,144' summit. *From village, take Route 44 west, go under I-91, then turn left (south) and follow signs to park entrance.*

Wolcott. (NE) Wooden railroad bridge, across Lamoille River, still in use. *Route 15, 2 miles east of center.*

Woodstock. (SE) Billing Farm and Museum. Active dairy farm and museum of late nineteenth-century farming. *From center, take Route 12 north to entrance right (east) by River Road. Admission.*

Site List by Subject

New Hampshire: Acworth, Canterbury, Effingham, Enfield, Franklin, Grafton, Hillsboro, North Conway, Stark
Vermont: Brookline, Calais, Chelsea, Glover, Newfane, Plymouth, Royalton, Springfield, Strafford, Tunbridge, Washington, Woodstock

8. Valley Mills and Valley Industrial Villages

Connecticut: New Preston, Riverton
Maine: Bethel, Dexter, Harrison, Lebanon, Newfield
Massachusetts: Bernardston, Colrain, Gilbertville, Hinsdale, Leverett, New Marlboro, Rowe, Russell, Townsend, Windsor, Worthington
New Hampshire: Acworth, Alstead, Bennington, Berlin, Harrisville, Haverhill, Hillsboro, Stoddard, Suncook, Wilton
Vermont: Barnet, Bridgewater, Brookfield, Calais, East Montpelier, Groton, Hartland, Jericho, Johnson, Northfield, Orwell, Putney, Reading, Readsboro, Springfield, Tunbridge, Wallingford, Weston, Whitingham, Windsor

9. Transportation Artifacts

Connecticut: Canaan
Maine: Fryeburg, Greenville, Guilford, New Portland, Newry, Phillips, Porter
Massachusetts: Chesterfield, Conway, North Adams, South Carver
New Hampshire: Claremont, Contoocook, Conway, Greenville, Holderness, Lincoln, North Conway, Stark, White Mountain National Forest
Vermont: Brookfield, Clarendon, Hartland, Randolph, Readsboro, Wardsboro, Wolcott

10. Lumbering and Mining

Connecticut: Canaan, Cornwall
Maine: Albany, Byron, Chesuncook, Greenville, Katahdin Iron Works, Millinocket, Onawa, Patten, West Paris
Massachusetts: Leverett

11. Summer Boarders and Sportsmen

Connecticut: Norfolk
Maine: Greenville, Poland, Rangeley
Massachusetts: Royalston
New Hampshire: Bretton Woods, Canaan, Dixville Notch, Franconia, Hancock, Jaffrey, Mount Vernon, North Conway, Washington, White Mountains National Forest, Wilton
Vermont: Chester, Clarendon, Grafton, Townshend

12. Twentieth-Century Business

Maine: Rumford
Massachusetts: Russell
New Hampshire: Ashland, Berlin
Vermont: Cabot, Morrisville, Mount Holly, Pittsford, Plymouth, Putney, Saint Johnsbury, Springfield, Weston, Windsor, Woodstock

13. The Auto Age

Massachusetts: North Adams, Shelburne
New Hampshire: Pinkham Notch
Vermont: Burke, Manchester, Windsor

14. Hiking and Skiing

Connecticut: Cornwall, Litchfield
Maine: Mount Katahdin
New Hampshire: Franconia Notch, Jaffrey, Pinkham Notch
Vermont: Killington, Stowe

Notes

Introduction

1. U.S. Department of the Interior, *The National Atlas of the United States of America* (Washington, D.C., 1970), map p. 63.
2. Attributed, *On the Old Man of the Mountain,* quoted in John Bartlett, *Familiar Quotations,* ed. Emily Morison Beck, et al., 15th ed. (Boston, 1980).

1. Landforms

1. See various comments in Moses F. Sweetser, ed., *The White Mountains: A Handbook for Travelers*, various eds., (Boston, ca. 1870s–1900s).

a. All quotations are from Sereno E. Dwight, "Description of the Eruption of Long Lake and Mud Lake, in Vermont . . . ," *American Journal of Science and Arts* 11 (Oct. 1826): 39–54.

2. The Indians before the Coming of the White Man

1. Dean R. Snow, *The Archaeology of New England* (New York, 1980), 157.
2. William Wood, *New England's Prospects* (London, 1634), ed. Alden T. Vaughan (Amherst, Mass., 1977), 82.
3. W. L. Grant, ed., *Original Narratives of Early American History: Voyages of Samuel de Champlain* (New York, 1907), 55.
4. Snow, *Archaeology,* 33.
5. Wood, p. 80.
6. Samuel G. Drake, *Tragedies of the Wilderness; or, True and Authentic Narrative of Captives Who Have Been Carried Away by the Indians* (Boston, 1846), 98.

a. Charles G. Leland, *The Algonquin Legends of New England: or, Myths and Folk Lore of the Micmac, Passamaquoddy, and Penobscot Tribes* (Boston, 1884), 134.
b. F. G. Speck, "Mammoth or Stiff-legged Bear," *American Anthropologist* 37 (1935): 162.

3. Early European Contacts and Settlements: 1524–1675

1. Giovanni da Verrazano, *Voyages* (Boston, 1920), 11.
2. Ibid.
3. William Wood, *New England's Prospects* (London, 1634; Amherst, Mass., 1977), 118.
4. W. L. Grant, ed., *Original Narratives of Early American History: Voyages of Samuel de Champlain* (New York, 1907), 60.
5. Ibid., 162.
6. Ibid.
7. John Smith, *A Description of New England.* In *Mass. Hist. Colls.* 3rd ser., vol. 6 (1837): 107.
8. Dean R. Snow, *The Archaeology of New England* (New York, 1980), 34.
9. Wood, *Prospects,* 107.
10. Ibid., 81.
11. John Winthrop, *The History of New England, 1630–1649;* also, Journal, 2 vols., ed. James K. Hosmer (New York, 1908), 1:29, 224.
12. Jeremy Belknap, *The History of New Hampshire* (Dover, N.H., 1831), 11–12.
13. Ibid., 11.
14. Ibid., 12.
15. Reuben G. Thwaites, ed., *The Jesuit Relations and Allied Documents . . . 1610–1791,* 73 vols. (Cleveland, 1896–1901), 34:57.

a. Winthrop, *History,* 2:62–63.
b. Ibid., 2:85–86.

4. Indian Wars and Colonial Settlements: 1675–1763

1. For a record of Brookfield's problems, see John Pynchon, *Hampshire County Court Records (Wastebook), Apr. 1663–Jan. 1672.* At Connecticut Valley Historical Society Library, Springfield, Mass.
2. Thomas Wheeler, *A Thankful Remembrance of God's Mercy . . . at Quabaug or Brookfield* (Cambridge, Mass., 1676; reprinted in New Hampshire Historical Society *Collections,* Concord, N.H., 1827), 2:11–12.

3. Ibid., 14.
4. Samuel G. Drake, *Tragedies in the Wilderness* (Boston, 1846), 23.
5. Ibid., 53.
6. Fr. Sebastien Rale as quoted in William Kip, *The Early Jesuit Missions in America* (New York, 1846), p. 54.
7. Ibid., 58 & 7.
8. [Robert Rogers], *Reminiscences of the French War* (Concord, N.H., 1831), 27.
9. As quoted in Charles A. Hanna, *The Scotch-Irish* (New York, 1902), 19.
10. As quoted in Allan Healy, *Charlemont, Massachusetts, Frontier Village and Hill Town* (Charlemont, Mass., 1965), 12.
11. As quoted in Francis Parkman, *A Half Century of Conflict*, 2 vols. (Boston, 1892), 2:265.
12. As quoted in John R. Cueno, *Robert Rogers of the Rangers* (New York, 1959), 101.
13. Robert Rogers, *Journals of Major Robert Rogers. Reprinted from the Original Edition of 1765* (New York, 1961), 106–107.
14. Ibid., 111.
15. Ibid., 107.
16. Ibid., 112.
17. Ibid.

a. *Narrative of Titus King of Northampton, Mass.: A Prisoner of the Indians in Canada 1755–1758* (Hartford, 1938), 6–7.
b. Ibid., 17.

5. Settling the Hills: The Revolution and Postwar Problems: 1763–1791

1. General J[ames] Warren, "Observations on Agriculture," *American Museum* 2 (1788): 347.
2. George Washington, letter of Dec. 5, 1791, to Arthur Young, as quoted in Samuel Blodget, Jr., *Economica* (Washington, D.C., 1806), 91.
3. [Nathaniel Shatswell Dodge], *Sketches of New England, or, Memories of the Country. By John Carver, Esquire, Justice of the Peace and Quorum* (New York, 1842), 152.
4. Horace Bushnell, "The Age of Homespun," in his *Work and Play: or Literary Varieties* (New York, 1864), 392.
5. Jared Eliot, *Essays on Field Husbandry in New England.* (Boston. 1760), 23–24.
6. Timothy Dwight, *Travels in New York and New England*, 2 vols. (Reprint, Cambridge, Mass., 1969), 2:321.
7. As quoted in Zadock Thompson, *History of Vermont, Natural, Civil and Statistical, in Three Parts . . .* (Burlington, 1853), part 2, p. 45.
8. Ibid., 2:44.
9. François Jean Chastellux, *Travels in North America*, 2 vols. (London, 1788), 1:34.
10. Hosea Beckley, *The History of Vermont: With Descriptions, Physical and Topographical* (Brattleboro, 1846), 113.
11. Luigi Castiglioni, as quoted in Thomas D. S. Bassett, *Outsiders inside Vermont* (Canaan, N.H., 1976), 40–41.
12. Elias Smith, as quoted in Bassett, *Outsiders*, 35–36.
13. Nathan Perkins, as quoted in Bassett, *Outsiders*, 44.
14. Percy W. Bidwell, *The History of Agriculture in the Northern United States to 1860* (Washington, D.C., 1925), 82.
15. François, Duc de La Rochefoucauld-Liancourt, *Travels through the United States of North America*, 2 vols. (London, 1799), 1:385.
16. Dwight, *Travels*, 2:321–322.
17. Beckley, *Vermont*, 114.
18. Dwight, *Travels*, 2:86–87.
19. Beckley, *Vermont*, 32.
20. Nathan Perkins, as quoted in Bassett, *Outsiders*, 43.

a. Nathan Perkins, as quoted in Bassett, *Outsiders*, 44–45.
b. Nathan Perkins, *A Narrative of a Tour through the State of Vermont from April 27 to June 1, 1789* (Reprint, Rutland, Vt., 1964), 34.
c. James B. Wilbur, *Ira Allen, Founder of Vermont 1751–1814*, 2 vols. (Boston and New York, 1928), 2.
d. Ibid., 6.
e. Ira Allen, as quoted in Bassett, *Outsiders*, 24.
f. As quoted in James T. Adams, *New England in the Republic, 1776–1850* (Boston, 1926), 106–107.
g. Thompson, *Vermont*, 1:34.
h. Ibid., 1:64.
i. Ibid., 3:81.
j. Ibid., 2:76.
k. Ibid., 3:82.

6. Hill Town Portraits during the Golden Age: 1790–1840

1. Hosea Beckley, *The History of Vermont: With Descriptions, Physical and Topographical* (Brattleboro, 1846), 188–189.
2. Samuel Eliot Morison, *The Oxford History of the United States 1783–1917*, 2 vols. (London, 1927), 1:79–80.
3. Ibid.
4. William Tudor, *Letters on the Eastern States* (Boston, 1821), 234–235.
5. Claude Simpson, ed., *Nathaniel Hawthorne: The American Notebooks* (Columbus, 1972), 149.
6. Timothy Dwight, *Travels in New York and New England*, 2 vols. (Reprint, Cambridge, Mass., 1969), 2:321.
7. Ibid.
8. Walter Prichard Eaton, Litchfield Hills (n.p., n.d., ca. 1915), 5.
9. Quoted in Alain C. White, *The History of the Town of Litchfield, Connecticut, 1720–1920* (Litchfield, Conn., 1920), ch. 10.
10. Ibid., 132.
11. Moses F. Sweetser, ed., *The White Mountains: A Handbook for Travelers . . .* (Boston, 1888), p. 416, quoting Henry Tudor, *Narrative of a Tour in North America*, 2 vols. (London, 1834).
12. Sereno Edwards Dwight, Letter of April 4, 1826, *American Journal of Science . . . Collections* 11 (Oct. 1826): 39.
13. Daniel A. Metraux, *Craftsbury: A Brief Social History* (Craftsbury, Vt., 1890), 16.
14. John Lambert, *Travels in Lower Canada and North America*, 2 vols. (London, 1810), 2:498–499.
15. *The Shorter Oxford English Dictionary*, 2nd. ed. (London, 1939), s.v. "bee."

a. Charles Dudley Warner, *Being a Boy* (Boston, 1878), 159–160.

7. The Move Downhill: Newfane, Vermont, and Harrisville, New Hampshire

1. Hosea Beckley, *The History of Vermont...* (Brattleboro, 1846), 37–38.
2. Ibid., 39, 36.
3. Abby M. Hemenway, *Vermont Historical Gazetteer*, 5 vols. (Burlington-Brandon, 1868–1891), 5:460.
4. Beckley, *Vermont*, 122–123.
5. Ibid., 124.
6. Benjamin F. Taylor, *The World on Wheels and Other Sketches* (Chicago, 1874), 241.
7. Charles Dudley Warner, *Being a Boy* (Boston, 1878), 101–102.
8. Ibid., 57.
9. Ibid., 113–15.
10. Ibid., 110.
11. [Nathaniel Shatswell Dodge], *Sketches of New England: Or, Memories of the Country. By John Carver, Esquire, Justice of the Peace and Quorum* (New York, 1842), 77.
12. Rowland E. Robinson, *Silver Fields: And Other Sketches of a Farmer Sportsman* (Boston, 1921), 144.
13. Anonymous, "Factory Life in New England. By T. Throstle, Gent.," *Knickerbocker Magazine* 30 (Dec. 1847):516.
14. *New Hampshire Sentinel* [Keene], Aug. 30, 1843.
15. Anonymous, "Manufacturing Corporations and Manufacturing Villages," *New England Magazine* (May 1849), 253.
16. Robinson, *Silver Fields*, 148–149.
17. *Vermont Chronicle* [Windsor], Oct. 17, 1834.

a. Hemenway, *Vermont*, 5:462.
b. Ibid.
c. *The Witness* [Putney, Vt.], 1 (Sept. 25, 1839):78.
d. Donald E. Byrne, Jr., *No Foot of Land: Folklore of American Methodist Itinerants* (Metuchen, N.J., 1975), 286.
e. Hemenway, *Vermont*, 4:372.
f. As quoted in Byrne, *No Foot*, 289.

8. Lumbering and Mining

1. Timothy Dwight, *Travels in New York and New England*, 2 vols. (Reprint, Cambridge, Mass., 1969), 2:161.
2. Jeremy Belknap, *The History of New Hampshire*, 3 vols. (Boston, 1813), 3:135.
3. John S. Springer, *Forest Life and Forest Trees: Comprising Winter Camp-Life among the Loggers, and Wild-Wood Adventure; with Descriptions of Lumbering Operations on the Various Rivers of Maine, and New Brunswick* (New York, 1851), 56.
4. Ibid., 56–57.
5. Henry David Thoreau, *The Maine Woods*, arranged by Dudley C. Lunt (New York, 1950), 95.
6. Lawrence T. Smythe, "The Lumber Industry in Maine," *New England Monthly*, N.S., 25 (Jan. 1902):632.
7. Zadock Thompson, *History of Vermont, Natural, Civil and Statistical, in Three Parts . . .* (Burlington, 1853), part 3, p. 11.
8. Ibid.
9. Ibid.
10. Rowland E. Robinson, *Vermont: A Study of Independence* (Boston, 1892), 362.

11. Ray Bearse, ed., *Vermont: A Guide to the Green Mountain State* (Boston, 1968), 159. The New American Guide Series.

a. Samuel A. Drake, *The Heart of the White Mountains: Their Legend and Scenery* (New York, 1881), 115–116.
b. Nathaniel Hawthorne "The Great Carbuncle: A Mystery of the White Mountains," *The Token* (Boston, 1837): 156. Reprinted in *Twice-Told Tales* (Boston: 1837).
c. Ibid., 175.

9. Rural Decline, 1860–1920

1. Edith Wharton, *Summer* (New York, 1917; reprinted New York, 1981), 1–2.
2. Ibid., 45–46.
3. Anonymous, "The Decay of Rural New England," *The Saturday Review*, Oct. 18, 1890, 454.
4. Alvan F. Sanborn, "The Future of Rural New England," *The Atlantic Monthly* 80(1897): 78.
5. Ibid.
6. Anonymous, "Decay of Rural New England," 454.
7. "A Non-Resident American," "Village Life in New England," *Littell's Living Age* (1881): 40.
8. Wharton, *Summer*, 177.
9. Quoted in Harold F. Wilson, *The Hill Country of Northern New England* (New York, 1936), 99.
10. Clifton Johnson, *Highways and Byways of New England* (New York, 1915), 291–292.
11. Kate Waller Barrett, "Discussion," *Papers and Proceedings: Eleventh Annual Meeting, American Sociological Society . . . 1916*. Vol. 11: *The Sociology of Rural Life* (Chicago, 1917), 40.
12. Sanborn, "The Future of Rural New England," 77.
13. Wharton, *Summer*, 84.
14. Harriet M. Rice, "The Young Women and the Farm," *Fifteenth Vermont Agricultural Report for the Year 1895* (Burlington, Vt., 1896), 193.
15. Sanborn, "The Future of Rural New England," 81.
16. Anonymous, "The Decay of New England," *The Nation*, May 27, 1869, 410.
17. Wharton, *Summer*, 32.
18. Clifton Johnson, *A Book of Country Clouds and Sunshine* (Boston, 1896), 167–168.
19. Edward A. Ross, "Folk Depletion as a Cause of Rural Decline," *Papers and Proceedings: Eleventh Annual Meeting, American Sociological Society . . . 1916*, vol. 11: *The Sociology of Rural Life* (Chicago, 1917), 24.
20. Wharton, *Summer*, 43.
21. For further discussion, see Wilson, *Hill Country*, 152.
22. Johnson, *Book of Country Clouds*, 172.
23. Anonymous, "The Decay of Rural New England," 454.
24. J. B. Harrison, "The Abandoned Farms of New England," *Granite State Monthly*, N.S., 3(1890): 154–155.

a. William C. Kitchin, *A Wonderland of the East: Comprising the Lake and Mountain Region of New England and Eastern New York* (Boston, 1920), 269–271.
b. H. P. Lovecraft, "The Dunwich Horror," *The Dunwich Horror and Others*, selected by August Darleth, ed. S. T. Joshi (Sauk City, Wis.: 1963), 155–157.

10. Summer Boarders and Sportsmen

1. Charles Hallock, *The Fishing Tourist: Angler's Guide and Reference Book* (New York, 1873), 89.
2. Ibid., 91.
3. [Nathaniel S. Dodge], *Sketches of New England: Or Memories of the Country. By John Carver, Esquire* (New York, 1842), 87.
4. G. M. Davison, *The Traveller's Guide through the Middle and Northern States, and the Provinces of Canada* (Saratoga Springs, 1837), 373–374.
5. Anonymous, "A Ramble among the White Mountains," *The Worcester Magazine and Historical Journal* 1, no. 1 (Oct. 1825): 1.
6. John Neal, "Animal Magnetism," *The New York Mirror*, 16 (1839), no. 33 (Feb. 9), p. 257. Also see nos. 34 (Feb. 16), pp. 265–266; 35 (Feb. 23), p. 273; 36 (March 2), pp. 281–282; 37 (March 9), pp. 289–290; 38 (March 16), pp. 297–298).
7. *The New York Mirror*, 16 (1839), no. 36 (March 2), p. 282.
8. John R. Spaulding, *Historical Relics of the White Mountains* (Boston, 1855), 16.
9. Dodge, *Sketches of New England*, 93.
10. W. Williams, *Appleton's Northern and Eastern Traveller's Guide* (New York, 1852), 60–61.
11. James R. Osgood & Co., *New England: A Handbook for Travelers* (Boston, 1875), 235.
12. Wallace Nutting, *New Hampshire Beautiful* (Framingham, Mass., 1923), 66.
13. Wallace Nutting, *Massachusetts Beautiful* (Framingham, Mass., 1923), 242, 245.
14. Moses F. Sweetser, ed., *The White Mountains: A Handbook for Travelers*, 9th ed. (Boston, 1888), 272.
15. Ibid., 86.
16. Ibid., 31.
17. Boston and Maine Railroad, *Among the Mountains* (Boston, 1897), 13–14.
18. Hallock, *Fishing Tourist*, 95.
19. Clifton Johnson, *Highways and Byways of New England* (New York, 1915), 6.
20. Anonymous, *Boston and Maine Railroad: Fishing and Hunting* (Boston, 1902), 6.
21. William C. Prime, *I Go A-Fishing* (New York, 1873), 303.
22. Anonymous, *Boston and Maine Railroad: Fishing and Hunting*, 9.
23. Prime, *I Go A-Fishing*, 180.
24. Ibid., 181.
25. Anonymous, *Boston and Maine Railroad: Fishing and Hunting*, 5.

a. Nathaniel Hawthorne, "The Ambitious Guest," *New England Magazine*, 8(June 1835): 425–431 (collected in *Twice-Told Tales*, 1837).
b. Dodge, *Sketches of New England*, 93.
c. Neal, "Animal Magnetism, 289.
d. Dodge, *Sketches of New England*, 108–109.
e. William B. Swett, *Adventures of a Deaf Mute* (Marblehead, Mass., 1875), 25–26.

11. Twentieth-Century Improvements and the Depression: The 1920s and 1930s

1. Harold F. Wilson, *The Hill Country of Northern New England* (New York, 1936), 346–347.
2. Arthur H. Gleason, "New Hampshire: a State for Sale at $10 an Acre," *Country Life in America* 19(Nov. 1905): 53.
3. Allen Chamberlain, *Vacation Tramps in New England Highlands* (New York, 1919), 163–164.
4. *New England Homestead*, 61(Aug. 20, 1910): 146, quoted in Wilson, *Hill Country*, 263.
5. Wilson, *Hill Country*, 265.
6. See Daniel A. Metraux, *Craftsbury: A Brief Social History* (Craftsbury, Vt., 1890).
7. R. C. Estall, *New England: A Study in Industrial Adjustment* (New York, 1966), 43.
8. Dorothy Canfield Fisher, "Vermont, Our Rich Little Poor State," *The Nation* 114(May 31, 1922): 644.

12. The Touring Car in the Landscape

1. John T. Faris, *Roaming American Highways* (New York, 1931), 284.
2. William C. Kitchin, *A Wonderland of the East: Comprising the Lake and Mountain Region of New England and Eastern New York* (Boston, 1920), 243.
3. The White [Automobile] Company, *White Route Book Number Three: The Main Touring Route from New York to Boston . . .* (Cleveland, 1907), 90.
4. Almon C. Judd, *The Ideal Tour* (Waterbury, Conn., 1908), 4.
5. Judd, *The Ideal Tour*, 1910 ed., 6.
6. Judd, *The Ideal Tour*, 1914 ed., 3.
7. Frederic J. Wood, *The Turnpikes of New England* (Boston, 1919), 66.
8. George W. Seaton, *What to See and Do in New England* (New York, 1940), 15.
9. Anonymous, *Six-Day Triangular Tour Including Motor Trip in the Gray Line Touring Limousine "Berkshire"* (Boston, ca. 1920s).
10. New England Hotel Association, *New England Tours for 1915* (n.p., n.d.).
11. Wallace Nutting, *Maine Beautiful* (Framingham, Mass., 1924), 27.
12. Kitchin, *Wonderland of the East*, 267.
13. Wallace Nutting, *Massachusetts Beautiful* (Framingham, Mass., 1923), 186.
14. Ibid., 189.
15. Seaton, *What to See and Do in New England*, 17.
16. Nutting, *Massachusetts Beautiful*, 158, 161.
17. Ibid., 162.
18. Wallace Nutting, *New Hampshire Beautiful* (Framingham, Mass., 1923), 286.
19. Thomas D. Murphy, *New England Highways and Byways from a Motor Car: "Sunrise Highways"* (Boston, 1924), 6–7. The "See America First" Series.
20. Wallace Nutting *Vermont Beautiful* (Framingham, Mass., 1922), 114–117.
21. Nutting, *New Hampshire Beautiful*, 94.
22. Catherine B. Mayo, ed., *Three Essays by Lawrence Shaw Mayo: An Appreciation: With a Bibliography* (Boston, 1948), "The White Mountains in Three Centuries," 59.
23. Charles H. Towne, *Jogging around New England* (New York, 1939), 137–138.

24. Seaton, *What to See and Do in New England*, 15.
25. Towne, *Jogging Around New England*, 142–143.
26. Nutting, *Massachusetts Beautiful*, 98.

13. New England Outdoors: Hiking and Skiing

1. Nathaniel Hawthorne "The Great Carbuncle: A Mystery of the White Mountains," *The Token* (Boston, 1837). Reprinted in *Twice-Told Tales* (Boston, 1837).
2. Henry David Thoreau, *The Maine Woods*, arranged by Dudley C. Lunt (New York, 1950).
3. Allen Chamberlain, *Vacation Tramps in New England Highlands* (New York, 1919), 137.
4. Ibid., 148–149.
5. Ibid., 161.
6. Ibid., 158.
7. Ibid., 157.
8. Walter C. O'Kane, *Trails and Summits of the White Mountains* (Boston, 1925), 29. The Riverside Outdoor Handbooks.
9. W. Storrs Lee, *The Green Mountains of Vermont* (New York, 1955), 156.
10. As quoted in Odell Shepard, *The Heart of Thoreau's Journals* (Boston, 1927; reprinted New York, 1961), 91, 37.
11. Chamberlain, *Vacation Tramps in New England Highlands*, 114–115.
12. Ibid., 53.
13. O'Kane, *Trails and Summits of the White Mountains*, 5.
14. Fred H. Harris, "Skiing Over the New Hampshire Hills," *National Geographic* 27, no. 2(Feb. 1920):160.
15. United States Forest Service, *Tuckerman: White Mountain National Forest* (Concord, N.H., n.d. [ca. 1970]).
16. Lawrence Dame, *New England Comes Back* (New York, 1940), 247.
17. Charles E. Crane, *Winter in Vermont* (New York, 1941), 227.
18. Ibid., 200.
19. Quoted in David Maunsell et al., *Gazetteer of Vermont Heritage* (Chester, Vt., 1966), 80.
20. Crane, *Winter in Vermont*, 266.

14. The Hills Today

1. Lisa Alther, *Kinflicks* (New York, 1975), 281.
2. Ibid., 293.

Bibliography

Town and local histories listed are those recommended for the overall insight they can give to the person reading for a general understanding of New England history.

General Works

Adams, James T. *Album of American History*, 4 vols. New York, 1944–1948.

———. *The Founding of New England*. Boston, 1921.

———. *New England in the Republic*, 1776–1850. Boston, 1926.

———. *Revolutionary New England, 1691–1776*. Boston, 1923.

Allen, Richard S. *Covered Bridges of the Northeast*. New York, 1986.

American Guide Series. State and regional guidebooks to interesting and historical sites. First published in the 1930s, by the Federal Writers' Project of the Works Project Administration. *Berkshire Hills* (New York, 1939); *Connecticut* (Boston, 1938); *Here's New England!* (Boston, 1939); *Maine* (Boston, 1937); *Massachusetts* (Boston, 1937); *New Hampshire* (Boston, 1938); *Vermont* (Boston, 1937). Some have been recently revised and reprinted. Unfortunately, only the modern volume on Maine approaches the comprehensiveness of the first edition. Beware, however, of local tales and location name sources recorded in the 1930s editions. Like many federal workers during the Depression, the researchers seemed to have been paid by the shovelful.

Baker, George P. *The Formation of the New England Railroad Systems*. Cambridge, Mass., 1937. Small line consolidation.

Banks, Ronald F. *A History of Maine: A Collection of Readings on the History Of Maine 1600–1976*. Dubuque, Iowa, 1976.

Bassett, Thomas D. S. *Outsiders inside Vermont: Three Centuries of Visitors' Viewpoints on the Green Mountain State*. Canaan, N.H., 1967.

Beard, Frank, Bette Smith, et al. *Maine's Historic Places: Properties on the National Register of Historic Places*. Camden, Me., 1982.

Beck, Horace P. *The Folklore of Maine*. Philadelphia and New York, 1957. Contains both history and fiction.

Belknap, Jeremy. *The History of New Hampshire*. Dover, N.H., 1831.

Bidwell, Percy W., and Falconer, John I. *History of Agriculture in the Northern United States 1620–1860*. Washington, D.C., 1925.

Black, John D. *The Rural Economy of New England: A Regional Study*. Cambridge, 1950.

Botkin, B. A. *A Treasury of New England Folklore*. New York, 1947. A comprehensive attempt to classify tales and make them sociologically useful.

Brown, Ralph H. *Regional Geography of the United States*. New York, 1948.

Clark, Victor S. *History of Manufactures in the United States, 1607–1860*. Washington, D.C., 1916.

Committee for a New England Bibliography. Bibliographies of New England history: *Connecticut* (Hanover, N.H., 1986); *Maine* (Boston, 1977); *Massachusetts* (Boston, 1976); *New Hampshire* (Boston, 1979); *Vermont* (Boston, 1981). In preparation: *New England*. The most comprehensive bibliography of New England. Entries are by state, county, and town. Exceptionally useful are the volumes for which the research team went beyond the standard card catalogues and included the less obvious material, such as nineteenth-century magazine articles and books, which, although not written as historical texts, are today historically valuable for their information on a locale.

Congdon, Herbert W. *Old Vermont Houses: The Architecture of a Resourceful People*. New York, 1946.

Crofut, Florence S. *Guide to the History and Historical Sites of Connecticut*. 2 vols. New Haven, 1937.

Davis, W. T. *The New England States*. Boston, 1897. Industrial studies.

Day, Clarence A. *Farming in Maine, 1860–1940*. Orono, Me., 1963.

———. *A History of Maine Agriculture, 1604–1860*. Orono, Me., 1954.

Dunbar, Seymour, *A History of Travel in America*. New York, 1915. Has never been superseded.

Dwight, Timothy. *Travels in New England and New York*. New Haven, 1821–1822. Reprinted in 4 vols., Cambridge, 1969. Yale President Dwight was a most knowledgeable observer, and his insightful descriptions are mixed with many a derisive comment befitting the personality of this Puritan throwback.

Fiske, John. *The Beginnings of New England*. Boston, 1898.

———. *New France and New England*. Boston, 1904.

Godin, Alfred J. *Wild Mammals of New England*. Baltimore, 1977.

Hall, Benjamin H. *The History of Eastern Vermont*. New York, 1858.

Harlow, Alvin F. *Steelways of New England*. New York, 1946.

Hawthorne, Nathaniel. *Nathaniel Hawthorne: The American Notebooks*. Ed. by Claude M. Simpson. Columbus, Ohio, 1972. Modern edition of an 1868 volume. Travel diary and source for many of his works.

Hemenway, Abby M. *Vermont Historical Gazetteer*. 5 vols. Burlington-Brandon, Vt., 1868–1891.

Hill, Ralph N. *Yankee Kingdom: Vermont and New Hampshire*. New York, 1960.

Holland, Josiah G. *History of Western Massachusetts . . . and Separate Histories of its One Hundred Towns*. 2 vols. Springfield, Mass., 1855.

Howard, Andrew R. *Covered Bridges of Connecticut: A Guide* (Unionville, Ct., 1985); *Covered Bridges of Maine: A Guide* (Unionville, Ct., 1982); *Covered Bridges of Massachusetts: A Guide*. (Unionville, Ct., 1983).

Irland, Lloyd. *Wildlands and Woodlots: The Story of the New England Forest*. Hanover, N.H., 1982.

Johnson, Charles W. *The Nature of Vermont*. Hanover, N.H., 1980.

Johnson, Clifton. *Highways and Byways of New England*. New York, 1915.

———. *New England: A Human Interest Geographical Reader*. New York, 1917.

———. *New England and Its Neighbors*. New York. 1902. A native New Englander, Johnson sees turn-of-the-century New England as an insider and provides the best insights and descriptions. As a traveling photographer, he did not spend all his time in libraries, but got out into the country to really see the landscape. All his works are highly recommended.

Krause, John, and Fred Bailey. *Trains of Northern New England*. New York, 1977.

Kulik, Stephen, et al. *The Audubon Society Field Guide to the Natural Places of the Northeast: Inland*. New York, 1984. Contains both natural and historical information about locales.

Lindahl, Martin L. *The New England Railroads*. Boston, 1965.

Mathews, Lois K. *The Expansion of New England*. Boston, 1909. About movements of the New England population.

National Register of Historic Places, 1972. Washington, D.C., 1972 (and later supplementary volumes). List sites designated as "historic" throughout the country.

Randall, Peter E., ed. *New Hampshire's Land: How the Glaciers Shaped It, How the Weather Affects It and How We Use It*. Hanover, N.H., 1976.

Robinson, Rowland E. *Silver Fields: And Other Sketches of a Farmer Sportsman*. Boston, 1921.

Robinson, William F. *Abandoned New England: Its Hidden Ruins and Where to Find Them*. Boston, 1976.

Speare, Eva A. *Colonial Meeting Houses of New Hampshire*. Littleton, 1955.

Steele, Frederic L., and Albion R. Hodgdon. *Trees and Shrubs of Northern New England*. Concord, N.H., 1971.

Thompson, Zadock. *History of Vermont, Natural, Civil and Statistical, in Three Parts, with an Appendix*. Burlington, Vt., 1853.

Tolles, Bryant F., Jr. *New Hampshire Architecture: An Illustrated Guide*. Hanover, N.H., 1979.

Tree, Christina, *How New England Happened*. Boston, 1976.

Tuckerman, Henry T. *America and Her Commentators: With a Critical Sketch of Travel in the United States*. New York, 1864. The classic discussion, anthology, and bibliography of American travel accounts.

Untermeyer, Louis, ed. *An Anthology of New England Poets*. New York, 1948.

Westveld, Marinus, et al. "Natural Forest Vegetation Zones of New England," *Journal of Forestry* 54(1956):332–338. Contains map.

Williamson, William D. *The History of the State of Maine . . . 1602 . . . 1820*. 2 vols. Hallowell, Me., 1832.

Wilson, Harold F. *The Hill Country of Northern New England 1790–1930*. New York, 1936. An excellent economic and social study of all phases of northern New England's rural hill life.

Chapter 1

Barrell, Joseph. "The Piedmont Terraces of the Northern Appalachians," *American Journal of Science* 199(1920):227–258; 327–351; 407–428.

Billings, Marland P. *Bedrock Geology*. Vol. 2 of *The Geology of New Hampshire*. Concord, N.H., 1956.

Fenneman, Nevin M. *Physiography of Eastern United States*. New York, 1938.

Flint, Richard F. *Glacial and Pleistocene Geology*. New York, 1957.

———. *Glacial and Quarternary Geology*. New York, 1971.

———. *Glacial Geology of Connecticut*. Hartford, 1930.

Goldthwaite, James Walter, et al. *Surficial Geology*. Vol. 1 of *The Geology of New Hampshire*. Concord, N.H., 1969.

Hussey, Arthur M. *Bibliography of Maine Geology, 1672–1972*. Augusta, Me., 1974.

Jorgensen, Neil. *A Guide to New England's Landscape*. Barre, Mass., 1971. The modern popular classic on New England geology.

Kurten, Bjorn, and Elaine Anderson. *Pleistocene Mammals of North America*. New York, 1980.

Ludlum, David M. *The New England Weather Book*. Boston, 1976.

Rodgers, John. *The Tectonics of the Appalachians*. New York, 1970.

Stewart, David P. *The Glacial Geology of Vermont*. Bulletin 19 of Vermont Geological Survey. Montpelier, Vt., 1961.

Stewart, David P., and Paul MacClintock. *The Surficial Geology and Pleistocene History of Vermont*. Bulletin 31 of Vermont Geological Survey. Montpelier, 1969.

Sullivan, Walter. *Continents in Motion*, New York, 1974. Plate tectonics, with a chapter on the New England Appalachians.

Thompson, Betty F. *The Changing Face of New England*. New York, 1958. Still the popular classic on how the landscape developed.

Thompson, W. F. "The Shape of New England Mountains," *Appalachia* 33(1960–1961):145–159; 316–335; 458–478.

Chapter 2

Alger, Abby L. *In Indian Tents: Stories Told by Penobscot, Passamaquoddy, and Micmac Indians*. Boston, 1897.

Daniels, Thomas E. *Vermont Indians*. Orwell, 1963.

De Forest, John. *History of the Indians of Connecticut . . . to 1850*. Hartford, 1852.

Funk, Robert E. "Early Man in the Northeast and the Late-Glacial Environment," *Man in the Northeast* 4 (1972): 7–39.

Gookin, Daniel. "Historical Collections of the Indians in New England, 1792," *Massachusetts Historical Collections* 1 (1806).

Haviland, William A. *The Original Vermonters: Native Inhabitants, Past and Present*. Hanover, N.H., 1981.

Huden, John C. *Archaeology in Vermont*. Rutland, Vt., 1971. Includes annotated bibliography.

Leland, Charles G. *The Algonquin Legends of New England, or, Myths and Folk Lore of the Micmac, Passamaquoddy, and Penobscot Tribes*. Boston, 1884.

Peabody Museum of Archeology and Ethnology. *A Cultural Overview of the Green Mountain National Forest, Vermont*. Cambridge, Mass., 1978.

Russell, Howard S. *Indian New England before the* Mayflower. Hanover, N.H., 1980. Indians as revealed by early explorers.

Salisbury, Neal. *The Indians of New England: A Critical Bibliography*. Bloomington, Ind., 1982.

Snow, Dean R. *The Archaeology of New England*. New York, 1980. Comprehensive and definitive.

Speare, Eva A. G. *Indians of New Hampshire*. Littleton, N.H., 1965.

Speck, Frank G. *Penobscot Man: The Life History of a Forest Tribe in Maine*. Philadelphia, 1940.

Trigger, Bruce G. *The Northeast*. Vol. 15 of *Handbook of the North American Indians*. Washington, D.C., 1979. Part of the Smithsonian Institution's monumental and definitive survey.

Tunis, Edward. *Indians*. New York, 1959. Popular book with historically accurate sketches by the author/artist.

Willoughby, Charles C. *Antiquities of the New England Indians, with Notes on the Ancient Cultures of the Adjacent Territory*. Cambridge, Mass., 1935.

Wright, H. E., Jr., and David G. Frey, eds. *The Quarternary of the United States*. Princeton, 1965. Deglaciation and early man.

Young, William R., ed. *The Connecticut Valley Indian: An Introduction to Their Archaeology and History*. Springfield, Mass., n.d. Extensive bibliography. Lists western New England tribes, village sites, etc. Also includes Glacial Age information.

Chapter 3

Bailey, Alfred G. *The Conflict of European and Eastern Algonkian Cultures, 1504–1700*. St. John, N.B., 1937.

Kimball, James. "The Exploration of the Merrimack River, 1638, by Order of the General Court of Massachusetts, with a Plan of the Same," *Historical Collections of the Essex Institute* 14, no. 3 (1878):153–171.

Moloney, Francis X. *The Fur Trade in New England, 1620–1676*. Cambridge, Mass., 1931.

Neal, David. *The History of New England*. 2 vols. London, 1747.

Vaughan, Alden T. *New England Frontier: Puritans and Indians, 1620–1675*. Boston, 1965.

Wood, William. *New England's Prospect*. London, 1634.

Chapter 4

Albion, Robert G. *Forest and Sea Power: The Timber Problem of the Royal Navy*. Cambridge, 1926.

Bailey, Alfred G. *Conflict of European and Eastern Algonquin Cultures, 1504–1700*. Toronto, 1969. Predominantly Canadian, but of some American interest.

Browne, William B. *The Mohawk Trail: Its History and Course . . . Together with an Account of Fort Massachusetts and of the Early Turnpikes over Hoosac Mountain*. Pittsfield, Mass., 1920.

Charlton, Mary F. "The Crown Point Military Road," *Vermont Historical Society Proceedings* 2 (December, 1931): 163–193. Includes map.

Clark, Charles E. *The Eastern Frontier: The Settlement of Northern New England: 1610–1763*. Hanover, N.H., 1983.

Crown Point Road Association. *Historical Markers on the Crown Point Road*. Springfield, Vt., 1965.

Cueno, John R. *Robert Rogers of the Rangers*. New York, 1959.

Fiske, John. *New France and New England*. Boston, 1904.

Griffin, Simon G. *A History of the Town of Keene*. Keene, N.H., 1904. Excellent account of an early outpost settlement.

Hanna, Charles A. *The Scotch-Irish, or the Scot in North Britain, North Ireland, & North America*. 2 vols. New York and London, 1902.

Healy, Allan. *Charlemont, Massachusetts: Frontier Village and Hill Town*. Charlemont, Mass., 1965.

Kellaway, William. *The New England Company, 1649–1776: Missionary Society to the American Indians*. New York, 1961.

Kip, William I. *The Early Jesuit Missions in North America*. New York, 1846.

Leach, Douglas E. *The Northern Colonial Frontier, 1607–1763*. New York, 1966.

Leger, Mary C. *The Catholic Indian Missions in Maine, 1611–1820*. Washington, D.C., 1929.

McManis, Douglas R. *Colonial New England: A Historical Geography*. New York, 1975. An excellent overview.

Pierce, Ken J. *A History of the Abenaki People*. Burlington, 1977.

Roy, Louis E. *Quaboag Plantation, alias Brookefield: A 17th Century Massachusetts Town*. West Brookfield, 1965.

Shea, J. D. G. *History of the Catholic Missions among the Indian Tribes of the United States, 1529–1854*. New York, 1855.

Varney, George J. "The Scotch-Irish and the Bay State Border," *New England Magazine* n.s. 16 (1897): 347–352.

Vetromile, Eugene. *The Abenakis and Their History, or, Historical Notices on the Aborigines of Acadia*. New York, 1866. Read with caution.

Wood, Sumner G. *Ulster Scots and Blandford Scouts*. West Medway, Mass., 1928.

Woodbury, Gordon. "The Scotch-Irish and Irish Presbyterian Settlers of New Hampshire," New Hampshire Historical Society, *Proceedings* 4 (1899–1905): 143–162.

Chapter 5

Allen, Ethan. *The Narrative of Ethan Allen (1779)*. New York, 1961.

Batchellor, Albert S. *The Ranger Service in the Upper Valley of the Connecticut, and the Most Northerly Regiment of the New Hampshire Militia in the Period of the Revolution*. Concord, N.H., 1903.

Bushnell, Horace. "The Age of Homespun," *Work and Play: or Literary Varieties*. New York, 1864.

Codman, John. *Arnold's Expedition to Quebec*. New York, 1901.

Eliot, Jared. *Essays on Field Husbandry in New England*. Boston, 1760.

Fox, Dixon R. *Yankees and Yorkers*. New York, 1940.

Hoyt, Edwin P. *The Damndest Yankees: Ethan Allen and His Clan*. Brattleboro, Vt., 1976.

Jones, Matt B. *Vermont in the Making, 1750–1777*. Cambridge, Mass., 1939.

Lamson, Genieve. "Geographic Influence in the Early History of Vermont," Vermont Historical Society, *Proceedings, 1921–1923*: 75–138.

Maine State Library. *Maine Forest*. Augusta, Me., 1924.

Meeks, Harold A. "An Isochronic Map of Vermont Settlements," *Vermont History* 38 (Spring, 1970): 95–102. Displays state with settlement dates in contour.

Minot, George R. *The History of the Insurrection in Massachusetts, in the Year 1786, and the Rebellion consequent Thereon*. Worcester, Mass., 1788. Shays's Rebellion.

Mitchell, Isabel S. *Roads and Road Making in Colonial Connecticut*. New Haven, Conn., 1933.

Perkins, Nathan. *A Narrative of a Tour through the State of Vermont from April 27 to June 12, 1789*. Reprint. Rutland, Vt., 1964.

Randall, Peter E., ed. *New Hampshire Years of Revolution, 1774–1783*. Hanover, N.H., 1976.

Roberts, Kenneth. *Northwest Passage*. New York, 1937. Rogers' Rangers.

Rosenberry, Lois M. K. *Migrations from Connecticut Prior to 1800*. New Haven, Conn., 1936.

Smith, Justin H. *Arnold's March from Cambridge to Quebec . . . with Reprints from Arnold's Journal*. New York, 1903.

Taylor, Robert J. *Western Massachusetts in the Revolution*. Providence, R.I., 1954.

Van de Water, Frederic F. *The Reluctant Republic: Vermont, 1724–1791*. New York, 1941.

Woodman, Cyrus, ed. *Memoirs and Journals of Rev. Paul Coffin*. Portland, Me., 1855. Journals of late eighteenth-century travels across northern New England.

Chapter 6

Beckley, Hosea. *The History of Vermont: With Descriptions, Physical and Topographical.* Brattleboro, Vt., 1846. Much first-person material: descriptions, incidents, observations.

Bidwell, Percy W. "Rural Economy in New England at the Beginning of the Nineteenth Century," *Transactions of the Connecticut Academy of Arts and Sciences* 20 (April, 1916): 241–399. Excellent. Treats southern New England and should be considered the companion to Black's *Hill Country of Northern New England.*

Fobes, Charles B. "Paths of the Settlement and Distribution of Population in Maine," *Economic Geography* 20 (1944): 65–67.

Hurd, D. Hammond. *History of Hillsborough County, New Hampshire.* Philadelphia, 1885. Discusses reasons for hilltop settlements.

Metraux, Daniel A. *Craftsbury: A Brief Social History.* Craftsbury, Vt., 1980.

Phelps, Charles S. *Rural Life in Litchfield County.* Norfolk, Conn., 1917.

Pressey, Edward P. "The Rise of the Tide of Life to New England Hilltops," *New England Magazine* n.s. 22 (1900): 695–711.

Rosenberry, Lois K. M. *Migrations from Connecticut after 1800.* New Haven, Conn., 1936.

Stowe, Harriet B. *Poganuc People.* New York, 1878. Litchfield, Connecticut, in the early nineteenth century.

White, Alain C. *The History of the Town of Litchfield, Connecticut, 1720–1920.* Litchfield, Conn., 1920.

Chapter 7

Anonymous. "Factory Life in New England. By T. Throstle, Gent.," *Knickerbocker Magazine* 30 (December, 1847): 511–517.

Anonymous. "Manufacturing Corporations and Manufacturing Villages," *New England Magazine* 7 (May, 1849): 240–244.

Armstrong, John B. *Factory under the Elms: A History of Harrisville, New Hampshire, 1774–1969.* Cambridge, Mass., 1969.

Bishop, John L. *A History of American Manufactures from 1608 to 1860.* 2 vols. Philadelphia, 1861, 1864.

Chase, Edward E. *Maine Railroads: A History of the Development of the Maine Railroad System.* Portland, Me., 1926.

Cole, Arthur H. *American Wool Manufacture.* 2 vols. Cambridge, Mass., 1926. Chronicles movement from cottage industry to small mills to factories.

Davison Publishing Company. *Davison's Textile Blue Book.* New York, 1887–1933, annually. Lists all active New England textile mills, with handy map of towns.

[Dodge, Nathaniel S.] *Sketches of New England. Or, Memories of the Country. By John Carver, Esquire, Justice of the Peace and Quorum.* New York, 1842. Articles on the New England countryside by a New Hampshire–born essayist for *Knickerbocker* magazine.

Dunwell, Steve. *Run of the Mill.* Boston, 1978.

Goldthwaite, James Walter. "A Town That Has Gone Downhill," *The Geographical Review* 17 (October, 1927): 527–552. Lyme, New Hampshire, area.

Holland, Josiah G. *Farm Life in New England.* Boston, 1858. By a Springfield, Massachusetts, newspaperman.

Huxtable, Ada L. "New England Hill Village: Harrisville, New Hampshire," *Progressive Architecture* 38 (July, 1957): 139–140.

Lapham, William B., and Silas P. Maxim. *History of Paris, Maine, from Its Settlement to 1880.* Paris, Me., 1884. Much of the early frontier life, and hill vs. valley settlement.

Le Blanc, Robert G. *Location of Manufacturing in New England in the 19th Century.* Hanover, N.H., 1969. Excellent account of the hows and whys of the shape of New England's industrial growth.

Marlowe, George F. *Coaching Roads of Old New England.* New York, 1901. Covers routes from Boston northwest across Massachusetts into Vermont and New Hampshire.

Parks, Roger N. *Roads and Travel in New England 1790–1840.* Sturbridge, Mass., 1967.

Stillwell, Lewis D. *Migration from Vermont (1776–1860).* Montpelier, Vt., 1948.

Warner, Charles D. *Being a Boy.* Boston, 1878. Excellent account of early nineteenth-century life in the Berkshire Hills.

Wilgus, William J. *The Role of Transportation in the Development of Vermont.* Montpelier, Vt., 1945.

Wood, Frederic J. *The Turnpikes of New England.* Boston, 1919.

Wood, Joseph S. "The Road Network in Vermont, 1796–1824," *Vermont Geographer* 2 (1975): 53–64.

Zevin, Robert B. *The Growth of Manufacturing in Early Nineteenth Century New England.* New York, 1975.

Chapter 8

Abbott, Collamer M. "Gold in Them Thar Hills," *New England Galaxy* 10 (Fall, 1968): 14–21. Plymouth, Vermont, Rooks Mine.

———. *Green Mountain Copper: The Story of Vermont's Red Metal.* Randolph, Vt., 1973.

Anonymous. "Gold Hunting in Berkshire," *Berkshire Hills* 2 (June 1, 1902): 1–4.

Anonymous. "Life Among the Loggers," *Harper's New Monthly Magazine* 20 (1859–1860): 437–454.

Barker, Fred C. *Lakes and Forest as I have Known Them*. By famous Maine guide, with a chapter on his early years as a logger.

Belcher, Fran. A series of White Mountains logging and logging railroad articles in *Appalachia* 33 (1960–1961).

Coolidge, Philip T. *History of the Maine Woods*. Bangor, Me., 1963.

Cornwall, L. P., and Jack W. Farrell. *Ride the Sandy River: A Trip into the Past on What Was America's Largest Two-Foot Gauge Railroad*. Edmonds, Wash., 1973.

Eckstrom, Fannie H. *The Penobscot Man*. Boston, 1904. Loggers and the logging industry.

Harte, Charles, and Herbert Keith. *The Early Iron Industry of Connecticut*. New Haven, Conn., 1935. Lists furnace locations in Connecticut and adjoining areas of eastern New York and western Massachusetts.

Hempstead, Alfred G. *The Penobscot Boom: And Development of the West Branch of the Penobscot River for Log Driving, 1825–1931*. Orono, Me., 1931.

Lillard, Richard G. *The Great Forest*. New York, 1947. Good general information on American forests.

Meyer, T. R., and Glenn W. Stewart. *Minerals and Mines*. Vol. 2 of *The Geology of New Hampshire*. Concord, N.H., 1969.

Moody, Linwood, W. *The Maine Two-Footers: The Story of the Two-Foot Gauge Railroads of Maine*. Berkeley, Cal., 1959.

Morrill, Philip, et al. *Maine Mines and Minerals*. 2 vols. Also his *Mineral Guide to New England, New Hampshire Mines and Mineral Locations*, and *Vermont Mines and Mineral Locations*. East Winthrop, Me., n.d. All are available from Winthrop Mineral Shop, East Winthrop, Maine. Exhaustive lists for the rockhound.

Pike, Robert G. *Tall Trees, Tough Men*. New York, 1967. Extremely readable.

Robinson, Rowland W. "In the Marble Hills," *The Century* 40 (September, 1890): 743–751.

Smith, Beth R. "The Plymouth Gold Rush," *Vermont Life* 6 (Winter, 1969): 49–51.

Smith, David C. *A History of Lumbering in Maine, 1861–1960*. Orono, Me., 1972.

Smythe, Lawrence T. "The Lumber Industry in Maine," *New England Monthly Magazine* 25 (January, 1902): 629–648. The tough-customer character of the loggers.

Springer, John S. *Forest Life and Forest Trees: Comprising Winter Camp Life among the Loggers, and Wild-Wood Adventure, with Descriptions of Lumbering Operations on the Various Rivers of Maine and New Brunswick*. New York, 1851.

Thoreau, Henry David. *The Maine Woods*. Boston, 1864.

Wight, Denham B. *The Wild River Wilderness*. Littleton, N.J., 1971. Classic account of a typical lumbering community.

Chapter 9

American Sociological Society. *Papers and Proceedings: Eleventh Annual Meeting . . .* Vol. 11. *The Sociology of Rural Life*. Chicago, 1917. An excellent assembly of papers and discussions on the sociological effects of rural abandonment.

Anonymous. "Village Life in New England," *Littell's Living Age* 148 (1881): 35–40. Observations on an 1880 visit by a lady who left her hometown in the early 1830s.

Galpin, Charles J. *Rural Social Problems*. New York, 1924.

Hartt, Rollin L. "A New England Hill Town," *The Atlantic Monthly* 83 (1899): 561–574; 712–720.

Howard, John R. "Social Problems of Rural New England," *Proceedings of the National Conference of Charities and Correction* (1911): 471–472.

Johnson, Clifton. *A Book of Country Clouds and Sunshine*. Boston, 1896. Well illustrated with Johnson's photographs. Rural decline in central Massachusetts.

Klimm, Lester E. *The Relation between Certain Population Changes and the Physical Environment in Hampden, Hampshire, and Franklin Counties, Massachusetts, 1790–1925*. Philadelphia, 1933.

Rice, Harriet, M. "The Young Women and the Farm," *Fifteenth Vermont Agricultural Report for the Year 1895* (Burlington, Vt., 1896), pp. 193–204.

Wharton, Edith. *Ethan Frome*. New York, 1911.

———. *Summer*. New York, 1917.

Wilson, Harold F. *The Hill Country of Northern New England 1790–1930*. New York, 1936. Contains an excellent bibliography of turn-of-the-century articles and books on farm abandonment.

Chapter 10

Anonymous. "A Ramble among the White Mountains," *The Worcester Magazine and Historical Journal* 1 (Oct. 1825–April 1826), no. 1, pp. 1–7.

Baker, Fred C. *Lakes and Forests as I Have Known Them*. Boston, 1903. Experiences of a guide who developed the Rangeley Lake region as a resort.

Bangor & Aroostook Railroad. *In the Maine Woods: A Guide for Sportsmen*. Bangor, issued annually in first few decades of the twentieth century. Anthologies of sportsmen's narratives.

Bolles, Frank. *At the North of Bearcamp Water: Chronicles of a Stroller in New England from July to December*. Boston, 1893. New Hampshire region.

Brown, William R. *Our Forestry Heritage: A History of Forestry and Recreation in New Hampshire*. Concord, N.H., 1958.

Bryan, Clark W. *Carriage Driving in and Near unto Western Massachusetts*. Springfield, 1892.

Drake, Samuel A. *The Heart of the White Mountains: Their Legend and Scenery*. New York, 1881.

Farrar, Charles A. J. *Through the Wilds: A Record of Sport and Adventure in the Forests of New Hampshire and Maine*. Boston, 1892. Farrar also wrote the Farrar's Illustrated Guide Book series, covering northern Vermont and New Hampshire and northwestern Maine.

Foster, William H. *New England Grouse Shooting*. New York, 1942.

Hallock, Charles. *The Fishing Tourist: Angler's Guide and Reference Book*. New York, 1873.

Hawthorne, Nathaniel. *Tales of the White Hills*. Boston, 1889. Collected stories.

Hitchcock, Charles. *Mt. Washington in Winter, or the Experiences of a Scientific Expedition upon the Highest Mountain in New England, 1870–71*. Boston, 1871.

Hubbard, Lucius L. *Summer Vacations at Moosehead Lake and Vicinity: A Practical Guide-Book for Tourists: Describing Routes for the Canoe-Man over the Principal Waters of Northern Maine, with Hints to Campers, and Estimates of Expenses for Tours*. Boston, 1879. The first of Hubbard's Maine Guides.

Kenison, Frank R. *The Enterprise of the North Country of New Hampshire*. New York, 1980.

Koier, Louise. "Those Wonderful Waters," *Vermont Life* 10 (Summer, 1957): 56–60. Chronicles and lists all mineral-spring hotel sites in Vermont.

Lowell, James R. *A Moosehead Journal*. Boston, 1864.

Neal, John. "Animal Magnetism," *The New York Mirror, a Weekly Journal Devoted to Literature and the Fine Arts*, vol. 16 (1839), nos. 33 (Feb. 9), p. 257; 34 (Feb. 16), pp. 265–266; 35 (Feb. 23), p. 273; 36 (March 2), pp. 281–282; 37 (March 9) pp. 289–290; 38 (March 16), pp. 297–298. Six-chapter account of a visit to Crawford Notch.

Prime, William C. *I Go A-Fishing*. New York, 1873.

Robinson, Rowland E. *In New England Fields and Woods*. Boston, 1896.

Smith, Warren. *Berkshire Days on the Boston & Albany*. New York, 1982.

Stevens, Charles W. *Fly-Fishing in Maine Lakes: or, Camp-Life in the Wilderness*. Boston, 1881.

Sweetser, Moses F., ed. The *White Mountains: A Handbook for Travelers*. Boston, various editions, ca. 1870s–1900s.

Swett, William B. *Adventures of a Deaf-Mute*. Marblehead, 1875. A White Mountain guide.

Taber, Edward Mackham. *Stowe Notes: Letters and Verses*. Boston and New York, 1913. Artist's journal of his life in rural Stowe, Vermont.

Wight, Denham B. *The Wild River Wilderness*. Littleton, N.H., 1971.

Winthrop. Theodore. *Life in the Open Air and Other Papers*. New York, 1862. Maine lakes and mountains.

Chapter 11

American Geographical Society of New York. *New England's Prospect*. New York, 1933.

Artman, Charles E. *The Industrial Structure of New England*. Washington, D.C., 1930. Also covers agriculture.

Black, John D. *The Rural Economy of New England*. Cambridge, Mass., 1950. A study of rural adjustment in the twentieth century.

Dame, Lawrence. *New England Comes Back*. New York, 1940.

Devino, William S. *A Study of Textile Mill Closings in Selected New England Communities*. Orono, Me., 1966. Life after the mill closed.

Dunnack, Henry E. *Rural Life in Maine*. Augusta, Me., 1928.

Eisenmenger, Robert W. *The Dynamics of Growth in New England's Economy 1870–1964*. Middletown, Conn., 1967.

Estall, R. C. *New England: A Study in Industrial Adjustment*. New York, 1966.

———. *New England: A Study in Industrial Development*. New York, 1966.

Kinnard, William N., Jr., ed. *The New England Region: Problems of a Mature Economy*. Storrs, Conn., 1968.

Lamson, Genieve. *A Study of Agricultural Populations in Selected Vermont Towns*. Burlington, Vt., 1931.

New England Regional Planning Commission. *Basic Data for a Tentative and Preliminary Plan for New England: Designed to Stimulate Criticism, Suggestion and Eventually Action*. Boston, 1935.

Pearson, John W. *Changes in Manufacturing in Rural Towns of New Hampshire, 1915–1931*. N.p., 1932.

Vermont Commission on Country Life. *Rural Vermont: A Program for the Future, by Two Hundred Vermonters*. Burlington, Vt., 1931.

Wilder, Thornton. *Our Town*. New York, 1938. A play about a New Hampshire mill town.

Woodworth, Harry C. *Nute Ridge: The Problem of a Typical Backtown Community*. Durham, N.H., 1927. Illustrations.

Chapter 12

Chase, Mary E., and the Editors of *Look*. *New England*. Boston, 1947.

Dole, Nathan H., and Irwin G. Gordon. *Maine of the Sea and Pines*. Boston, 1928.

Faris, John T. *Roaming American Highways*. New York, 1931.

———. *Seeing the Eastern States*. Philadelphia, 1922.

Kitchin, William C. *A Wonderland of the East: Comprising the Lake and Mountain Region of New England and Eastern New York*. Boston, 1920. By a retired professor at the University of Vermont.

Murphy, Thomas D. *New England Highways and Byways from a Motor Car: "Sunrise Highways."* The See America First Series. Boston, 1924.

Nutting, Wallace. *Connecticut Beautiful*. Framingham, Mass., 1923.

———. *Maine Beautiful*. Framingham, Mass., 1924.

———. *Massachusetts Beautiful*. Framingham, Mass., 1923.

———. *New Hampshire Beautiful*. Framingham, Mass., 1923.

———. *Vermont Beautiful*. Framingham, Mass., 1922.

Towne, Charles H. *Jogging around New England*. New York, 1939. The author was a well-known literary and magazine editor of his day.

Chapter 13

(A variety of hiking guides published by commercial presses and hiking organizations is readily available at bookstores and sporting-goods stores.)

Baldwin, Henry I., ed. *Monadnock Guide*. Concord, N.H., 1970. A nature, literary, and hiking guide.

Baxter, Constance. *Greatest Mountain: Katahdin's Wilderness*. San Francisco, 1972.

Bowles, Ella S. *Let Me Show You New Hampshire*. New York, 1938.

Bujaucius, Gerald A., et al. *The Impact of the Ski Industry in Vermont*. Montpelier, Vt., 1977.

Chamberlain, Allen. *Vacation Tramps in New England Highlands*. New York, 1919.

Crane, Charles E. *Let Me Show You Vermont*. New York, 1937.

———. *Winter in Vermont*. New York, 1941.

Dame, Lawrence. *New England Comes Back*. New York, 1940.

Dudley, Charles M. *60 Centuries of Skiing*. Brattleboro, Vt., 1935.

Faris, John T. *Roaming the Eastern Mountains*. New York, 1932.

Hagerman, Robert. *Mansfield: The Story of Vermont's Loftiest Mountain*. Canaan, N.H., 1971.

Lee, W. Storrs, ed. *Footpath in the Wilderness: The Long Trail in the Green Mountains of Vermont*. Middlebury, Vt., 1941.

———. *The Green Mountains of Vermont*. New York, 1955.

O'Kane, Walter C. *Trails and Summits of the Green Mountain*. The Riverside Outdoor Handbooks. Boston, 1926.

———. *Trails and Summits of the White Mountains*. The Riverside Outdoor Handbooks. Boston, 1925.

Olton, Charles and Percy. *Ski Tracks*. New York, 1936.

Peattie, Roderick, ed. *The Berkshires: The Purple Hills*. New York, 1948.

———. *The Friendly Mountains: Green, White, and Adirondack*. New York, 1942.

Shepard, Odell. *The Harvest of a Quiet Eye*. Boston and New York, 1927. A college professor's walks across northern Connecticut. A local classic.

Stiles, Percy G. *Wayfaring in New England*. Concord, N.H., 1920.

Torrey, Bradford. *Footing It in Franconia*. Boston, 1901.

Towne, Charles H. *Jogging around New England*. New York, 1939.

Whiting, Charles G. *Walks in New England*. New York, 1903.

Chapter 14

Bevins, Malcolm I. *The Outdoor Recreation Industry in Vermont*. Burlington, Vt., 1964.

Clark, Lewis E. *Trends in Maine Agriculture, 1954–1964*. Orono, Me., 1966.

Harris, Seymour. *The Economics of New England: Case Study of an Older Area*. Cambridge, Mass., 1952.

Niederfrank, Evlon J. *The Massachusetts Hill Towns in Wartime*. Upper Darby, Pa., 1945. The Berkshire Hills.

Osborn, William C. *The Paper Plantation: Ralph Nader's Study Group Report on the Pulp and Paper Industry in Maine*. New York, 1974.

Partridge, Cora C. "Snowmobile Country," *Vermont Life* 29 (Winter, 1974): 2–5.

Smith, Dwight A. *Northern Rails: A Complete Guide to the Railroads of Maine, New Hampshire and Vermont*. N.p., ca. 1967.

Tree, Christina. *Maine: An Explorer's Guide*. Woodstock, Vt., 1984.

———. *Massachusetts: An Explorer's Guide*. Woodstock, Vt., 1981.

———, and Peter Jennison. *Vermont: An Explorer's Guide*. Woodstock, Vt., 1983.

Especially Useful Maps and Atlases

Bennison, Allan P., et al. *Map No. 10: United States Geological Highway Map Series: Geological Highway Map of the Northeastern Region . . . American Association of Petroleum Geologists*. P.O. Box 979, Tulsa, OK 74101, 1976. All-in-one collection of bedrock maps, geological cross sections, glacial deposits, and locations of fossils, museums, mineral diggings, etc.

DeLorme Publishing Company. *The Maine Atlas and Gazetteer*. Freeport, Me., 1984. *The New Hampshire Atlas and Gazetteer*. Freeport, Me., 1984. *The Vermont Atlas and Gazetteer*. Freeport, Me., 1983. Three excellent road/nature/historical/recreation guides to northern New England. In addition to their text information, the 60-some large maps in each volume are sufficiently detailed (I would say from the best of my experience using them) to show every passable dirt road in the state. For anyone bumping down an unpaved road in northern New England, these atlases are a great reassurance that the rutted tracks one is following will not suddenly end in a swamp just around the bend ahead.

DeLorme Publishing Company. *Trail Map and Guide to the White Mountain National Forest: With 250 Up-to-Date Trail Descriptions*. Freeport, Me., 1983.

Marshall Penn-York Co., Inc. *Visual Encyclopaedia: Southern New England Atlas*. Syracuse, 1983. The closest substitute for a DeLorme atlas to the lower New England states. This large map is extremely useful for backcountry touring, as it lists the names of many smaller connecting roads, allowing the rural visitor to navigate the landscape successfully without the usual dependence on numbered routes or dead reckoning.

The National Survey Map of New England. Chester, Vt., 1978. Laminated wall map for the New England enthusiast. Also comes sectioned off into an atlas edition, *Yankee Magazine's Travel Maps of New England*.

Works Important for Their Illustrations

Boston and Maine Railroad: The Charles River to the Hudson; Mountains of New England; New England Lakes; Picturesque New England; Rivers of New England. Boston, ca. 1900. A series of oblong picture books in wrappers, containing New England scenes photographed by Henry G. Peabody.

Bryant, William C. *Picturesque America*. 2 vols. New York, 1872.

Chamberlain, Samuel. *Ever New England*, *The New England Scene*, and many other of his books of photographs taken between the 1930s and 1960s.

Colby College Art Museum. *Maine and Its Artists, 1710–1963, an Exhibition. . . .* Waterville, Me., 1963.

Griffiths, Thomas M., and Arthur M. Griffiths. *A Pictorial History of the State of Maine*. Lewiston, Me., 1970.

Heinrich, Roy F., and Herbert M. Stoops, artists. *The Story of Vermont in Pictures*. Montpelier, Vt., 1937.

Hill, Ralph, ed. *Vermont Album: A Collection of Early Vermont Photographs*. Brattleboro, Vt., 1974.

Hubbard, Lucius. *Woods and Lakes of Maine*. Boston, 1884. Illustrations by William L. Taylor.

Jennison, Keith. *Vermont Is Where You Find It*; *The Maine Idea*; *New Hampshire*; *Green Mountains and Rock Ribs*. New York, 1941–1954. Picture books comprising photos from WPA, FSA, and New England commercial photographers.

Keyes, Donald H. (exhibition curator). *The White Mountains: Place and Perceptions*. Hanover, N.H., 1980. Publication accompanying an exhibition of White Mountain pictures. Excellent collection of images with a good short historical introduction.

Kingsley, Elbridge, and Frederick Knab. *Picturesque Worcester*. 2 vols. Springfield, Mass., 1895. A continuation of Warner's "Picturesque . . ." series. Vol. 2 is of rural towns.

Lipke, William C., and Philip N. Grime, eds. *Vermont Landscape: Images 1776–1976*. Burlington, Vt., 1976. Also includes some excellent essays.

Newhall, Nancy. *Time in New England*. New York, 1950. Photographs by Paul Strand.

Orton, Vrest. *And So Goes Vermont*. Weston, Vt., 1937.

Peladeau, Marius B. *Chansonnetta: The Life and Photographs of Chansonnetta Stanley Emmons, 1858–1937*. Waldoboro, Me., 1977. Genre photography in the Kingfield, Maine, region.

Resch, Tyler, ed. *Berkshire: The First Three Hundred Years, 1676–1976*. Pittsfield, Mass., 1976.

Rinhart, Floyd and Marion. *Summertime: Photographs of Americans at Play, 1850–1900*. New York, 1978.

Sandler, Martin W. *This Was New England*. Boston, 1976.

Sweetser, Moses F. *Views of the White Mountains*. Portland, Me., 1879.

Warner, Charles F., ed. *Picturesque Berkshire*. 2 vols. 1893. *Picturesque Franklin*. 1891. *Picturesque Hampden*. 2 vols. 1891. *Picturesque Hampshire*. 1890. All published in Northampton, Mass. Counties of western Massachusetts. Profusely illustrated with photographs and drawings.

Whitehill, Walter M. *Massachusetts*. New York, 1976.

Wilder, Elizabeth F., ed. *Maine and Its Role in American Art*. New York, 1963.

Wilmerding, John. *American Light: The Luminist Movement, 1850–1875*. New York, 1980.

Sources of Illustrations

Illustrations that appear on the following pages are photographs or ephemera from the author's personal collection: 26, 27, 59, 82, 91 (bottom left), 92, 99 (top), 113, 115, 117 (both ills.), 118 (both ills.), 119, 120, 121 (both ills.), 123, 129 (top), 130 (top right and left), 134, 135, 137, 141, 142 (top), 145, 147, 157, 162, 163.

Illustrations reproduced courtesy of the following sources:

American Indian Archaeological Institute, Washington, Conn. (W.F.R. photos): 13 (both ills.), 18, 19

American Museum of Natural History, New York, Department of Library Services (neg. 333916): 17

Dartmouth College Archives, Baker Library, Hanover, N.H.: 159 (left)

Hood Museum of Art, Dartmouth College, Hanover, N.H., Gift of Paul Sample, Class of 1920: 138

Library of Congress, Washington, D.C., F.S.A., Photograph #45158-D by Jack Delano: 146

Litchfield Historical Society, Litchfield, Conn.: 65 (top)

National Gallery of Art, Washington, D.C., Andrew W. Mellon Fund: 126

Phillips Historical Society, Phillips, Me.: 103

Proctor Free Library, Proctor, Vt.: 140

University of Vermont, Bailey/Howe Library:
    Collamer Abbott Collection: 96
    Dexter Collection: 56 (both ills.), 57 (left)
    Special Collections: 100
    Wilbur Collection: 84 (bottom), 95 (bottom)

Vermont Historical Society, Montpelier, Vt.: 86, 101, 105, 111

Wesleyan University, Science Library, Middletown, Conn.:
    from *American Journal of Science*, vol. 14 (1828): 4–5, 6–7; vol. II (1826): 10
    from Edward Hitchcock, *Final Report of the Geology of Massachusetts* (Amherst, Mass., 1841): 20, 79

Woodstock Historical Society, Woodstock, Vt. (property of): 80, 161

Yale University Library, New Haven, Conn.:
    from William Allen, *The History of Norridgewock* (Norridgewock, Me., 1849): 35 (bottom)

Illustration Sources:

Abbott, Jacob, *American History* (New York, 1850): 15, 40

Adams, James C., *Nature Studies in Berkshire* (New York, 1899): 39

Barber, John W., *Historical, Poetical and Pictorial American Scenes* (New Haven, Conn., 1851): 24, 32, 57 (right)

Barrell, Joseph, *American Journal of Science*, vol. 199 (1920): 9

Boston and Maine Railroad, Fishing and Hunting (Boston, 1902): 129 (bottom)

Boston and Maine Railroad, *The White Mountains of New Hampshire* (Boston, 1910): 158

Champlain, Samuel de, *Les Voyages* (1613): 23

Chisolm Brothers, *Views of the White Mountains* (Portland, Me., 1912): 125

Coolidge, A. J., and J. B. Mansfield, *A History and Description of New England, General and Local* (Boston, 1859): 68 (bottom)

Crockett, Walter H., *The Green Mountains of Vermont*, Vermont Publicity Department (Montpelier, Vt., 1928): 156 (top)

Devens, R. M., *Our First Century* (Springfield, Mass., 1882): 63

Every Saturday (January 28, 1871): 89

Farmer, John A., *A Catechism of the History of New Hampshire* (Concord, N.H., 1849): 116

Franklin, James, *The Rebels Rewards or English Courage Displayed. Being a full and true Account of the Victory obtained over the Indians at Norridgewock, on the Twelfth of August last, by the English Forces under the Command of Capt. John Harmon* (Boston, 1724): 37

Grand Trunk Railroad, *Mountains of New England and the Sea* (Portland, Me., 1906): 130 (bottom)

Hager, Albert D., *Report on the Geology of Vermont* (Claremont, N.H., 1862): 99 (bottom)

Hazen, Edward, *Popular Technology* (New York, 1850): 77

Howe, Henry, *Historical Collections of Ohio* (Columbus, Ohio, 1888): 87

Jahns, R. H., and M. E. Willard, *American Journal of Science*, vol. 240 (1942): 8 (bottom)

Kittredge, George L., *The Old Farmer and his Almanack* (Cambridge, Mass., 1920): 14

The Ladies Repository (January 1849): 29

London Magazine (1755): 48

Lossing, Benson J., *Our Country* (New York, 1877): 16, 28, 33 (bottom), 41, 51

Maine Central Railroad, *The Lakes and Woods of Maine* (ca. 1910): 131

Marshall, John, *The Life of George Washington* (London, 1804–1807): 50

Matthews, L. K., *The Expansion of New England* (Boston, 1909): 34 (adapted)

New England Regional Planning Commission, District No. 1, *Basic Data for a Tentative Plan for New England* (Boston, National Resources Board, 1935): 150

Report of the Commissioner of Agriculture for the year 1864 (Washington, D.C., 1865): 81

Rogers, Robert, *Journals of Major Robert Rogers. Reprinted from the Original Edition of 1765* (New York, 1961): 43

Rosebrook, G., and L. Rosebrook, *Trips in Northern New Hampshire* (Lancaster, N.H., ca. 1930): 94–95 (top)

Rowlandson, Mary, *A Narrative of the Captivity, Sufferings, and Removes of Mary Rowlandson* (Boston, 1778): 33 (top)

Scribner's Monthly (December 1877): 91 (bottom)

Sewall, Joseph S., *New Homes Under Old Roofs* (New York, 1916): 149 (both ills.)

Shepard, Odell, *Harvest of a Quiet Eye* (Boston, 1927): 153, 155

Sweetser, M. F., *Picturesque Maine* (Portland, Me., 1880): 91 (top)

Swett, William B., *Adventures of a Deaf-Mute* (Marblehead, Mass., 1875): 128

Taber, Edward M., *Stowe Notes. Letters and Verses* (Boston, 1913): 165
Thompson, Zadock, *History of Vermont* (Burlington, Vt., 1853): 49, 58 (all ills.)
United States Department of the Interior, *The National Atlas of the United States of America* (Washington, D.C., 1970): 3
Warner, Charles F., *Picturesque Berkshire* (Northampton, Mass., 1893): 106, 156 (right)
Whitcombe Summit Company, *Beautiful Mohawk Trail* (North Adams, Mass., n.d.): 142, 144

Index

165; in Vermont, 144, 148, 152, 155, 156–157, 160–164
Townsend, Vermont, 73
Trapp family, 161, 164, 169
Tuckerman, Edward, 117
Tuckerman's Ravine (New Hampshire), 7, 116, 158–159
Tuftonborough, New Hampshire, 80
Tunbridge, Vermont, 11
Tunxis tribe, 14
turnpikes, 67, 68, 76
Twain, Mark, 78

Umbagog, Lake, 51
Underhill, Vermont, 55
Underhill Range (Vermont), 169
unions, 100

Vermont: farming in, 83–85, 107, 108, 111, 133, 134, 137; granite industry in, 98–102; hiking in, 152, 155, 156–157; Indians in, 12, 14, 16, 23, 29, 51; lumber industry in, 89, 94; mining in, 94–97; Revolutionary War in, 51, 52; roads in, 145, 152, 155; settlement of, 48–49, 53–61, 68–71, 73–75, 76; skiing in, 160–164; tourism in, 144, 148, 152, 155, 156–157, 160–164
Vermont: A Guide to the Green Mountain State, 101–102
Vermont Copper Mine, 95
Vermont Valley, 2, 49, 51
Vernon, Vermont, 39
Verrazano, Giovanni de, 21
Vershire, Vermont, 94, 95

Wabanaki culture, 14, 19
Wampanoag tribe, 31
Ward, Hannah, 83
Warner, Charles Dudley, 69, 77–78
Warner, Seth, 49
Warren, Massachusetts, 37
Washington, George, 47, 49, 66
Washington, Mount (New Hampshire), 6, 7, 9, 27, 117–124, 158–160
Waterbury, Connecticut, 105, 140
Waterbury, Vermont, 135
Waterbury River, 162
Weathersfield, Vermont, 45, 59, 62
weaving, 77
Wentworth, Benning, 60

Wentworth-by-the-Sea (Portsmouth, New Hampshire), 141
West Brookfield, Massachusetts, 30–32
West Dummerston, Vermont, 82
Western Summit, 143
Westfield, Massachusetts, 105
Westfield River, 8, 79, 93, 107
West Rutland, Vermont, 99
Wharton, Edith, 104, 107–109, 112
Whitcomb Summit, 143, 147
White, Franklin, 27, 118
White, H. L., 97
White Hills: Their Legends, Landscape and Poetry, The, 123
White-Horse Ledge (New Hampshire), 122
White Mountain National Forest, 154
White Mountains: beaver dam in, 25; geological history of, 4, 5, 6, 7, 9; hiking in, 152–154; history of, 18, 27, 28; legend of, 97; skiing in, 157–160; tourism in, 114–124, 125, 126–127, 128, 157–160
White River, 11, 98
White River Junction, Vermont, 80
Willard, Mount (New Hampshire), 121
Willey house, 116, 120
Williamstown, Massachusetts, 143
Williamstown Gulf, 98
Williamsville, Vermont, 113
Willoughby, C. C., 14
Winchester, New Hampshire, 147
Windham, Vermont, 74
Windham County, Vermont, 73
Winnipesaukee, Lake, 26, 160
Winnipesauke settlement (New Hampshire), 16
Winooski River, 16, 135
"Winter Costume at Stowe," 165
Winthrop, John, 27
Winthrop, Theodore, 154
wolves, 58
Wood, T. H., 159
Wood, William, 21
woodcutting industry, 88–94
Woodstock, Vermont, 53–55, 80, 160, 161
wool industry, 81, 83–85, 135, 136
Worcester, Massachusetts, 37, 63, 140
Worcester Range, 162
Woronoco, Massachusetts, 93, 105
Wyachtonok tribe, 14, 29

Young, Brigham, 85

Edited by Terry Reece Hackford
Editorial coordination by Dorothy Oehmler
Jacket and text design by Dianne Schaefer
Production coordinated by Christina M. Holz
Composition by DEKR Corporation
Text printing by Arcata Graphics/Halliday
Jacket and insert printing by John P. Pow Company, Inc.
Binding by Horowitz/Rae Book Manufacturers, Inc.